P9-BYM-584

MONEY
AND BANKING

About the Author

DR. HERBERT SPERO, late Associate Professor of Economics at the City College of New York, taught courses in money and banking, monetary theory, and the business cycle. He also taught at the American Institute of Banking, the educational division of the American Bankers' Association.

Dr. Spero had professional banking experience in both the investment and the commercial banking fields and engaged in research work for professional banking organizations. He wrote numerous articles on financial topics for professional and trade journals—for example, *Journal of Political Economy, Barron's, Bankers' Magazine, Banking Law Journal,* and *Trusts and Estates*—was co-author of *American Financial Institutions* and author of *Reconstruction Finance Corporation Loans to the Railroads.*

Professor Spero earned his B.B.A. degree at the City College of New York, his M.C.S. at New York University, and his Ph.D. at Columbia University.

COLLEGE OUTLINE SERIES

MONEY
AND BANKING

SECOND EDITION

By Herbert Spero

Barnes & Noble, Inc. • **New York**
Publishers • *Booksellers* • *Founded 1873*

©

SECOND EDITION, 1953

COPYRIGHT, 1949, 1953, 1955

By BARNES & NOBLE, INC.

All rights reserved

Reprinted, 1966

L. C. Card Number: 55–12478

This book is an original work (No. 69) in the original College Outline Series. It was written by a distinguished educator, carefully edited, and produced in the United States of America in accordance with the highest standards of publishing.

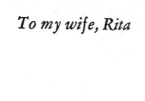

To my wife, Rita

Table of Contents

Charts, Figures, and Tables

Preface

This Outline seeks to survey the field of money and banking and to provide the student with an understanding of the basic principles of American financial institutions and developments. Included in the original survey was consideration of current international monetary and banking developments, such as the Bretton Woods' organizations designed to achieve currency and economic stabilization. A new chapter in the second edition discusses American financial policy following World War II.

In this new edition a number of minor changes have been made throughout the text. The references have been revised and moved to the back of the book, and a new series of objective questions, with answers, has been added.

The material should enable the student to grasp in summary form the fundamental principles set down in more elaborate fashion in his text, and facilitate an understanding of these principles.

The author is greatly indebted to Professor S. J. Flink, Chairman of the Department of Economics at Rutgers University, whose suggestions for improving the manuscript were invaluable. The Outline was first suggested by the author's colleague, Dr. Alexander V. Brody, of the Economics Department of the City College of New York. The preface would be incomplete without acknowledgment of the helpful comments of Mr. Oscar Lasdon, Associate Editor of *The Banking Law Journal*, and of the kindly assistance of my wife.

—Herbert Spero

TABULATED BIBLIOGRAPHY OF STANDARD
TEXTBOOKS ON MONEY AND BANKING

This *College Outline* is keyed to standard textbooks in two ways:

1. If you are studying one of the following textbooks, consult the cross references here listed to find which pages of the *Outline* summarize the appropriate chapter of your text. (Roman numerals refer to the textbook chapters, Arabic figures to the corresponding *Outline* pages.)

2. If you are using the *Outline* as your basis for study and need a fuller treatment of a topic, consult the pages of any of the standard textbooks as indicated in the Quick Reference Table on pp. xiv-xvi.

Chandler, Lester V. *The Economics of Money and Banking.* Fourth ed. New York: Harper & Row, 1964.
> I (1–10); II (47–55); III (11–20); IV (56–64); V (92–102); VI (73–91); VII (125–138); VIII (103–116); IX (117–124); X (114–115, 117); XII–XIV (140–152); XVII (29–37); XVIII–XIX (38–46); XX–XXIII (21–28); XXIV–XXV (229–235).

Haines, Walter W. *Money, Prices, and Policy.* New York: McGraw-Hill Book Co., Inc., 1961.
> I–III (1–10); V–VI (125–139); VII (56–59, 65–81, 92–97); VIII (47–49); IX–XII (103–116); XIII (60–63, 97–102); XIV (49–54); XV (153–162, 215–228); XVI (85–87, 163–192); XVII (45–46, 193–200, 204–214); XVIII (11–20); XIX (22–27); XXI (140–142); XXIV (142–146); XXV–XXVII (146–151); XXIX (146); XXX–XXXV (117–124, 233–235); XXXVI–XXXIX (29–46, 229–233).

Halm, George N. *Economics of Money and Banking.* Revised ed. Homewood, Ill.: Richard D. Irwin, Inc., 1961.
> I (1–10); II–III (140–150); IV (1–20); V (65–72); VII–X (140–152); XI (122–124); XII (103–122); XIII (56–59, 65–67, 92–93); XIV (47–49, 93–95); XV (21–28, 125–139); XVI–XVIII (103–116, 233–235); XIX–XX (90, 146–151); XXI–XXII (47–55, 73–91); XXIII–XXVIII (140–152); XXIX–XXXIV (29–37); XXXV–XXXVI (38–46); XXXVII (229–233).

Harriss, C. Lowell. *Money and Banking.* Second ed. Boston: Allyn and Bacon, Inc., 1965.
> I (1–9, 11–19); II (65–67); III (56–63, 69–72); IV (73–91, 185–186, 202–204, 220); V (73–84); VI (47–54); VII (85–90); VIII (63, 97–102); IX (103–106); X (106–115); XI (117–122); XII (153–162); XIII–XVII (140–146, 146–151); XVIII (29–37); XIX (11–13, 29–37); XX (38–46, 229–233); XXIII (122–124); XXIV (117–122); XXV (229–235); Appendix A (21–28, 125–139); Appendix B (141–142).

Hart, Albert Gailord, and Peter B. Kenen. *Money, Debt, and Economic Activity.* Third ed. Englewood Cliffs, N. J.: Prentice-Hall, Inc., 1961.

    Intro. (1–10); I (47–48, 54); II (125–139); III (56–64, 92–102); IV (65–69); V (99–102, 110–115, 137–138, 185–214); VI (103–116); VII (73–79, 153–176, 192–193, 215–228); VIII–XVI (140–152); XVII–XVIII (29–37); XIX (38–46, 229–233); XXII (233–235); XXIII (117–122); XXIV (122–124); XXV (233–235).

Kent, Raymond P. *Money and Banking.* Fifth ed. New York: Holt, Rinehart and Winston, 1966.

    I (1–9); II (11–19); III (15, 30–31); IV (18–19); V (21–27, 38–39); VI (47–54, 65); VII (65–72, 132–133); VIII (51–52, 67–72); IX (56–63, 92–97); X (97–99); XI (100–102); XII (88–89, 92, 95–97); XIII (73–90); XIV (92–93, 114); XV (93–95, 117–122); XVI (73–79, 113, 216–217); XVII (75–87, 95–96); XVIII (85–87); XIX (125–139); XX–XXI (103–115); XXII (117–122); XXIII–XXV (140–152); XXVI (103–105); XXVII (78–79, 117–122); XXVIII (122–124); XXIX (229–235); XXX (29–37); XXXI (81–83); XXXII (32–35); XXXIII (38–46); XXXIV (153–162); XXXV (215–227); XXXVI (163–176); XXXVII (202–213); XXXVIII (185–200).

Klise, Eugene S. *Money and Banking.* Third ed. Cincinnati: South-Western Publishing Co., 1964.

    I (1–4); II (4–9); III (21–27); IV (11–20); V (47–55); VI–VII (56–72); IX (103–110); X (110–116); XI–XII (117–124); XIII–XIV (140–152); XV (163–169); XVII (146–152); XXIII (229–236); XXIV (87–91); XXVI–XXVII (92–97, 73–87); XXVIII (153–160, 215–227); XXIX (185–201, 163–176); XXX–XXXI (29–46).

Kreps, Jr., Clifton H. *Money, Banking and Monetary Policy.* New York: The Ronald Press Co., 1962.

    I (1–4); II (5–9); IV (11–19); V–VII (21–27); VIII (56–57); IX–XI (125–138); XII (57–59); XIII (65–69); XVI–XVII (73–90); XIX (103–115); XX (69–72); XXI (140–151); XXIV–XXV (117–124); XXVI–XXVIII (125–138); XXIX–XXX (229–236).

Prather, Charles L. *Money and Banking.* Eighth ed. Homewood, Ill.: Richard D. Irwin, Inc., 1965.

    I (1–10); II (21–27); III (7–8, 11–19); IV (47–54); V (66, 84, 146); VI (125–138); VII (65–72, 103–104); VIII (56–63, 92–97); IX (65–69, 99–102); X (92–97); XI (73–81, 84); XII (85–90); XIII (104–106, 233–235); XIV–XV (103–115); XVI (114, 119–120); XVII (140–151); XVIII (146–151); XIX (117–122); XX (122–124); XXI (140–151); XXII (163–169, 174–176); XXIII (177–184); XXIV (183, 185–201); XXV (202–214); XXVI (215–227); XXVII (178–184); XXIX–XXXII (30–37, 38–46, 229–235).

Pritchard, Leland J. *Money and Banking.* Second ed. Boston: Houghton Mifflin Co., 1964.

    I–II (1–9); III (21–28); IV (11–20); V (56–63); VI (63–64); VII (60–63); VIII (47–55); IX (90–97); X (73–84); XI (65–67); XIII–XIV (125–139); XV (103–110); XVI (110–116); XVII (117–122); XVIII (122–124); XX (29–31); XXI–XXII (31–37); XXIV (12–15, 22–24); XXV–XXVII (38–46); XXVIII–XXX (140–151); XXXII (153–162); XXXIII (185–228).

Thomas, Rollin G. *Our Modern Banking and Monetary System.* Fourth ed. Englewood Cliffs: Prentice-Hall, Inc., 1964.

    I–II (1–9); III (10–19); IV (21–27); V (56–63); VI (47–54); VII (59–60, 87–93); VIII (65–69, 99–102); IX (67–72); X (92–95); XI–

XII (73–84); XIII (85–90); XIV (56–59, 125–138); XV (56–63, 125–138); XVI (103–115); XVII (117–124); XIX–XX (140–151); XXI (117–124); XXII–XXIV (140–151); XXV (66, 84, 146); XXIX (103–106, 117–120, 234–235); XXX (35–37, 81–84); XXXI–XXXIII (29–35); XXXIV (229–235); XXXV (38–46).

Whittlesey, Charles R., Arthur M. Freedman, and Edward S. Herman. *Money and Banking*. New York: The Macmillan Co., 1963.

I (1–9); II–III (11–20); IV (47–55); V (56–64); VI (65–72); VII (73–90); VIII (92–102); IX (163–176); X–XI (21–28); XII (103–116); XIII–XIV (117–124); XV–XIX (140–152); XXIV (229–236); XXVI–XXVII (97–99, 125–139); XXVIII (29–36); XXIX–XXX (38–46).

Chapter in Money & Banking	Chapter Title	Chandler	Haines	Halm	Harriss
I	Development of Money Systems	I	1–3	I, 4	*3–16*
II	Monetary Standards	3	18	4	*16–23*
III	Monetary History of the U. S.	*471–539*	19	15	*527–553*
IV	The International Money System	17	*36–38*	29–34	*18–19*
V	International Monetary Reorganization	18	39	35–36	20
VI	Credit and Credit Institutions	2	8, 14	14, 21–22	6
VII	Commercial Banking—Organization and Internal Management	4	13 *101–104*	13	3, 7
VIII	Bank Deposits and Checks	4	*104–119*	5, 13	2
IX	Commercial Bank Loans and Investments	5	16 *107–108*	21–22	4–5, 7
X	Bank Management, Supervision, and Deposit Insurance	6	*111–112* *218–224*	13–14	*122–126* *139–145*
XI	The Federal Reserve System	8	9–12	12, 16–18	9–11
XII	Federal Reserve Credit Operations and Treasury Monetary Policy	9	30–35	11–12	23–25
XIII	History of United States Commercial Banking	7	5–6	15	App. A
XIV	Money, Bank Credit, Prices, and National Income	15	21 24–27 29	2–3, 19–20 Parts III, VII	13–17 App. B
XV	Savings Banks	322, *591–592*	248–255	307	*197–207*
XVI	Investment Banks and the Securities Exchanges; Investment Trusts	*247–249*	16	*307–308*	*207–221*
XVII	Trust Companies	*308–310*, *117–118*	280–281		150, 210 *502–503*
XVIII	Urban Real-Estate Finance	*249–250*, *277*, *145–147*	*291–296*		*207–209* *215–221*
XIX	Farm Credit		278, 288–291		*78–79* *207–209*
XX	Consumer Finance	*124–131*, *202–203*, *475–476*	15		12
XXI	American Financial Policy	*531–594*	*584–594* *689–729*	37 *223–228*	20, *25–26*

See pp. xi-xiii for

Roman figures indicate chapters.

Hart & Kenen	Kent	Klise	Kreps	Prather	Pritchard
Intro.	1	1	1–3	1	1
343–351	2–4	1–2	4	3	4
	5	3–4	5–7	2	2–3
17–18	30–32	725–735	4–5 70–71, 62–72	28–29	20
19	33	735–769	7	31	21–27
1	6	87–105	11–12, 27–28 203–206, 534–547	4	8
3–4	9, 11–13	6	8	8	5
4	7–8 15	7	13 237–259	7, 9	11
119–129	16, 18	27	13, 17 223–224, 326–349	11–12	9–10
3	14, 17, 10	26	8, 9, 13 149–151, 253–258	10, 12	6–7
6 74–82	21	9	19 367–379	14	15
23–24	22, 26–28	10–12	19, 25 369–374, 493–508	15–16	16–18
2 82–85	19	22–23	9–11 154–211	6	12–13
Part II	23–25	13–16	21–23	17–18, 21	28–31
107–118	34	28	11–13	569–571	32
120–122	36	29	18	23	33
	741–750	719–724		27	83, 602–616
81–82 108–111	38	698–712	15, 16 285, 321–324	24	205–206, 168, 626–634
80–81	37	705–708	16 310–315	25	
58. 115	35	684–696	16 315–321	26	622–624, 631–642
22, 25 351–370	29, 33	31	28 539–557	13, 22	19

list of complete titles.

Italic figures indicate pages. Roman figures indicate chapters.

Chapter in Money & Banking	Chapter Title	Thomas	Whittlesey Freedman Herman		
I	Development of Money Systems	*1–2*	I		
II	Monetary Standards	*3*	2		
III	Monetary History of the U. S.	*4, 34*	10		
IV	The International Money System	*30–33*	28		
V	International Monetary Reorganization	*35–36*	29–30		
VI	Credit and Credit Institutions	*6*	4		
VII	Commercial Banking—Organization and Internal Management	*5, 7*	5		
VIII	Bank Deposits and Checks	*8–9*	6		
IX	Commercial Bank Loans and Investments	*11–14*	7		
X	Bank Management, Supervision, and Deposit Insurance	*10, 20*	8, 26		
XI	The Federal Reserve System	*16*	12		
XII	Federal Reserve Credit Operations and Treasury Monetary Policy	*17, 20–21, 28*	13–14		
XIII	History of United States Commercial Banking	*15*	3, 11		
XIV	Money, Bank Credit, Prices, and National Income	*22–25*	15–19		
XV	Savings Banks	*5*	*43–44, 163–166*		
XVI	Investment Banks and the Securities Exchanges; Investment Trusts	*5*	*155–173*		
XVII	Trust Companies	*5*	*173–181*		
XVIII	Urban Real-Estate Finance	*5, 12*	*62–63, 165–171, 175*		
XIX	Farm Credit	*12*			
XX	Consumer Finance	*5*	*62, 171–173*		
XXI	American Financial Policy		24–25		

See pp. xi-xiii for list of complete titles.

⊞

Development of Money Systems

Money and banking is a study of: (1) the functions these institutions perform in modern society; (2) their development, evolution, and growth; (3) the problems they bring to the businessman and community.

FUNCTIONS OF MONEY

Money renders many services in modern economic life. These services facilitate the production, exchange, and consumption of goods and services—the aim of a smoothly operating society. Only if goods and services are produced in a steady flow and sold to the consumer can we say that our productive organization is being used wisely. How does money aid this flow of commodities to the market?

Medium-of-Exchange Function. Our producers sell their output for dollars and cents. They readily accept this money since they know it can be used in turn to buy whatever goods and services they may wish. Everyone in the United States has confidence in the exchangeability of the dollar. Its general acceptability leads to its wide use as a medium of exchange. Production is stimulated when manufacturers know that the money they receive for their output can be used to purchase whatever they wish. Similarly, wage earners, landlords, and capitalists readily accept money for their services, their land, and their capital when the dollar payments will be exchangeable for goods and services offered them.

Standard-of-Value Function. Money—in the United States, the dollar—is the unit by which we measure value or the worth of goods and services. If a pair of shoes is priced at $10 while a wallet can be had for $5, it is fair to conclude that buyers and sellers consider the wallet only half as valuable as the shoes. In other words, prices expressed in money terms reflect our appraisal of the many goods and services offered for sale.

Money also serves as a unit or money of account, a measure of the money value of goods and services not offered for sale but representing personal and business assets.

Closely allied in function to the monetary unit is near-money like debts receivable, commodities, and securities readily convertible into money. Their utility as near-money changes with variations in their money price and the consequent general public unwillingness to accept them.

Dollar price is the measuring rod of value—yet not a perfect standard of value. Changes in the gold content of the dollar, the amount of money and credit in circulation, and the quantity of goods offered for sale affect the stable value of the dollar and cause price fluctuations.

Money is used more often as a standard of value than as a medium of exchange. People compare the money prices of competitive goods they consider buying before coming to a decision. In many instances, decisions reached are not effectuated. Under these circumstances, money does not change hands for goods. Thus, money is used more frequently as a standard of value than as a medium of exchange.

Store-of-Value Function. People store up money for future use. Savings banks and life insurance companies are outstanding examples of institutions which safekeep the public's unspent buying power. Under normal circumstances, a savings bank depositor can draw upon his account with the assurance that the money stored up or saved will buy about the same quantity of goods and services as when it was deposited. During inflationary periods money loses purchasing power and is a poor store of value. People then buy valuable goods with their depreciating money and avoid currency and bank deposits representing claims on currency as a means of storing value and unspent buying power. This was the experience of many nations during the turbulent years of World Wars I and II. Stability of a money's buying power is essential to its use as a store of value.

Standard of Deferred Payments. General confidence in the purchasing power of money is the basis of its use in money loan transactions. The debtor, borrowing for productive or consumptive use, accepts money because of his confidence in its buying power.

The lender, in turn, agrees to accept payment in currency because of his confidence in its future purchasing power when the loan is repaid.

If prices advance during the life of the loan, the borrower is adversely affected because his newly acquired funds purchase less than he anticipated. A decline in prices works to the borrower's advantage because then the borrowed money buys more goods.

Price fluctuations help or hinder a borrower's ability to repay a debt. When prices advance, a borrower is in a better position to meet a money obligation, for his goods are marketed at a higher figure than when his debt was contracted. Banks and other creditors lend more willingly in periods of rising prices, for their debtors are likely to be better able to repay their money debts. A sharp price decline may cripple the debtor's capacity to repay and in turn embarrass the creditor who is not repaid.

Thus, while money is the standard of deferred payment, price changes affect debtors and creditors and interfere with the currency's function as a standard of deferred payment.

IMPORTANCE OF MONEY TO ECONOMIC LIFE

The Importance of Money to Production. Businessmen produce and trade for a money profit on their invested capital. When profit can be earned easily, as during World War II and the prosperous '20's, the amount of money put into new plant and equipment grows by leaps and bounds. This money investment benefits society, for the flow of goods and services to consumer markets broadens.

The Importance of Money to Exchange and Consumption. Money's general acceptability and wide use as a medium of exchange stimulate the movement of goods from producer to consumer. The consumer's money income, called a wage, salary, interest, or rent, enables him to satisfy his desires by exchanging this income for goods and services.

The smooth system of money exchange raises community living standards as production increases and is marketed for the generally accepted money.

The Importance of Money to Society. The nation-wide use of a common money, payable for all commodities and services, assures people of the ready exchangeability of their common medium of exchange. Then, each person is satisfied to work in some specialized position for a money income. Division of labor is typical of modern society and increases production, trade, and human welfare.

Certain unfavorable social and economic developments are outgrowths of a money society. Money income and money price often become the yardsticks for judging people and things. A desire for a money profit often induces manufacturers to retain outworn production techniques for fear of the cost of modernization. Labor-management disputes frequently arise out of the contending parties' claims to a large money income. The dispute may shut down factories and halt production. The drive for a money income may result in exhaustion of natural resources without any provision for replacement. Business concerns concentrate on their own money welfare, ignoring the antisocial results of a lack of industry-wide planning and co-operation. In depressions, each firm fights for its own life, regardless of the effect its actions have on its competitors, workers, and the national economy.

During the 1930's, the money and banking system was vital to the government's efforts to stimulate business activity by pump priming. This program was strongly criticized by the wealthier and more conservative people who feared higher taxes accompanying persistent unbalanced budgets.

GROWTH OF THE MONEY SYSTEM

Barter and Commodity Currency.   Barter—the direct exchange of goods for goods—was the first stage of monetary development. It was quickly replaced by commodity currency, some generally accepted good. For example, during the early American colonial period, the settlers used tobacco, rice, lumber, fish, wool, and cattle, among other useful goods, as their mediums of exchange and standards of value.

Both barter and commodity currency were cumbersome systems of exchange for these reasons: (1) People could not easily arrange exchanges since it was difficult to find people who owned and were willing to part with their possessions for what was offered in trade. (2) Frequently there was no coincidence of wants. (3) Different ideas of the value of goods in terms of other goods prevailed in the colonies. (4) Commodities were not generally acceptable in unlimited quantities, for traders were interested only in specific amounts of goods, and there was no easy flow of commodities. Consequently exchanges were not easy to work out. (5) Many items, like cattle, wheat, and tobacco, were not divisible, were not easily transported, or had little value even in large amounts and so were not convenient mediums of exchange. (6) Commodity money was hardly a suitable store of value since items like grain and meat easily spoiled and the owners often found that their wealth was shortly of little value.

Coins and Coinage. Coins were the first type of modern money. The earliest coins were not standardized. They were made of silver, gold, or copper. Before the development of modern coinage in Europe, metallic money appeared in bullion form. Each transaction required weighing and testing the metal for its quality. This cumbersome procedure interfered with trade; but the difficulty was eliminated when kings, goldsmiths, and bankers stamped the weight and fineness on metallic money. Thus, standardized coinage was born. Today a thin dime is worth as much as a new dime. In olden times, a new coin was worth more than an old one.

Today governments have the sole power of coining money. They create and control its coinage. The problem of a heterogeneous money system has been eliminated. Governments today do not control the process for the profit (*seigniorage*) in it as was true of many feudal lords.

Standard coins were made from a standard metal like gold according to mint rules and regulations. Public confidence in adherence to these rules and regulations meant confidence in the government issuer. The money value of a standard coin was equal to its bullion value.

The standard coin in the United States before 1934 was the gold dollar consisting of 25.8 grains of gold, 9/10 fine. Anyone could bring gold to the mint for coinage. In this sense "free" coinage existed. The Treasury abandoned "free" coinage of gold in 1934. Unlimited coinage of standard silver dollars had been abandoned in 1873.

Subsidiary or *token coins* are made of a standard or cheaper metal. Their money value is greater than their bullion value. Subsidiary money is readily exchangeable for standard money. The government safeguards its standard metal reserves by limiting the amount of token coin and by agreeing to redeem it in standard money. The amount of subsidiary coins depends upon the business community's needs. The government determines the subsidiary money needs of the people and coins the requisite amount but does not permit "free" coinage of this type of currency. United States subsidiary money consists of silver dollars and other silver coins, as well as bronze, copper, and nickel coins.

Paper Money. Paper money is the chief type of American money in circulation. The growth of trade in volume and value demanded a more suitable medium of exchange than coins. Paper money is easier to handle than coin and can be issued in varying denominations. Moreover, its value as money is not reduced by the reduction of its metallic content through constant handling.

In the United States, there are different types of paper money. Now they are all issued by the government or its agent, the Federal Reserve System.

Since 1934, gold certificates, called *representative* money, have been issued by the Treasury to the federal reserve banks to serve as their monetary reserves. Prior to 1934, they were in active circulation, but were called in during the bank holiday of 1933. Each gold certificate has a 100 per cent reserve in gold behind it. It is for this reason that it is called *representative money.*

Silver certificates are also representative money, for they are supposed to represent an equal value in silver. However, the face value of the bills is greater than the bullion value behind them. Hence, people accept them, in part, on the credit of the United States government.

Credit money is the major type of paper currency in circulation. Federal reserve notes have the characteristics of this type of circulating medium for they are not fully backed by gold. The reserve consists of only 25 per cent in gold certificates; the remainder is made up of promissory notes of banks and businessmen and United States government securities.

Still another type of credit money is the United States note. It is secured by a partial gold reserve in the Treasury and by the credit of the government.

Federal reserve bank notes, secured chiefly by government bonds, and national bank notes, similarly collateraled, are also credit money. Faith in the government is the basis of their general acceptability. In 1945, the power of federal reserve banks to issue bank notes was repealed. In 1935, the Treasury called in the bonds securing national bank notes. Since these dates, the amount of both these notes outstanding has declined.

DEPOSIT CURRENCY

Definition.   The bulk of the money in circulation in the United States consists of demand deposits. This deposit currency is bank credit or deposited funds against which depositors draw checks or drafts. Convertible into cash on demand, checks are drawn by individuals; drafts, by banks. Large business transactions are ordinarily settled with deposit currency. Such currency is used so frequently in American business life that the United States is said to have a *credit economy*. Since the major medium of exchange in the country is the bank check or draft, our attention must be focused on banking operations as well as on money.

LEGAL TENDER AND LAWFUL MONEY

Legal Tender.   Legal tender is the type of money creditors must accept in settlement of their claims. Since 1933, all types of money except demand deposits have been called legal tender.

Lawful Money.   Lawful money differs from legal tender in that it is not necessarily acceptable in payment of debts. Gold certificates, prior to 1933, were legal tender. Since then, they have not been in general circulation and are now held by the federal reserve banks as security for their liabilities.

MONEY IN CIRCULATION AND DEPOSIT CURRENCY

Types and Amount.   Table I below lists as of June, 1952, the different types and amounts of money in circulation and the

TABLE I
MONEY IN CIRCULATION AND BANK DEMAND DEPOSITS
June 30, 1952 *

	Amount (in millions)
Gold	$ 38
Federal Reserve Notes	24,605
Standard Silver Dollars	191
Silver Bullion	
Silver Certificates and Treasury Notes of 1890	2,089
Subsidiary Silver Coin	1,093
Minor Coin	393
United States Notes	318
Federal Reserve Bank Notes	221
National Bank Notes	77
Demand Deposits	108,650

* Source: *Federal Reserve Bulletin*, August, 1952, pp. 897, 899.

amount of demand deposits of all banks in the United States. The dominance of demand deposits in thc money system is very evident.

Chart I shows the changing nature of the money in circulation between 1914 and 1947.

CHART I: Money in Circulation in the United States, by Major Types, 1914, 1929, 1947

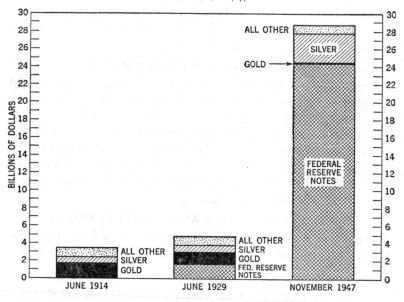

Sourccs: *Annual Report of the Secretary of the Treasury*, 1945, p. 677; *Federal Reserve Bulletin*, Jan., 1948, p. 61.

QUALITIES OF A GOOD MONEY

Acceptability and Cognizability. The prime requisite of a sound money is general acceptability. Acceptability and its use as a medium of exchange, store of value, and standard of deferred payments generally grow out of the money commodity's utility. Such acceptability grows in part out of the maintenance of an adequate metallic reserve to meet all likely demands for conversion into gold and in part out of a government guaranty of the note issue. This guaranty assures a limit on the note issue and vests it with legal tender power—the power to pay debts.

Stability of Value. Utility gives the money value. It is vital that this value be stable or show only minor fluctuations. Otherwise, the money will not be widely accepted, for people always hold their wealth in goods that retain their value. If a nation's money shows marked and erratic value changes, the community will not favor it as a standard of value and medium of exchange. European and Asiatic experiences during and following World Wars I and II illustrate this truth.

Elasticity of Supply. The money supply must be sufficient to facilitate business. An inadequate money supply starves trade channels and forces resort to other means of exchange like barter.

The central banking system, like the federal reserve banks in the United States, is the only issuer of bank notes. It must judge and adapt the supply of federal reserve notes to the needs of business.

Portability. Money must be portable for daily dealings. Even large transactions can be effected if the money has a high value in small bulk.

Durability. In passing from hand to hand the money commodity must retain its value. Otherwise, wear and tear will cause deterioration of this value and destroy the monetary usefulness of the good.

Uniformity of Value: Gresham's Law. All types of metallic money in circulation declared equal in value or purchasing power by the government must actually be kept equal in value or buying power. If they are not, the undervalued money will be hoarded, exported to places where its true value is recognized, or melted down for sale in the bullion market, while the overvalued, cheaper money will be kept in circulation. This is known as Gresham's law and is named after Sir Thomas Gresham, master of England's mint in the sixteenth century. This law can apply to a money system composed of all types of moneys. The general disrepute of the cheaper money interferes with its monetary services.

Divisibility. Money is used to settle transactions of varying amounts. Therefore, moneys of different denominations must be issued to accommodate debtors and creditors. To insure the exchangeability of one money form for another, all types of money must be kept equal in value.

REVIEW QUESTIONS

1. Why are demand deposits considered the equivalent of money?
2. What services does money perform in our modern economic life?
3. How does barter differ from commodity currency?
4. What are standard coins? How do they differ from subsidiary coins?
5. List the different types of credit money in circulation today.
6. How does lawful money differ from legal tender?
7. What is Gresham's law?
8. Why is stability of value an outstanding quality of a good money?
9. How does near-money differ from money?

✠

Monetary Standards

We have indicated that in the United States the dollar is the unit by which we measure values. It has been shown also that the prime requisite of a sound money is its general acceptability which, in turn, grows out of the money commodity's utility. Today, the United States adheres to a gold unit. The American dollar is backed by a fixed quantity of gold. Between 1879 and 1933 this country was on a gold coin standard. Since 1934 it has operated on a managed gold bullion standard.

Prior to 1873, the United States used a bimetallic standard, with both gold and silver money as standards of value. During the depression of the 1930's, many authorities advocated a managed standard, with the money unit freed from any tie to gold and manipulated to maintain business stability.

TYPES OF MONEY STANDARDS

The Gold Standard. The gold standard is the typical standard of the world, especially in the Western Hemisphere. There are four general types of gold standards: (1) the gold coin standard; (2) the gold bullion standard; (3) the managed gold bullion standard; (4) the gold exchange standard. What are the characteristics of each of these standards?

THE GOLD COIN STANDARD. Under this standard: (1) A fixed gold content is established for the money unit. (Prior to 1934, when the United States was on a gold coin standard, the dollar was valued at 23.22 pure gold grains.) (2) The government is prepared to mint gold bullion into gold coins for the general public. Therefore, free coinage is another characteristic of this type of standard. (3) The fixed relationship thus established between the monetary unit and a fixed quantity of gold keeps the monetary unit equal in value to the gold bullion contained therein. (4) People can do as they wish with their gold—export it, hoard it, or use it for any personal or business purpose. (5) The gold coin is declared legal tender and must be accepted in settlement of all obligations. (6) Credit money, at most only partially backed by a gold reserve, is redeemable in gold coin.

THE GOLD BULLION STANDARD. This standard differs slightly from the gold coin standard. Similar to it: (1) the money is given a fixed gold content (since 1934, when the United States adopted a modified version of a managed gold bullion standard, the dollar has been valued at 13.714 grains of gold); (2) a government buys and sells all offerings of gold at a fixed price; (3) but due to the large units in which the gold is sold, the public is limited in its ability to buy the yellow metal; (4) once acquired, the gold may be hoarded, sold, used for industrial purposes, and for the discharge of debts; (5) the government accepts credit money in exchange for gold.

Unlike the gold coin standard, the gold bullion standard: (1) makes gold bars legal tender for all obligations, private and public; (2) causes gold coins to be withdrawn from circulation and converted into gold bars. There is no free coinage of gold.

THE MANAGED GOLD BULLION STANDARD. This managed standard is tied to gold. There is a fixed quantity of the yellow metal behind each money unit, but it cannot be obtained for general circulation. Therefore, there is no free gold market. The Gold Reserve Act of 1934, as we shall see, established a managed gold bullion standard in the United States. This legislation gave the government power to decrease the gold content of the dollar to stimulate business activity through hoped-for price rises resulting from the devaluation.

THE GOLD EXCHANGE STANDARD. This standard may be likened both to the gold coin and gold bullion standards, in that: (1) the money unit is declared equal to a fixed quantity of gold; (2) a free gold market is maintained, permitting the public to do as it wishes with its gold stock, with no limitations on the importation, exportation, hoarding, or ability to obtain gold from mining companies or the mint; (3) credit money may be used to purchase from the government gold drafts (claims on gold) which are convertible into gold abroad.

The outstanding characteristic of this money system, the characteristic which distinguishes it from the gold coin and the gold bullion standards, is that paper money is redeemed with gold drafts drawn on a foreign bank in a country on the gold coin or bullion standard. These drafts are direct claims on gold reserves or short-term investments held in the latter nation. However, the government or its central bank manages the uses to which these drafts are put.

Silver Standards. There could be standards similar to those based on gold. Thus, a silver coin, a silver bullion, and a silver exchange standard are possible.

Silver standards are of no practical significance today. England, the leading manufacturing and trading nation of the eighteenth and nineteenth centuries, led the way in abandoning silver as the basis of a money system when it gave up the silver coin standard in the latter part of the eighteenth century.

Bimetallism. The money system of a country is called bimetallic when: (1) two metals at a fixed ratio, one to the other, are the standards of value (the two metals ordinarily chosen have been gold and silver); (2) the government stands ready to buy gold and silver at fixed prices, while the standard coins composed of either gold or silver are legal tender.

The United States demonetized silver in 1873, while in the same year, the Latin Monetary Union, made up of France, Italy, Belgium, and Switzerland, which had agreed in 1865 freely to coin both gold and silver at a ratio of 15½ to 1, limited the coinage of five-franc silver pieces.

The Managed Paper Standard. Critics of the gold standard maintain that it hampers business activity. It limits the issue of currency when business requires more money because the gold reserve is severely depleted and the government fears it may be unable to maintain the value of its currency equal to gold. On the other hand, a large gold reserve encourages currency expansion beyond business requirements. Therefore, some monetary authorities urge that the money system be managed without regard to the gold reserve but with an eye primarily on business needs. There are two types of managed money.

FIAT MONEY. Fiat money is the first type. It is totally unsecured currency, issued by government order, without gold or silver backing, and without any promise of redemption. Its value is not kept equal to gold or silver, and its exchange value depends upon the government's ability to limit the quantity to prevent severe depreciation. In other words, the supply of this money is governmentally managed to meet the requirements of business.

INCONVERTIBLE PAPER MONEY. A second type of managed currency is inconvertible paper money. The continued circulation and ready acceptability in the past of such paper money—for example, greenbacks and continental currency—bearing a promise to pay specie on demand, but which could not be redeemed, depended upon two factors: (1) the specie reserve of the government; (2) the credit position of the government based, in part, on the size of its metallic reserve and its likely use to redeem what is at the moment irredeemable paper money.

ADVANTAGES AND DISADVANTAGES OF DIFFERENT MONEY STANDARDS

Advantages of the Gold Standard. Gold standard advocates defend the gold standard on these grounds:

ACCEPTABILITY. People accept gold, and money based on gold, because of the metal's utility. All moneys and deposit currency in gold standard nations are in general circulation because people realize that the paper money issues and bank deposits are readily convertible into gold. In the case of temporarily irredeemable paper money, its circulation and general acceptability rest in good part on the public's opinion of the government's ultimate capacity to resume redemption.

AUTOMATIC LIMITATION ON MEDIUMS OF EXCHANGE. Minimum gold reserve requirements for paper money issues and bank deposits serve as automatic brakes on the overissue of paper money and bank credit. General public confidence in the mediums of exchange is maintained if minimum reserve requirements are adhered to.

A CHECK ON INFLATION AND DEFLATION. The automatic limitation on a government's issue of money and bank credit prevents an excessive issue relative to the supply of goods and services. Hence, inflation is unlikely. Conversely, a decline in business activity need not result from a shrinkage in gold reserves. If a nation's gold stock is inadequate, its reserve requirements can be reduced and the throttling influence of a too rigid gold reserve stipulation minimized or eliminated. At the same time, general public confidence in the country's mediums of exchange can be maintained.

Again, during periods of depression the cost of mining gold declines. Since the mint price of the yellow metal is fixed, gold production increases, for mining company profits are on the rise. The stimulus resulting from this relation between the cost of mining and the selling price of gold provides a broader gold base and the foundation on which to finance a rising volume of business. In good times when costs of mining are on the upswing, gold production is discouraged, for mining profits are not so attractive. Nevertheless, the volume of bank credit outstanding mounts during prosperity and pushes prices upward until bank reserves are exhausted, or the supply of goods and services catches up with demand, or some outside factor disturbs general business optimism.

It should be noted that the total quantity of newly mined gold each year is small relative to the outstanding supply. Therefore, economic dislocations are not a likely outgrowth of changes in the supply of gold.

BASIS OF AN INTERNATIONAL MONEY SYSTEM.   In the past, currencies have been based on gold. The general acceptability of this precious metal and its stable value has led to its adoption as an international standard of value and medium of exchange. The gold value of gold currencies fixes their value relative to one another and provides a stable base for international dealings.

STIMULUS TO INTERNATIONAL INVESTMENT AND TRADE.   Since gold currencies are widely accepted, adherence to the gold standard encourages international trade and investment. Importers, exporters, bankers, and investors will gladly put their funds to work if their contracts call for payment in gold-secured money.

UNIFORM INTERNATIONAL PRICE SYSTEM.   A free gold market permits freedom of gold import and export. If country A has a lower price level than its neighbor country B, country A will receive gold in partial payment for its heavy sales to B in excess of purchases from B. The newly received gold is the basis for issues of new money and credit which force up country A's price level; country B's price level is depressed as money and bank credit are contracted due to a loss of gold. Thus, country A's and country B's price levels fluctuate around the same point as gold moves into and out of their treasuries. Movements of gold affect prices internationally, and make for automatic adjustments in international prices.

Disadvantages of the Gold Standard.   The following criticisms are leveled at the gold standard: (1) Confidence in money exists only when confidence is not needed. But during a recession this confidence crumbles. Then the public demands gold for its money and bank deposits, exhausts the metallic reserves of the government, and forces a suspension of the gold standard. (2) When the gold standard is suspended, there is no automatic limitation on the supply of money and deposits. If the gold reserve shrinks, a government does not necessarily obey the dictates of the automatic gold standard, but contrives to maintain the supply of money in circulation in spite of its shrinking gold reserve. A fixed gold reserve requirement can be reduced or suspended, or the treasury may refuse to export gold in settlement of international debts. (3) The gold standard is not as automatic as its advocates would have us believe. A loss of gold does not necessarily mean a contraction in the supply of money and bank credit and a drop in the price level. Nor does an increase in gold reserves indicate an automatic increase in money and bank credit in circulation with a corresponding advance in prices. Consequently, the expected international adjustment of prices will not occur. (4) The accumulation of gold reserves without a corresponding growth in business activity lays the groundwork for speculation and its excesses, followed by a crash in money prices. (5) While fixed gold contents in monetary units assure foreign exchange stability, they do not assure internal price stability. A nation with a large gold reserve can expand its supply of money and credit and inflate its price level. Loss of gold necessitates deflation as money and credit is withdrawn from circulation.

Advantages of the Gold Coin Standard. (1) Free coinage and the maintenance of a free gold market keep the market value of gold and the face value of coins equal. When the market value of the bullion in a gold coin rises above the face value of the coin, the metal in the coin is melted down and sold as bullion. The effect is to equalize the market value of gold and the now relatively scarce gold coin. (2) All forms of paper money and bank credit money are redeemable in gold coin, and so equality of value is established among the mediums of exchange.

Disadvantages of the Gold Coin Standard. (1) Few people use gold coins, and no real domestic purpose is served by the coinage and circulation of gold money. (2) Gold is rarely used domestically in ordinary trade. The gold coin is small, has a high value, and is not convenient for trade transactions. (3) A period of monetary crisis (like that in the United States in 1933, when individuals hoarded gold coins) rapidly strips the treasury of its metallic reserves and minimizes the capacity of the government to meet extraordinary gold demands.

Advantages of the Gold Bullion Standard. This standard overcomes the disadvantages of the gold coin standard: (1) The country is freed from the burden of gold coinage. (2) It is better prepared to cope with the gold drain. This is especially true since the government sells gold only in bar form having a high value. In the United States a gold bar can only be had for $14,000, putting it beyond the reach of the average man. Thus while a free gold market exists, for all practical purposes most individuals do not have access to the nation's gold reserves.

Disadvantages of the Gold Bullion Standard. (1) Since most individuals do not have access to the gold reserves of a country, the volume of money and credit is not responsive to the automatic operation of the gold standard. The only people who can withdraw gold are the well-to-do, bankers, and wealthy corporations. Under these circumstances, a limited group influences the automatic operation of the gold standard. (2) Therefore, it has been said that the "gold bullion standard is a rich man's standard, operating above, and out of the reach of, the man of small means." [1]

Advantages of the Gold Exchange Standard. (1) Since gold reserves, in part, are held abroad, they earn interest. (2) Gold movements to settle international obligations are minimized, for there are reserves abroad available for this purpose. (3) Since gold movements are sharply curtailed, the cost of shipping the valuable metal in settlement of debts is lowered. (4) The maldistribution of gold following World War I and its concentration in the United States and France forced the adoption of a money system which temporarily enabled most countries to adhere to a type of gold standard. A return to the pre-1914 money system seemed effected.

Disadvantages of the Gold Exchange Standard. (1) This gold standard eliminates the so-called automatic operation of the gold standard. No longer does the money and credit supply of a nation respond to changes in its domestically owned and held gold reserves. When a nation keeps its monetary reserves partially in another country, both nations use this reserve as a basis for the issue of money and credit. (2) The country holding the gold reserves

---

[1] Spahr, W. E., *The Case for the Gold Standard* (New York: Economists' National Committee on Monetary Policy, 1940), p. 28.

and investments must always be prepared to export gold if the owner desires to withdraw its gold reserves. (3) The net result of this latter action is to force liquidation of bank credit based, in part, on foreign reserves, and initiate a general contraction of the medium of exchange. (4) This deflation may be avoided by refusing to meet foreign obligations, thereby freezing the reserves of the depository nation and so embarrassing it, as well as compelling a general abandonment of the gold standard by failing to meet gold commitments abroad.

Advantages of Bimetallism. (1) The inadequate supply of gold relative to the money and credit issues of governments and banks apparently argued for a bimetallic system in the 1920's. (2) Some advocates believe that a bimetallic system would be more stable in value than a monometallic system based on gold. The metallic reserves would be larger and not so easily influenced by a marked increase in the supply of these reserves. (3) The value of the monetary reserves also would be more stable because the production of gold and silver varies in opposite directions. More gold is produced in depression periods when silver output is declining, since silver is a by-product largely of industrial metals like copper whose production rises in good times when gold-mining costs advance and discourage gold production. The monetary reserves of a nation would always be supplemented from one or the other sources. An increase in the monetary reserves would have a negligible effect on the value of the total reserve. (4) Gresham's law would not be permanently operative since a flood of the overvalued money into the market would depress its value there, bring it into line with its mint value, and lead to a resumption of its use as a money.

Disadvantages of Bimetallism. The monetary history of the United States in the nineteenth century indicates that a bimetallic system becomes a de facto monometallic system. Discrepancy between the mint and market values of the two metals tends to drive the undervalued metal out of circulation. The net result is a money system based on only one metal.

Advantages of Managed Money. (1) Freedom from adherence to a metallic reserve permits expansion of the currency to meet trade requirements. (2) The inflationary and deflationary consequences of an automatic gold standard are avoided. (3) Only in periods of severe inflation and general loss of confidence in the buying power of paper money has the public shown a preference for metallic currency. (4) It is cheaper to print paper money than to coin metallic money.

Disadvantages of Managed Money. (1) The lack of a tie-up to a metallic reserve encourages the overissue of paper money and bank credit, especially in periods of shrinking tax receipts and rising governmental expenses. Printing-press money is an easy but unsound way out. (2) Foreign exchange rates are not fixed by the metallic content of currencies. The net result is erratic fluctuations in these prices disturbing to international finance, trade, and investment. Competitive monetary depreciation might easily be used by each nation in a fight for world trade.

PROPOSED MONETARY REFORMS

Dissatisfaction with price fluctuations and their hardships on debtors and creditors has led to proposals aimed at stabilizing the purchasing power of the gold dollar.

The Compensated Dollar. If prices rise, injuring creditors and creating business unsettlement, the gold content of the dollar should be raised to offset the upswing in prices and restore the old equilibrium. If prices fall, the gold content should be lowered to raise prices. The late Professor Irving Fisher of Yale University was the leading advocate of this proposal.

The Tabular Standard. Again, the desire to maintain equity between debtors and creditors prompted this proposal. As prices rise, creditors should be repaid a greater number of dollars than they lent; if prices fall, debtors should pay fewer dollars than they borrowed in settlement of their obligation. Business and personal contracts would be more satisfactory to all parties. They would not penalize either the borrowers or the lenders.

Lehfeldt Gold Subsidization Plan. When the demand for gold exceeds the supply, gold output should be increased by government subsidization. When the supply exceeds the demand, the output of gold should be reduced. The agency to stimulate or retard gold production would be an international syndicate of gold producers. Professor Lehfeldt of South Africa has urged this scheme.

REVIEW QUESTIONS

1. How does the gold coin standard differ from the gold bullion standard and the gold exchange standard?

2. What major criticism of the gold standard is made by the advocates of a managed currency?
3. What is inflation? Deflation?
4. How do gold movements aid in creating uniform international prices?
5. How does foreign exchange stability differ from internal price stability?
6. What type of monetary standard does the United States enjoy today? Why?
7. What international dangers always face the nation holding the reserves of a gold exchange standard country?
8. Mention two periods of American history when the United States issued unsecured paper money.

🅷

Monetary History of the United States

The United States has used different types of monetary standards during its life as a colony and as an independent nation.

COLONIAL SYSTEMS OF EXCHANGE

Barter, Hard Money, and Paper Currency. The early settlers
rapidly exhausted their own gold and silver resources through the
purchase of basic necessities in England. Whatever gold and silver
were obtained in international trade quickly moved to England in
exchange for goods and services. Barter was the order of the day,
with Spanish pieces of eight the leading form of hard money.
Massachusetts tried to meet the need for metallic money by the
coinage of the "pine tree shilling," but the British forbade this
issue after some three decades. The colonists also resorted to fiat
money. "Bills of credit" and "loan bills" were issued by colonial
governments to such excess that they depreciated rapidly. The
British government put a halt to these issues shortly before the
Revolution. This prohibition was only another irritant to the already sorely beset colonists and aggravated their grievances against
England.

Money Issue of the Continental Congress. The war with Britain and its attendant expense forced the Continental Congress to
print paper money supposedly redeemable in gold, silver, or Spanish dollars. The promise was not kept, but it at least indicated that
the dollar rather than the pound would be the money unit of the
United States. The federal and state governments issued increasing
amounts of these pieces of paper while the hope of redemption
grew dimmer. The money depreciated sharply in value to the van-
ishing point. Finally, it ceased to circulate as a medium of exchange.

UNITED STATES MONETARY HISTORY, 1792-1933

The United States has enjoyed the advantages and disadvantages of bimetallism, the gold standard, and unsecured or fiat standards since the thirteen colonies organized as an independent nation in 1789 and gave to Congress the sole power to coin money and regulate its value. A brief summary of American monetary history is offered below.

Bimetallism, 1792–1862. Bimetallism was established by the Coinage Act of 1792. Since the silver dollar consisted of 371.25 grains of fine silver while the gold dollar was made up of 24.75 grains of fine gold, the mint ratio of silver to gold was 15 to 1. This ratio undervalued gold when the market price of silver declined. Under the circumstances, gold tended to disappear from the United States. An attempt was made to remedy the divergence between mint and market values of the two metals in 1834 when the gold weight of the dollar was cut officially to 23.2 grains. The new ratio between silver and gold was 16 to 1. However, silver was now undervalued, and it was profitable to export it to those places and markets where it was quoted at a higher price. The result was a disappearance of silver money from the currency system of the United States and a forced reliance upon gold. While legally bimetallism had been the official monetary system since 1792, in practice the United States had operated on a monometallic base— first silver and then gold.

Fiat Money, 1862–1879. Gold payments were suspended by the banks immediately upon the outbreak of the Civil War. The Treasury sought to finance the war, in part, through the issue of greenbacks, more properly called *United States notes*, not redeemable in gold. Their large issue and the lack of confidence in their ultimate redeemability led people to hoard gold. Naturally, the paper money depreciated in value. In 1875, the Specie Resumption Act called for the redemption of greenbacks in gold, beginning in 1879, putting the United States on a gold standard. Few of these notes were presented, and those that were, had to be reissued to comply with a legislative act of 1878.

The Gold Coin Standard, 1873–1918. The government abandoned free coinage of the silver dollar in 1873. In subsequent years, this action was called the *crime of '73*, although at the time the silver interests did not object since their output could be sold at a higher figure on the market than at the mint. However, new discoveries of silver in addition to a general world-wide abandonment of the bimetallic standard depressed silver's value and aroused a demand that the government do something for this metal.

The agitation led to the Bland-Allison Act of 1878 and the Sherman Silver Purchase Act of 1890. The Bland-Allison Act ordered the Treasury to buy $2,000,000 to $4,000,000 of silver monthly. This metal was coined into silver dollars, or silver certificates were issued on the basis of the silver purchases. Gold redemption of this money was not specifically called for; therefore, the monetary standard was termed a "limping" standard. The Sherman act permitted redemption in gold of silver certificates growing out of the purchase of at most four and a half million ounces of silver monthly. The Bland-Allison Act was repealed in 1890, but the continued shower of silver into the Treasury in exchange for gold under the terms of the Sherman act was partly responsible for the panic of 1893. As a result, the Sherman act was repealed in that year.

The Gold Standard Act of 1900 definitely established the gold dollar as the American standard of value. All forms of money were redeemable in gold, and a fund of $150,000,000 was set up to redeem the Greenback and the Treasury notes of 1890.

Suspension of the Gold Coin Standard during World War I. The gold coin standard was suspended shortly after America's entry into World War I. The uncontrolled gold market was eliminated, and gold was not available freely for internal or export purposes. An opportunity to reduce outstanding silver certificates was offered the United States by the Pittman Act of 1918. This act authorized retirement of the silver-secured money whose backing had been sold to Britain for transshipment to India in payment for British purchases in that country. Federal reserve bank notes then replaced the retired silver certificates. However, the act also required certain purchases of silver from domestic mines as collateral for new silver certificates to replace the temporary federal reserve bank notes.

The Gold Coin Standard, 1919–1933. The United States returned to the gold coin standard in 1919. But the world-wide abandonment of this standard which had begun during World War I continued to prevail. There were several factors responsible for this monetary situation: (1) Trade restrictions paralyzed international commerce and made ineffective the automatic operation of the gold standard; price reductions in one nation, which ordinarily would follow gold exports and attract gold were offset by tariffs and quota restrictions imposed by other countries fearful of losing newly gained gold. (2) The wide adoption of the gold exchange standard in the 1920's minimized gold movements and further prevented the normal workings of the gold standard. (3) The gold exchange standard meant a concentration of gold reserves in nations on the gold coin and gold bullion standards. Such reserves could be withdrawn readily when the economic or political situation in the depository nations seemed unsound. (4) War debts and reparations payments, abetted by the American high tariff policy, meant a concentration of the yellow metal in the United States and an unstable type of gold standard abroad. Any unfortunate turn of events could easily drain off the meager gold reserves of other nations and threaten their gold standards. (5) The unequal distribution of the world's gold reserves meant a precarious type of international gold standard and encouraged the adoption of schemes to offset either a scarcity or a surplus of gold. (6) Overvaluation of the English currency made England an expensive market, reduced its exports, forced it off the gold standard, and weakened a strong advocate of the gold standard. (7) Trusts, cartels, trade associations, and labor unions were developed which controlled production and promoted a "sticky" price structure and so interfered with the price influence of the automatic gold standard.

These factors in the American economic picture added fuel to the flame: (1) Farm prices collapsed in 1920 and during the next decade continued at a low level. (2) Bank failures in the agricultural regions, resulting partly from the low price level, created uneasiness in domestic business and financial circles. (3) The stock market crash of 1929, and the downward plunge of American business activity accentuated the uneasiness.

Furthermore, when England, quickly followed by several other countries, abandoned the gold standard, rumor spread that the United States would follow suit. Financial panic spread throughout the nation—gold was exported in large quantities, withdrawn by Americans and hidden in their own bank vaults or homes, while bank failures were so large that bank holidays were declared in most states by March 4, 1933, when President Roosevelt took office. He declared a national bank holiday and suspended the gold coin standard.

THE MANAGED GOLD STANDARD, 1933 TO DATE

Since 1933 the United States has experienced monetary experimentation and management. The various governmental steps in this program are outlined below.

Emergency Banking Act of 1933. Through this act: (1) the government appropriated the nation's gold stock; (2) the Treasury, acting for the United States government in a new monetary role, was authorized to control the exportation of gold in coin, bullion, or certificate form; (3) the federal reserve banks were named the depositories of all gold coin, bullion, or certificates by May 1, 1933; (4) industrial firms were permitted to continue their use of gold, the government allowing limited possession of the yellow metal for industrial purposes; and (5) the issue of new federal reserve bank notes was authorized to strengthen the cash position of the banks faced with heavy withdrawals of deposits. The security for the note issue consisted 10 per cent of government bonds and 90 per cent of commercial paper. The authority for this note issue was terminated in 1945.

Thomas Inflation Amendment to the Agricultural Adjustment Act of 1933. This amendment: (1) allowed the government to devalue or reduce the gold content of the dollar by 50 per cent of 23.22 grains of gold—its metallic content on March 4, 1933; (2) authorized the President to fix the weight of the silver dollar at a definite ratio to the metallic content of the gold dollar and to provide for unlimited coinag of both silver and gold at this ratio; (3) gave the chief executive power to issue $3,000,000,000 of United States notes to help pay off the federal debt (a power revoked in 1945); (4) permitted foreign countries to pay off their war debts partly in silver if the President so ruled; (5) made all forms of money legal tender.

Elimination of the Gold Clause Obligation. Prior to 1933, debt contracts frequently provided that a debt be met in gold dollars of the weight and fineness at the time of the contract was written. On June 5, 1933, Congress ruled that such obligations need be paid off dollar for dollar in legal tender only. Since all moneys had been made legal tender, creditors could no longer demand gold.

Gold Devaluation. President Roosevelt adopted the monetary plan of Professor George F. Warren of Cornell University to raise commodity prices. Professor Warren believed the demand for gold had so outstripped its supply that the buying power of the metal and the value of the dollar based on it had increased in worth with a resultant price decline. The solution, Professor Warren claimed, called for a devaluation, lowering the buying power of the gold dollar and increasing prices. This devaluation was accomplished by raising the price of gold from $20.67 per fine ounce to $35. The number of gold grains in each dollar was thereby reduced from 23.22 to 13.714. This action was officially taken on January 31, 1934. However, the price level did not advance materially for some time.

The Gold Reserve Act of 1934. This act provided that: (1) the United States government become the legal owner of all gold and gold claims held by the federal reserve banks, the central banking and gold-holding organizations, the federal reserve banks being compensated at the old rate of $20.67 per ounce; (2) gold certificates paid over for the gold appropriated by the Treasury were to constitute reserves of the federal reserve banks; (3) devaluation of the dollar had to equal at least 60 per cent of the dollar's pre-1934 rate although the President could devalue the gold content of the dollar by 50 per cent of its old rate; (4) profit from the devaluation was to be allocated to the Treasury, $2,000,000,000 of which was designated for the stabilization of the dollar in international exchange; gold coins could no longer be circulated in the United States, nor could any currency of the United States be redeemed in gold, unless authorized by the Secretary of the Treasury with the approval of the President (a managed gold bullion standard was thus virtually established); (5) gold coins were to be melted down into gold bars.

SILVER LEGISLATION DURING THE 1930'S

Like the prices of all commodities, silver plunged downward in value so that in 1932 the ratio of silver to gold was 80 to 1.

Arguments Pro and Con Silver Legislation. Silver interests urged legislation to benefit the silver-mining industry on these grounds: (1) More money in circulation raises prices and helps hard pressed business and farm debtors. (2) Higher silver prices provide more employment since silver mines are reopened and create a greater demand for goods. (3) Far eastern countries, like China on a silver standard, have greater purchasing power as silver rises in value.

The answers to these arguments are as follows: (1) Improved business does not depend primarily upon an increased money supply. As business advances, it requires more money, but it does not get the initial impetus from a rise in the money supply. (2) The seven silver states have only a small population. A negligible number of jobs depend upon silver production. (3) A high price for silver drains far eastern nations of their silver reserves and weakens their economic structure. The major beneficiaries from a high silver price are silver-producing countries, not the users.

Silver Legislation. Nevertheless, silver legislation was on the New Deal agenda. In December, 1933, by virtue of his authority under the Thomas Inflation Amendment, the President directed the mint to purchase newly mined domestic silver at $1.29 a fine ounce, less a seigniorage charge of 50 per cent. The net result was a yield to the American silver interests of 64.4 cents for each ounce. In 1939, the government was authorized to purchase all domestically mined silver at 71.11 cents per fine ounce.

The Silver Purchase Act of 1934 ruled it to be the policy of the United States that the metallic reserves of the country consist of 25 per cent silver and 75 per cent gold. The Secretary of the Treasury was to buy both foreign and domestic silver at not more than $1.29 per ounce, with domestic stocks in the United States on May 1, 1934, being taken up at 50 cents per ounce, maximum. The mint could sell silver if its world price reached $1.29 per ounce, or if the value of the government's silver reserves exceeded 25 per cent of all its gold and silver reserves.

World War II forced the government to sell or lend for industrial purposes all its silver not needed for reserve purposes and to cease its accumulation of foreign silver. However, the United States Treasury had to hold the money value of silver equal to the face value of outstanding silver certificates. Silver sales were at no time to be made at less than 71.11 cents per fine ounce. But the return of peace found the Treasury directed to purchase domestically mined silver at 90.5 cents per fine ounce. Any silver in excess of reserve requirements for outstanding silver certificates could be sold at 91 cents a fine ounce.

REVIEW QUESTIONS

1. Why did bimetallism fail in the United States?
2. What provision of the Pittman Act of 1918 prevented the permanent reduction of outstanding silver certificates?
3. Explain how trade restrictions and cartels interfere with the automatic operation of the gold standard.
4. Why did American bank failures aggravate the gold breakdown of the early 1930's?
5. Why was gold devaluation urged by Professor Warren?
6. What type of gold standard has the United States today?
7. What was the purpose of the Silver Purchase Act of 1934?

⊠

The International Money System

An efficient money system is important to speed the flow of goods and services internationally. Each country has its own monetary unit—the United States, for example, employs the dollar, whereas Britain uses the pound sterling. What price do Americans pay for pounds when they are indebted to Englishmen, and what is the British price for dollars? Before we consider these questions, let us analyze the typical types of international transactions which result in international money exchange.

TYPES OF INTERNATIONAL TRANSACTIONS

Importing and Exporting. Since nations are interdependent, they import and export goods. The term *goods* covers the usual items like food-stuffs, clothing, industrial raw materials, industrial finished products, and precious metals like gold and silver.

Services. Similarly, the interdependence of nations requires the rendition of mutual services. Among these services are tourist accommodations, banking, insurance, and transportation.

Capital Items. Americans buy capital claims from foreigners just as the latter do from Americans. During the 1920's, American investors put billions of dollars into foreign securities, while the period of the Second World War witnessed additional acquisitions of foreign corporate and governmental securities. American corporations and private citizens own and have claims on huge amounts of industrial plants and equipment abroad. This trend was only a reversal of the situation prior to World War I when foreigners invested large sums in American industrial development and governmental securities. Such transactions are called capital transactions. They require that United States citizens use foreign moneys when they purchase foreign assets just as foreign citizens must use American dollars when they buy American assets.

THE BALANCE OF INTERNATIONAL PAYMENTS

Total exports and imports of goods, services, and capital items make up the balance of international payments of a nation. It differs from the balance of trade which consists only of imports and exports of goods. Since the balance of international payments of the United States implies a balance or equalization of foreign and American claims, a favorable balance of trade for the United States is counterbalanced by a flow of services and capital from the United States.

FOREIGN EXCHANGE RATES UNDER A GOLD STANDARD

Individuals, business organizations, and governments that engage in international trade realize that the balance of international payments will balance each year. But each party has separate foreign obligations to meet at various times during the year. These debts are payable usually in the domestic currency of the creditor. What determines the value of the creditor's currency in terms of the debtor's? Why do these foreign exchange rates—the price of one money in terms of another—fluctuate?

Mint Par of Exchange. Prior to the 1930's, international trade was conducted largely by nations operating on the gold standard. Since there was a fixed quantity of gold in different monetary units, the value of each currency unit in terms of any other could be determined by comparing their gold contents. Prior to 1931, the English pound was made up of 113.0015 grains of gold, while the dollar held 23.22 grains of the metal. Therefore, the mint par of exchange of the English pound in terms of the United States dollar was $4.8665.

Gold Points. Why do the rates of exchange of gold standard nations move above or below par? They deviate because the demand for a currency resulting from international transactions exceeds the supply growing out of international trade. How great a deviation from the par of exchange can occur? The cost of shipping gold determines the degree of deviation. The cost of shipment includes more than the charges for preparing the metal for shipment abroad, like carting, insuring, and weighing. It also includes the loss of interest while the metal is in transport and the profit of the bankers who handle the deal. In the case of the English pound, prior to 1931, these costs amounted in all to $.0225.

Therefore, the upper limit of fluctuation was $4.8890. This rate was called the *gold export point*. When the demand for British currency forced its value to this level, gold would be exported from the United States since it was as cheap to settle debts with the precious metal as it was to purchase British currency.

Gold would move to the United States from London when the demand for American dollars to meet international obligations forced up their price so that the English pound was quoted at $4.8465. In other words, the English pound had dropped in value relative to the American dollar and encouraged gold imports to the United States to settle international debts. The rate $4.8465 was known to Americans as the *gold import point*. The same costs of shipping gold apply in this situation as in computing the gold export point.

Gold Movements and International Equilibrium. Gold standard advocates maintain (1) that gold imports and exports readjust exchange rates and minimize gold shipments. The export of gold reduces the demand for foreign currencies and equalizes it with the supply of foreign moneys. They also maintain (2) that gold exports reduce a nation's gold reserves, decrease its supply of money and credit in circulation, force prices down, and make the gold exporting country an attractive market for purchases and business investment. Gold imports have the reverse effect upon the importing nation, making it a less attractive place for purchases and capital investment. The net result is an equalization of exports and imports. They believe (3) that trade restrictions, like tariffs, should be discouraged since they prevent a uniform international price level. Gold will not necessarily move to the cheaper markets, since high cost producers will protect their domestic markets by such devices and reduce imports.

FOREIGN EXCHANGE RATES UNDER A PAPER STANDARD

When nations abandon the gold standard and adopt fiat currency systems, there are no mint pars of exchange to serve as the basic values of moneys.

Purchasing Power Parity. How are international currency prices then determined? Exchange rates are fixed by purchasing power parities, the exchange rates at which the buying power of currencies is equalized internationally. For example, the old mint par of exchange of the British pound was $4.8665. What is the current dollar value of the English money, assuming no exchange control? It depends upon prices in England and in the United States. If the price index in the British Isles is 100, while the price index in the United States is only 50, the value of English currency in terms of dollars drops 50 per cent to offset the higher price level in England. The purchasing parity of the English pound then is $2.4338. At this rate the buying power of the dollar and the pound in both England and the United States are identical. It is computed as follows:

$$\frac{\text{price index number of the United States}}{\text{price index number of England}} \times \$4.8665.$$

An exchange rate above this level discourages American purchases in England and encourages British purchases in the United States. Such a development brings the exchange rate of the British pound into line with its purchasing parity.

Criticism of Purchasing Power Parity Theory. This view of foreign exchange rates is criticized on several scores: (1) A comparison of internal price levels of different countries means little if many of the items are not traded internationally. (2) International traders compare the prices of a good or service in different world markets rather than general price levels which have only academic significance to them. (3) A general price level index is misleading because divergent price movements of individual items may offset one another. (4) Trade obstacles, like tariffs, make international price comparisons difficult. (5) Since the close of the First World War, exchange rates have been influenced frequently by unstable political conditions and flights of capital.

TYPES OF FOREIGN EXCHANGE RATES AND CLAIMS

International business dealings require that debts growing out of them be settled ordinarily in the creditor's currency. Debtors purchase claims on foreign currencies through their banks to meet their international obligations.

The Banks and Foreign Exchange Claims. Banks own foreign exchange claims since they have deposits abroad with banking institutions against which they can draw bankers' bills. Exporters or other claimants to foreign funds sell their claims, called *commercial bills*, to banks.

Foreign Exchange Rates. The types of rates at which foreign exchange is bought and sold follow.

FREE RATE. This rate is determined by market forces without governmental control and interference. The price at which banks sell foreign exchange usually exceeds their buying rate and the difference constitutes their profit.

OFFICIAL RATE. The rate at which foreign exchange may be sold and bought according to governmental order.

SPOT RATE. The price at which claims to foreign exchange will be delivered immediately.

FORWARD RATE. The price at which claims to foreign exchange will be bought and sold for future delivery.

SIGHT RATE. The rate at which claims to foreign exchange will be sold if the instruments are payable immediately upon presentation to the parties upon which they are drawn.

CABLE RATE. The rate at which claims against a banker's balance abroad are sold. This rate is higher than the sight rate at which foreign exchange is sold by a bank because funds on deposit abroad are immediately withdrawn and are no longer available to the selling bank for investment as they would be if sold on a sight basis. The funds would then still be available to the seller while the sight draft is in transit.

TIME RATE. The price at which instruments, payable only after a certain period of time, are bought and sold.

MARKET RATE. The rate at which large amounts of foreign exchange are dealt in. This rate is usually lower than the over-the-counter rate.

OVER-THE-COUNTER RATE. The rate at which banks and foreign exchange dealers buy or sell small amounts of claims against foreigners from or to the general public.

FORWARD EXCHANGE

Stabilizing Influence. The effect of fluctuations in exchange rates may be overcome by foreign traders through forward exchange contracts—that is, agreements to buy and sell foreign exchange in the future. The banks providing the exchange protect themselves from exchange fluctuations in the following ways: (1) When foreign exchange is sold for delivery in the future, the danger of rate changes is offset by the purchase of similar exchange for delivery to the bank at the time it must comply with its forward selling contract. (2) If the forward sale cannot be offset by a forward purchase, the bank may buy spot exchange, invest the funds abroad, and thus be in a position to meet its forward sale commitment on the due date. (3) If a forward purchase cannot be matched by a forward sale, it may be counterbalanced by spot sales of balances held abroad. When the buyer of the forward exchange contract complies with its terms, the bank finds its foreign exchange balance restored to its former level.

Close Relation of Spot and Forward Rates. Spot rates and forward rates are always close to one another. If interest rates are high in the United States, relative to money costs elsewhere, businessmen and banks prefer to keep American currency and buy spot exchange to settle international obligations. The net effect of buying spot rather than forward exchange is to depress the value of forward exchange and raise the price of spot exchange. On the other hand, a low interest rate level in the United States encourages the purchase of forward exchange. Its price is raised, while the quotation on spot exchange drops as the demand decreases. If interest rates abroad are attractive, foreign banks sell forward exchange and buy spot exchange for investment purposes at high rates. When forward contracts mature, they sell the spot exchange, invest it abroad, and meet their forward obligations.

Exporters, believing that their claims can be discounted in the forward market only at an excessive figure, liquidate in the spot market, thus bringing spot and forward rates closer. Heavy purchases of forward exchange sold at a discount by banks and specu-lators drive up the price of forward exchange.

ARBITRAGE

Foreign exchange dealers profit by discrepancies in foreign exchange rates between two or more markets. An operation aimed at making such a profit is termed *arbitrage*. For example, the price of French francs in New York may rise above par, while the dollar rate in Paris remains at the par of exchange. A French dealer then buys francs in Paris with dollar exchange, while his agent sells French francs in New York at the high figure relative to the dollar. The sale of francs in New York is covered by the purchase of a corresponding number of francs in France. The difference between the purchase price and the sale price constitutes the profit on the transaction. The effect of this operation is to narrow and eliminate the discrepancy in rates between the American and French markets, for the sale of the French francs in New York depresses their value with the purchase of the francs in Paris raising their price.

CURRENCY DEPRECIATION

Advantage of Depreciation. England's abandonment of the gold standard in 1931, and the ensuing monetary chaos as one nation after another followed her example, brings up the question: what is the advantage of a depreciated currency? It temporarily stimulates exports, for the depreciated currency is a cheap unit in terms of other currencies. Assuming prices remain the same in the depreciator's markets, foreign exchange or foreign moneys have increased buying power there, and flow to that market in exchange for goods and services.

Disadvantages of Depreciation. (1) Currency depreciation by one nation encourages similar action by others who also seek to stimulate their sales abroad or at least to recapture their lost markets. (2) A competitive currency depreciation may easily become the rule and lead to international monetary chaos. (3) Currency depreciation may be offset by tariffs and trade agreements which block out the depreciator's goods from many markets. (4) Nations whose currencies have been depreciated increase their foreign debt burdens and ease the repayment problem of their foreign debtors. (5) The cost of goods purchased abroad rises and increases the domestic cost of living. (6) The price of home output is also on the rise, if only because depreciation increases the demand for goods turned out locally and forces up its price. (7) Similarly, the exchange rate of a depreciated currency may be pushed up by the attraction of a temporarily cheap money.

FOREIGN EXCHANGE CONTROL

The general breakdown of a stable system of international money during the 1930's led to foreign exchange control—governmental control over the international prices of monetary units.

TYPES OF CONTROL

Stabilization Funds. These funds sought to minimize government interference in the exchange markets and preserve the free exchange system.

When England abandoned the gold standard in 1931, it established the Exchange Equalization Account. Its purpose was to
maintain stable exchange and credit conditions and a sound domestic price level. For example, if pound sterling rose due to an inflow
of foreign capital, the Equalization Account used its funds, obtained by the sale of government securities, to buy foreign exchange and gold, thereby offsetting the advance in the price of
sterling. On the other hand, the foreign exchange and gold accumulations of the fund were sold to offset the depressing effect
on British exchange of an outflow of funds from England.

The Gold Reserve Act of 1934 created the American Stabilization Fund of $2,000,000,000 for the purchase of gold, foreign ex-
change, government securities, and such other credit instruments
as are considered necessary to stabilize the dollar. The great demand for American dollars during the 1930's, due to American political and economic stability as contrasted with conditions elsewhere, made unnecessary any great activity by the fund.

To create a focal point of exchange stability in the midst of
international monetary chaos, the United States, Great Britain,
and France signed the Tripartite Agreement in 1936. Each nation
agreed to sell gold at fixed prices to any stabilization fund, equalization fund, or central bank, if these latter were also willing to
sell it at fixed prices not to be changed unless twenty-four hours'
notice was first given. Thus, the dollar, the franc, and the pound
were moored to gold by fixing their gold prices. The tripartite
monetary accord was eventually joined by Switzerland, Holland,
Belgium, and the Bank for International Settlements.

When World War II opened in 1939, the Tripartite Agreement became of secondary importance as war considerations dominated the economic scene.

Direct Foreign Exchange Control. In this type of foreign exchange control governments direct operations in foreign exchange
and eliminate the free market. The techniques employed are:
(1) allocating foreign exchange according to the uses it serves
and the country which is able to make use of it; (2) centralization
of claims on foreigners by forcing exporters and owners of foreign
money claims to sell them to a government control organization
at a fixed price; (3) blocking the funds owed foreigners by means
of standstill agreements which prevent repayment of debts owed
abroad and require that the money be used by creditors for tourist

travel or purchases from the debtor. Frequently, creditors collect debts only in terms of the debtor's currency with the debtor's central bank serving as the clearing agent in these transactions.

Control of Foreign Trade. Foreign exchange at the disposal of a nation's citizens is regulated also by: (1) directly limiting the quantity or value of imports or indirectly controlling it by manipulating the foreign exchange price of a money; (2) licensing imports; (3) bilateral trade agreements with exporters in other countries or the governments of those countries; (4) barter agreements whereby goods are sold for goods rather than for money. The central bank holds the importers' funds which are then paid out to exporters in the same country.

REVIEW QUESTIONS

1. Why is the balance of international payments more significant than the balance of trade?
2. How are the gold points determined?
3. What is purchasing power parity?
4. Explain spot, forward, and cable rates of exchange.
5. What are the disadvantages of currency depreciation?
6. Explain three different techniques of foreign exchange control.

⊠

International Monetary Reorganization

World War II was in its last stages when forty-four nations met at Bretton Woods, New Hampshire, to establish: (1) a sound framework for postwar currencies and (2) a postwar international lending organization for reconstruction and development.

As noted in the previous chapter, monetary obstacles to world trade were: (1) currency depreciation; (2) foreign exchange and trade control; (3) a general lack of confidence in fiat money systems; (4) maldistribution of gold and its unavailability to debtor nations as a means of settling international obligations.

THE BRETTON WOODS AGREEMENTS

Under the terms of the Bretton Woods Agreements an International Monetary Fund and an International Bank for Reconstruction and Development were established.

Purposes. The purposes of the International Monetary Fund are: (1) restoration of an international trading system based on gold values for each member nation's currency; (2) modification of the gold values of currencies, as conditions warrant, to correct disequilibriums in international balances of payments; (3) fostering of international trade by a common pool of different gold standard moneys which serve as mediums of exchange in international dealings. This pool of moneys is used only when foreign exchange resources in private banking channels are exhausted.

The purposes of the International Bank for Reconstruction and Development are indicated in its name: (1) capital investment in productive projects contributing to the reconstruction and development of member nations; (2) stimulation of international trade through international loans.

Legal Organization. According to the Bretton Woods Agreements, both the fund and the bank were officially established in

December, 1945, for 80 per cent of the capital contributions or "quotas" had already been subscribed. Only 65 per cent of the capital of both institutions had to be subscribed.

INTERNATIONAL MONETARY FUND

How does the International Monetary Fund operate?

Capital. Each member nation contributes a quota of gold and domestic money based on its prewar national income and international trade position. The gold contribution must equal 25 per cent of a member's gold reserve or 10 per cent of its gold holdings and dollar balances, whichever is the smaller; the remainder of the contribution must be in domestic currency or nonnegotiable, noninterest-bearing notes payable at par on demand. If the situation calls for it, capital contributions of members may be changed after five years with their approval and that of the governors of the fund holding 80 per cent of the voting power.

In 1947 the total capital amounted to about $8,000,000,000. The United States, which has contributed over one-third of the capital and holds about one-third of the voting power in the fund, met its subscription to both the fund and the bank with $1,800,000,000 in the Exchange Stabilization Fund and by the sale of government securities and the use of other Treasury cash.

Management. The managers of this pool of money and gold are as follows:

THE BOARD OF GOVERNORS. This group is composed of single representatives from each of the member nations, appointed for five-year terms. The representatives meet annually and at such other times as five member countries or as many as hold 25 per cent of the total voting power request a meeting. A member nation may reappoint its delegate or remove its representative at its discretion. Each participant has 250 votes plus 1 vote for every $100,000 of its capital contribution. The Board of Governors completely controls the fund and a majority of the votes cast in most cases decides an issue.

EXECUTIVE DIRECTORS. There are twelve executive directors, five of whom are appointed by those member nations with the largest quotas, two by North and South American republics besides the United States, and five selected by the remaining members. These executive directors may be members of the Board of Governors if the nation or nations they represent so decide. Each director holds the votes of the member or members who appointed or elected him. All votes are cast as a unit by each director in his supervisory function. The number of executive directors can be increased by a vote of 80 per cent of the number of votes held by the Board of Governors.

MANAGING DIRECTOR. The managing director is selected by the executive directors and removable by them. He is chief of the fund's operating staff. While he may not be a governor or executive director, he is chairman of the executive directors and as such may cast a vote. He may also sit in with the Board of Governors, but in this role he does not vote.

Value of Currencies. Currency values are established as follows: (1) The par value of a member nation's currency is expressed in terms of gold or United States dollars. This can be changed if either the member nation or the fund holds it to be unsuitable. A new par value is then agreed on. If no value satisfactory to both parties is fixed, the member nation loses its member status. (2) The gold value of a member nation's currency is fixed by the declaration of the par value and by a limitation on the rates at which various types of foreign exchange can be bought and sold. (3) A change in the par value of a currency can result from a dis-equilibrium in a nation's balance of payments. If a country pro poses a change in the par value of not more than 10 per cent, the fund cannot object. However, any proposed change beyond 10 per cent must be approved by the fund with the Board of Governors casting a majority of all votes for the change. Members with 10 per cent or more of the capital subscriptions or quotas must give specific approval to the proposed change. If any change of more than 10 per cent is made over the objections of the fund, the member country becomes ineligible to use the fund and is liable to expulsion. A majority of the voting power in the Board of Governors is required to expel a member. (4) Like changes in the par values of all currencies may take place if the Board of Governors votes it by a majority of all votes cast, provided members holding 10 per cent or more of the total quotas also approve. However, a member can legitimately insist upon the maintenance of its old par value if it gives the fund seventy-two hours' notice. (The Bretton Woods Agreement Act of 1945 prohibits the President, or any other person or agency acting for the United States, to propose or agree to a modification of the United States dollar's par value or any world-wide change in the par values of all currencies without Congressional authorization.) (5) An increase in the par value of a currency necessitates a return to the member nation of an amount of currency equal to the rise in its gold value. Similarly, a decline in the par value calls for an increase in the currency contribution of the member nation.

Operation of the Fund. (1) The fund holds all types of currencies as a result of member nations' subscriptions to its capital or quota. (2) These currencies are bought and sold by the fund at established par values. Thus, dollar holdings of the fund are sold for pounds and vice versa. The net result is an increase in the moneys the fund buys and a decrease in those it sells. Only if the purchasers were to pay for foreign currencies in gold would there be no increase in the fund's holdings of the buyer's moneys. (3) During any one year a member cannot purchase foreign currencies as to increase the fund's portfolio of the buyer's money by over 25 per cent of the member's quota if the fund already holds 75 per cent of the member's quota. (4) At no time can the fund hold any one currency beyond 200 per cent of the quota. (5) These limitations on the use of the fund may be suspended, particularly if a member does not make constant and active use of it. (6) The fund may rebuild its supply of a scarce currency by borrowing or buying it with gold. In extreme circumstances, it may ration its shrinking supply of a money. The fund may recommend steps to prevent a continued drainage of a scarce money and may permit member nations to regulate transactions so as to protect its small supply. (The United States Congress has forbidden its delegates to declare the dollar a scarce currency without the previous approval of the Advisory Council on International Monetary and Financial Problems.) (7) The fund cannot be used to facilitate large capital movements. This rule is mitigated by the proviso that a currency can be purchased from the fund for capital transfers if the fund's holdings of the buyer's currency have been under 75 per cent of its quota for at least six months, and until the fund's holdings of the currencies to be purchased and sold reach 75 per cent of their quotas. (8) Exchange restrictions may be continued and elaborated during the period when the country is re-establishing a strong peacetime economy if the fund is notified. These restrictions must be removed when the fund deems it expedient. Otherwise the member nation may be dropped from the membership list.

This last action can only be taken by a vote of those members of the Board of Governors who hold a majority of the voting power. (9) At the close of each fiscal year, member nations repurchase such amounts of the fund's accumulation of their currencies as appears consistent with the year's increase in the fund's currency holdings and alterations in the reserve position of the members. Members also agree to repurchase their currencies held by other members if the holdings grew out of current trading operations and will facilitate payments on current account. Such purchases must be in gold or in the currencies of the nations selling the money. (10) Multiple currency arrangements or discriminations in currency transactions between nations are forbidden unless authorized either in the Bretton Woods Agreement or by the fund through a majority vote of the Board of Governors.

Advantages of the Fund. (1) The establishment of international trade equilibrium will minimize disturbing gold movements. (2) Assuming the automatic operation of the gold standard, the internal money policies of each member nation can be developed without fear of gold losses with their inevitable disturbing internal influences. (3) International trade equilibrium will promote international trade, for there will be little fear of changes in the values of currencies. Even if changes do occur, they will be limited in amount. Currency warfare will be a thing of the past. (4) High prices at home and a loss of foreign trade can be offset by changes in the par value of a money. (5) A nation's monetary reserves can be expanded by borrowing from the fund. Furthermore, the money value of a country's gold stock can be increased by fixing a lower gold value for its money unit.

Disadvantages of the Fund. (1) The attempt at currency rehabilitation may not be successful because it has not been preceded by economic rehabilitation. Since the end of World War II, the productive power of wartorn Europe and Asia has been at a low ebb. They cannot produce for themselves, much less export abroad. (2) What are the values of the currencies of war-ravaged areas? They depend upon costs of production, gold reserves, and the international price level. Until such factors are more clearly understood, fixing a nominal value for a currency will not invest it with a true value. (3) Under these conditions, the United States will be the market for world purchases. Nations will dump their paper currencies into the fund in exchange for sorely needed dol-

lars. Eventually, the fund will be made up of paper money of uncertain value. (4) Currency depreciation and monetary chaos will
quickly follow when the fund is confronted with demands for
changes in the par values of moneys within the 10 per cent limit
and as international distrust sets in because the fund is based
on shifting money values.

THE INTERNATIONAL BANK FOR RECONSTRUCTION
AND DEVELOPMENT

The International Bank finances or facilitates the financing of
capital investment in member nations and stimulates international
trade. How does the bank operate?

Capital. The authorized capital stock is $10,000,000,000 of cur-
rent American money. By May, 1947, more than $8,000,000,000
had been subscribed by forty-four nations, which must be members of the International Monetary Fund.

The bank's capital is divided into two parts: (1) a "loan fund"
made up of 20 per cent of all contributions; (2) a "guaranty
fund" of 80 per cent of the subscriptions, designed to protect the
bank's creditors. By May, 1947, 20 per cent of the "loan fund"
subscriptions had been called for payment, the "guaranty fund"
being callable only if needed to meet the bank's commitments.
Two per cent of the "loan fund" is payable in gold or United States
dollars; the remainder is payable in the currencies of the member
nations and cannot be used in loan operations to purchase other
currencies without the consent of the members making the contributions. Repayment of this remainder plus interest must be in
the currencies of the contributing nations, unless they consent
to another type of settlement. Thus, the immediately available, un-
encumbered "loan fund" is only 2 per cent of the total capital
subscription.

Bank Borrowings. But this subscription is intended to be only
a small part of the bank's total "loan fund." It is supplemented
many times over by borrowings from private investors in exchange
for the bank's bonds. However, the country in whose security-issue
markets the bonds are sold must consent to their sale. There are
no restrictions on the uses to which the borrowed loan capital can
be put.

Direct Loans, Participations, and Guaranties. There are three
types of commitments the bank may make: (1) direct loans out

of its own funds or borrowed capital; (2) participating loans with other lenders; (3) the guaranty of loans made by private investors through regular investment organizations.

These different types of commitments may be made only if the bank believes a borrower could not obtain financial assistance otherwise.

Borrowers. The borrowers may be member nations, political subdivisions thereof, and private business enterprises in the member nations. In the case of the latter, the bank is guaranteed against loss by the member nation, its central bank, or any other organization acceptable to the bank. Naturally, the borrower seeks to obtain currencies which it can spend easily. Thus, if England wants to buy goods in the United States with the proceeds of a loan, it will receive dollars from the bank.

Limitations on Lending Power. There are two types of limitations: (1) all loans and participations must not exceed the bank's paid-in capital, surplus, reserves, and borrowings; (2) loans, participations, and guaranties must not exceed the unimpaired subscribed capital, surplus, and reserves.

Analysis of Loan Applications. Loans will be approved if: (1) the borrower is a good risk; (2) he can obtain sufficient foreign exchange to discharge his obligations; (3) the security market in which the loan will be sold is receptive; (4) the loan is productive in the light of the borrower's and its neighbors' conditions (productivity depending largely on the loan's uses).

Management. The management of the bank is vested in: (1) a board of governors made up of a representative from each member nation; (2) an advisory council of at least seven people representing banking concerns, industry, agriculture, and labor, selected by the board of governors; (3) twelve executive directors who act for the board of governors, except in the case of membership, expulsion, and capital changes; (4) the president and his staff who conduct the daily affairs of the institution.

The executive directors are appointed by the member nations with the largest capital subscriptions, while the others are chosen by the governors representing the other members. The president is chairman of the executive directors.

Advantages. International investment is necessary to rehabilitate the war-devastated countries. Such investment must be government sponsored, since private capital, especially in the United

States, where people remember lending experiences after World War I, is wary of any international commitments.

Disadvantages. (1) Member nations may paralyze the objectives of the bank, rejecting loan proposals out of their own currency subscriptions or out of moneys borrowed in their capital markets. Furthermore, a member nation may kill off a suggested guaranty loan if the funds are obtained from its citizens. (2) The bank's loan program may be hampered by American trade and tariff policy. The bulk of the bank's borrowings will be in the United States capital market. Repayment to the American investor can be facilitated only if the United States readily admits foreign goods and services. Will American industry and labor approve such a policy?

PRE-BRETTON WOODS ORGANIZATIONS

The monetary and banking organizations conceived at Bretton Woods were preceded by two other internationally significant governmental organizations.

Bank for International Settlements. In 1930, the Bank for International Settlements was organized to: (1) facilitate international transactions; (2) further central bank co-operation; (3) collect and transmit German reparations to the creditors.

Its major function, being trustee and reparations agent, was ended by the Hoover international debt moratorium of 1931. At that time, it also ceased making loans to enable nations to adhere to the gold standard. During World War II, when Europe was under the domination of Germany and her satellites, the Bank for International Settlements ceased to play a role in the thinking of American and British banking authorities.

Export-Import Bank. This bank was organized in 1934 to facilitate export trade with Soviet Russia. Now it makes loans and guarantees credit grants to develop the foreign trade of the United States with all countries. In these ways private capital is encouraged while competition with it is avoided. Loans and guaranties are considered in the light of their ultimate repayment. Credits outstanding at any time cannot exceed three and a half times the bank's authorized capital of $1,000,000,000.

A tie-up with the International Bank for Reconstruction and Development exists through the National Advisory Council on International Monetary and Financial Problems. This council coordinates the long-term loan activities of the Export-Import Bank with those of the World Bank.

REVIEW QUESTIONS

1. What are three purposes of the International Monetary Fund?
2. Explain how a member nation may use the International Monetary Fund.
3. List and explain three advantages of the International Monetary Fund.
4. What criticisms can be made of the International Monetary Fund?
5. What is the major source of lending power of the International Bank for Reconstruction and Development?
6. What three types of international commitments may the World Bank make?
7. What is the function of the Export-Import Bank?

☒

CHAPTER SIX

Credit and Credit Institutions

The layman ordinarily thinks that paper money and hard coin are the chief mediums of exchange in the United States. But this is not the case.

The major medium of exchange is the bank check or draft usually drawn against credits set up for individuals, business organizations, and governments by banking institutions. Bank credit has a counterpart—business credit, extended by one business organization to another. America is truly a credit economy.

CREDIT AS A MEDIUM OF EXCHANGE

What Is Credit? It is the sale of goods, services, and money claims in the present in exchange for a promise to pay (usually in money) in the future. The debtor and creditor can agree, of course, to settle their transaction in something else of value—for example, stocks and bonds.

Who Wants Credit and Why? (1) Business organizations seek credit for long-term, fixed or investment capital purposes (like the expansion of plant and equipment) or for short-term, working or commercial capital purposes (for example, to increase the volume of current productive operations). Neither investment nor commercial credit would be sought and granted unless the borrowers and lenders believed it productive credit—that it would be repaid and have yielded a profit to all parties. (2) Local, state, and federal governments seek to borrow on their public credit when tax receipts are inadequate to meet current expenses or pay off maturing security issues. The issue of unsecured or partially covered legal tender paper money is a type of forced loan if the public must accept the government note for goods and services to the government. During World War II, the United States government in-

47

creased its outstanding obligations sharply. The buying power it obtained was unproductive credit, largely used for defensive purposes and not yielding an increased supply of civilian goods. In the 1930's, the government borrowed, largely for investment or capital projects to stimulate business activity. Its borrowings were intended to yield the community social benefits. (3) Individuals seek investment credit for home building. They hope their income over the years will enable repayment of their mortgage obligations. Lacking the necessary funds, people may also seek consumption credit to buy consumer goods like vacuum cleaners and refrigerators on the installment plan. The retailer selling these commodities receives only a down payment and extends intermediate retail credit for the remainder, which the seller hopes will be repaid within an agreed upon time. Such credit is also extended when people make daily purchases in local stores, settling on a weekly or monthly basis. (4) Individuals and business organizations use speculative credit when they seek to profit within a short time from anticipated price changes. Stock market operators are speculative credit borrowers. (5) Banks selling stock and accepting deposits become their stockholders' and depositors' debtors.

Credit Maturity. (1) Short-term credit runs usually for less than one year; (2) intermediate credit is granted ordinarily for from one to five years; (3) long-term credit matures in more than five years.

The Bases of Credit. The factors determining an applicant's credit position are as follows:

CHARACTER. Has he repaid his past debts? Is his personal and business reputation good? In the case of a government, are its officials cognizant of their responsibilities and have they discharged them? The character of bank management can be judged by the community standing of its officers and their readiness to meet their responsibilities.

CAPACITY. The balance sheet and profit and loss statement of a business enterprise, or the development of a country's natural resources plus a consideration of its budgetary and debt position are the tests of business or governmental capacity.

CAPITAL. How much money does the credit seeker have invested in his own business? Will the banker become virtually the chief capital contributor as a result of the loan? If so, the risk is not desirable, for lenders who intend to be merely creditors should not have the major financial stake in a business. Otherwise, they are the business and owe the money to themselves.

When the requirements of character, capacity, and capital are met, an unsecured loan may be granted. Only the best risks can obtain such loans.

COLLATERAL. Readily marketable assets are pledged when a creditor questions the credit standing of a would-be debtor. The loan is thus secured satisfactorily. Otherwise, the creditor may find he is holding a frozen or worthless asset. The most marketable collateral is traded on regularly organized exchanges which permits the creditor to sell it easily at a fair value. If the liquidated collateral does not cover a debtor's obligation, he is liable for the unpaid debt. If the collateral yields more than the indebtedness, the borrower receives this surplus. When a default occurs on an unsecured loan, all unsecured creditors, including banks, are general creditors.

COSIGNERS. If the borrower's business position and his collateral are insufficient to meet the creditor's requirements, the latter may still be satisfied by indorsements of one or more parties of sound financial rating.

INVESTMENT CREDIT INSTRUMENTS

Stock Certificates. Stock certificates, legally speaking, are evidence of ownership in a business enterprise. Practically, they are obligations of the issuer. Stock buyers, purchasing such claims or rights to an issuer's assets, believe the corporate shares will earn and pay an attractive dividend. The business management also desires to earn and pay large dividends. Poor earnings and small dividends reduce an issuer's credit prestige.

Stock certificates are sold for cash, services, or property considered equal in value to the par or stated value of the stock. If stock is not fully paid for, a holder can be assessed for the unpaid amount. Not all issued stock certificates remain outstanding. Stock donated to the corporation or purchased out of its surplus is called treasury stock.

PREFERRED STOCK. This stock is preferred as to: (1) a fixed earning rate; (2) assets in the event of liquidation. Since such stock has a preferred position, it usually lacks voting rights and has limited earning power.

Preferred stock may be cumulative or noncumulative, participating or nonparticipating; it may be both cumulative and participating. If it is cumulative, stockholders will receive all dividends owed, both past unpaid and current, before common stockholders receive any return; if it is participating, stockholders will share with the common stockholders in the remaining earnings after both have received stipulated returns depending upon the provisions of the stock issues.

COMMON STOCK.   This stock represents a claim on earnings and assets, after creditors and preferred stockholders have been satisfied.

Bonds.   These corporate and governmental obligations, issued ordinarily in $500 and $1,000 denominations, require payment of interest annually or semiannually and repayment of principal at maturity. Bonds may be classified according to security, method of redemption, or special features: (1) *Debenture bonds* are unsecured obligations issued ordinarily by the best governmental and business risks. (2) *Mortgage bonds* are secured by liens on specific pieces of property. An issuer may emit additional bonds beyond the amount of an initial issue if the mortgage is "open-end," permitting successive issues, all secured by the same liens. An "after-acquired" clause requires an issuer to add subsequently acquired property to the collateral. A "closed" mortgage prohibits additional emissions beyond the original issue but may contain the "after-acquired" clause. (3) *Collateral trust bonds* are usually issued by investment trusts and holding companies pledging other securities as collateral for these debts. (4) *Convertible bonds* give holders the privilege of exchanging their claims for stock certificates. (5) *Callable bonds* vest an issuer with authority to redeem them by calling in the security before the due date. (6) *Serial bonds* require issuers to redeem portions of bonded debt at specified periods. (7) *Sinking fund bonds* are redeemed out of a fund built up during the life of an issue for this particular purpose. (8) *Refunding bonds* refinance an outstanding issue falling due or called by an issuer. (9) *Savings bonds* were sold by the United States government, as early as 1935, to help finance budgetary deficits with the small man's savings. During World War II, and in the reconversion period, the objective has been to fight inflation by drawing purchasing power from circulation. Unlike most governmental and corporate bond issues, United States government savings bonds generally do not yield a fixed interest rate but appreciate in value during their life so that the return to the owner increases with his retention of the issue. The savings bonds have been sold for as little as $18.75.

Long-Term Notes. They are secured or unsecured obligations, usually maturing within ten years, and evidencing privately arranged or publicly sold "term" loans, to increase net working capital, refinance old debt, or reorganize and rearrange capital structures. On occasion, the money is used for plant expansion.

Commercial bank "term" loan financing during the 1930's developed because of: (1) the stagnant capital market of the early 1930's, especially for medium size and small borrowers; (2) the growth of intermediate credit grants by the Reconstruction Finance Corporation and the federal reserve banks in co-operation with commercial banks; (3) the unwillingness of business to run the risk of nonrenewable short-term loans; (4) the expenses and penalties of the Securities Act of 1933 discouraging borrowers from seeking intermediate private credit; (5) the low level of bank interest rates after 1929 encouraging such loans for debt and preferred stock retirement; (6) high taxes and high labor costs encouraging such bank loans to meet expenses and reduce wage obligations by substituting therefor less expensive fixed equipment; (7) the more lenient attitude toward long-term loans by bank examiners and the opening up of federal reserve bank rediscount facilities to paper representing such loans.

COMMERCIAL CREDIT INSTRUMENTS

Open-Book Accounts. They are the simplest type of commercial credits. Business creditors enter their customers' obligations on their books. Banks evidence their obligations to depositors by book credits on their own ledgers and in depositors' bankbooks.

Business debtors usually enjoy the privilege of discharging debts prior to maturity. If payment is made within ten days the debtor has a smaller obligation to meet than if he paid at maturity.

Promissory Notes. These notes are unconditional, secured or unsecured, written promises by a maker to a payee, agreeing to pay on demand, or after a short time, a specified sum of money. They usually bear interest, and more than one party may be liable on an instrument.

Promissory notes usually are discounted at commercial banks in exchange for short-term loans or turned over to businessmen in exchange for goods and services to be paid for in the near future. Short-term loans are used to secure working capital convertible into finished goods salable at a high enough price to pay off the loans and yield profit. Such loans are called self-liquidating since they provide borrowers with the means of liquidating obligations.

Bills of Exchange. A drawer directs an unconditional order in writing to a drawee directing him to pay on demand or at some future time a sum of money to order or to bearer.

Sight bills are payable on demand, while time bills are payable at a fixed or determinable future time. Domestic bills are drawn and payable within one country, as against inland bills drawn and payable within a single state of the United States and foreign bills arising out of trade transactions between parties in different countries. Bankers' bills are drawn by banks, on banks; commercial bills, by people or business concerns on banks; and trade bills are drawn by people or business enterprises on nonbanking organizations.

Trade and commercial bills finance commerce. Bankers' bills are often purchased for investment because of their excellent rating.

Acceptances grow out of time bills of exchange accepted in writing by debtors. They pay the drawers or the parties specified as payees on the due dates. If a bank accepts an instrument, it is known as a banker's acceptance. If a nonbanking organization accepts the liability, the bill is known as a trade acceptance.

Collateral Credit Instruments. They may serve as the basis of short-term credits, just as long-term credit instruments may require collateral to be marketed. The short-term collateral instruments are as follows:

Bills of Lading. Issued by railroads and steamship companies, they give the holders or parties named therein the right to claim goods transported by these carriers. When goods are transported from one country to another, bills of lading are ordinarily attached to the bills of exchange. They are released to the drawees upon discharge of their obligations. The money owed the sellers for the merchandise is frequently paid off out of bank loans on warehouse receipts evidencing the obligations of warehousemen to release goods upon their presentation.

Trust Receipts. These give banks a first lien on goods released to debtors who are then in a position to sell the goods and reimburse the banks.

NEGOTIABILITY, INDORSEMENT, AND PRESENTMENT

Negotiability. Credit instruments are negotiable by indorsement and delivery or merely by delivery. The new owner has a clear title if he gives adequate consideration for the instrument and believes there is no defect in his title.

The conditions of negotiability are: (1) a written instrument signed by the maker or drawer; (2) an unconditional promise or order to pay a definite sum of money on demand or at some future time; (3) a clause making the instrument payable to order or to bearer; (4) a naming of the drawee.

Indorsement. An indorsement is necessary if a credit instrument is a promise to pay to a specified party or is an order to pay to such a party. A special indorsement requires the signature of the party specified. A qualified indorsement carries the words "without recourse." A blank indorsement does not name any indorsee, whereas a conditional indorsement requires the occurrence of a particular set of circumstances.

Presentment. When a maker or drawee is presented with his obligation, presentment takes place. If the maker or the drawee who has accepted an obligation fails to pay or accept, he dishonors his obligation. If a debtor does not reside in the same state, the creditor must protest to hold the indorsers liable. If the debtor lives in the same state, a protest may be filed. A creditor protests his claim by a formal statement to the maker, drawee, and indorsers.

ADVANTAGES AND DISADVANTAGES OF CREDIT

Advantages. The credit system benefits both society and individuals for: (1) idle goods and services are transferred from creditors to debtors and put to work increasing business and national income; (2) specialization and division of labor are stimulated by a ready flow of goods and services from creditor to debtor; (3) consumptive credit broadens industry's market, increases production, and so helps reduce costs and raise the general living standard.

Disadvantages. There are many disadvantages of credit, however: (1) Future income may be so mortgaged by present purchases that the future market is narrowed or must be aided by constantly growing credit accommodations. (2) An overexpansion of credit and apparent prosperity may only be followed by a sharp deflation.

(3) Banking and business creditors may find their assets frozen when the business situation slumps. (4) Speculative credit is unproductive for it does not increase the community's supply of goods and services. (5) Short-term credit may be unwisely used for long-term purposes. During the 1920's, German banks borrowed abroad on short-term and then used the funds in long-term domestic commitments. When the short-term loans were called, the banks could not satisfy their creditors, resulting in the German standstill agreements.

CREDIT-GRANTING INSTITUTIONS

Banks grant credit to individuals, business organizations, and governments.

Commercial Banks. Using their deposits and stockholders' capital contributions, they grant credit to desirable applicants. This credit may be long-term or short-term, although the original concept included only short-term loans.

Savings Banks. On the basis of savings deposits they lend to their customers—usually for long-term investment purposes.

Investment Banks. They provide long-term credit to corporations and governments by selling their securities to the community's savers.

Consumer Credit Institutions. Such institutions as industrial banks, credit unions, personal finance companies, and installment finance companies lend their resources, obtained by the receipt of deposits, the sale of stock, or borrowings, on an intermediate credit basis to individuals who wish to purchase goods and services beyond their immediate personal income and savings.

Mortgage Banks. They finance the purchase of real estate in both city and farm areas with long-term and intermediate loans.

Department-store banking is typical of many banking organizations which engage in more than one lending activity and have a diversified portfolio.

REVIEW QUESTIONS

1. Distinguish between an investment capital purpose and a commercial capital purpose.
2. What five factors determine an applicant's credit position?
3. How do debenture bonds differ from mortgage bonds and collateral trust obligations? What is a sinking fund?

4. List and explain three different types of bills of exchange.
5. What are the conditions of negotiability of credit instruments?
6. How does the credit system contribute to an improved community living standard?
7. What are the dangers of a credit system?

Commercial Banking—Organization and Internal Management

The organization and management of commercial banks are of public concern since banks are business financiers and depositories of the public's funds. Bank failures, like those of the 1921–1933 era, cripple a bank's credit-granting powers, wipe out a good percentage of depositors' claims, and hamper economic development.

COMMERCIAL BANKING ORGANIZATION

"Free Banking" and a Dual Banking System. Prior to the late 1830's, legislative authority was necessary to open a state commercial bank. Graft and favoritism marked such procedure. Thereafter, state officials were appointed to charter banks if they complied with capital and other official minimum statutory requirements. The National Bank Act of 1863 vested the Comptroller of the Currency with authority to charter national banks.

Thus, a dual "free banking" system was set up—state authorities issuing charters to state banks and one federal authority supervising the federally organized banks.

Organization Procedure. National bank organization is typical of the procedure: (1) The organizers notify the Comptroller of the Currency of their intent, giving the name of the proposed institution and the city in which it will be located. The name must contain the word "national." (2) If the name is approved, the organizers are provided blank forms calling for the name, place, capital and surplus, and the cost of building or renting a place of business. The amount to be invested in the building cannot exceed paid-in capital unless the Comptroller allows a larger investment. This application must be signed by at least five people whose financial interest in the institution and whose banking and business experience are indicated. Three local governmental officials must also put their name to the application. (3) An examiner from the Comptroller's office reports on the need for a proposed bank, the likelihood of success, and the standing of the organizers and probable officers. Information is also provided by such co-operating banking agencies as the district federal reserve bank, the Federal Deposit Insurance Corporation, and the state banking organization. (4) When the Comptroller approves the application for a charter, the bank's stock is offered for sale at a price yielding the necessary capital and a surplus equal to at least 20 per cent of the capital. The shares must have a par value of not over $100, one-half paid in cash prior to the opening and the remainder within six months of the organization certificate's receipt. (5) Articles of association, prepared after the stock is sold, and filed with the Comptroller of the Currency become the bank charter. (6) An organization certificate indicating the capitalization, number of shares, names and addresses of shareholders, and the amount held by each is also filed with the Comptroller. (7) Stockholders elect directors who must be stockholders. If the bank's capital exceeds $50,000, each director must own at least $2,500 of stock. A national bank must have five and may have twenty-five directors. They are chosen for one year and are eligible for re-election if they live within the state or district where the bank is located or at least within fifty miles of it if they reside outside the state or district. Each shareholder may cast as many votes as he has shares times the number of directors to be chosen. Thus, provision is made for possible minority representation. (8) Directors, representing the community's leading business interests, choose the bank's officers and adopt bylaws which, along with the articles of association, determine the conduct of affairs. (9) Directors and officers determine loan and investment policy and are liable for losses resulting from evasion and neglect of their responsibilities. Shareholders may sue them to recover losses, and certain law violations make them liable to criminal penalties. (10) The Comptroller authorizes the opening of the bank by the issue of a certificate of authority. (11) A national bank must be a member of the Federal Reserve System. Therefore, the bank applies for stock in the district federal reserve bank.

National Bank Capitalization. The minimum capitalization of banks organized under national law varies with a city's population. Thus, the capital position is adjusted to business needs. Minimum capital requirements call for: (1) at least $50,000 in cities of less than six thousand population; (2) at least $100,000 in cities of six thousand to fifty thousand population; (3) at least $200,000 in cities of more than fifty thousand people. However, the Comptroller may allow a bank to issue only $100,000 of capital stock, if state-chartered banks in the same place are permitted to open with no more than this amount. National banks organized before 1933 and located in towns of less than three thousand population have been permitted to continue operations with only $25,000 capital, the legal minimum before 1933.

National Bank Surplus.   It must amount to at least 20 per cent of the capital stock at the time of organization and is provided through the sale of stock at a premium. The initial surplus covers organization expenses and losses that may be suffered during a bank's early life.

State Bank Capitalization.   State law generally permits banks to be organized under state jurisdiction with a smaller capital requirement than for national banks. The usual minimum is $25,000.

Preferred Stock.   The demoralized banking situation in 1933 resulted in the Emergency Banking Act of March 9, 1933, allowing national banks to issue 6 per cent cumulative preferred stock, preferred as to assets in the event of liquidation, and with such voting powers as the Comptroller fixed. This stock did not carry double liability. The Secretary of the Treasury was directed to ask the Reconstruction Finance Corporation, a government financial rescue agency during the early days of the depression, to purchase or lend on this preferred stock if a bank needed capital, such stock to be redeemed out of a retirement fund.

The issue of preferred stock in exchange for depositors' claims against depression-weakened institutions bulwarked the banking structure.

Double Liability.   Prior to 1933, bank stock generally carried a double liability obligation. However, attempts to collect the par value of their stock from failed bank stockholders were not productive, for these debtors, hard hit by depression losses, were unable to meet their obligations as the Great Depression deepened. So-called "protection" for bank creditors did not materialize when most needed.

Double liability was thus eliminated: (1) The Banking Act of 1933 held holders of national bank stock, issued after June 16, 1933, not subject to double liability. (2) The Banking Act of 1935 ended double liability on or after July 1, 1937, for all national bank stock issued before 1933 provided six months' notice was given to the local community. (3) Local legislatures eliminated state bank stock double liability for the most part. SUBSTITUTE FOR DOUBLE LIABILITY. But a public responsibility to protect depositors' funds was shown in 1935 when the federal government required a national bank to have a paid-in surplus equal to 20 per cent of capital in addition to allocating to surplus semiannually, before dividends are paid, one-tenth of its net profits until the surplus equals outstanding common stock.

BANK MANAGEMENT

President. The president is chosen by the directors and is a director, re-elected annually. Conversant with local business and credit conditions, his major task, in consultation with his vice-presidents, is lending his bank's funds and credit to the community's businessmen in line with the policy set down by the board of directors. Small loans are granted without deferment to the directors' opinions, but large loans are passed upon by the loan and discount committee of the board of directors.

The president is assisted by credit officers who analyze applicants' requests with the final decision resting with the president, other chief officers, and the loan and discount committee.

A small-town bank may have only an honorary or part-time president, usually one of the community's leading businessmen. If this is the case, the actual daily operations of the bank are supervised by another official, customarily called a vice-president or cashier, a hired executive.

Chairman of the Board. When the president finds his duties too burdensome to carry alone, two chief executive officers may help guide the destinies of the institution. Comparable to the president is the chairman of the board.

Vice-president. In a large city institution there are several vice-presidents, each in charge of a bank division serving a major industry with which he is thoroughly familiar or supervising specialized areas of operation like investments or consumer loans. Other vice-presidents may be in charge of bank branches.

Cashier. He combines the functions of the secretary, the treasurer, and the chief clerk in a small bank. As secretary, his chief function is that of preparing the bank's reports and making a record of the directors' meetings. As treasurer, he oversees the bank's assets. As chief clerk, he controls the bank's internal affairs.

Tellers. They receive deposits and pay them out. There are other tellers, like the note teller, whose functions are explained by their titles.

UNIT, BRANCH, AND GROUP BANKING

Unit Banking. The typical American bank is the local unit bank, an independent institution organized under federal or state law. There are thousands of unit banks in the United States.

HISTORICAL BASIS. Unit banking is typical for at least two reasons: (1) Our system of government is a dual system, with both federal and state administrative organizations vested with the power to charter banks. Regional and state feeling is high, with each administrative organization jealous of its power and resenting any curtailment of its authority. Bank chartering powers have been closely guarded, and banks organized in one state have not been permitted to operate in other states. (2) The prevalent fear of a money trust has worked against the concentration of banking power in a few hands.

Branch Banking. Economic circumstances have led to a modification of the national and state banking laws to permit a degree of branch banking in the United States.

A branch bank is an individual bank with city or state-wide branches controlled by the home office.

GROWTH OF BRANCH BANKING. (1) California authorized state-wide branch banking in 1909. (2) The federal government admitted state banks to the national banking system or the Federal Reserve System in 1918 even though they had branches; however, no new branches could be established. (3) In 1922, the Comptroller of the Currency allowed national banks to establish banking offices to receive and pay out deposits if the local state law did not prohibit this activity for state banks. (4) The McFadden Act of 1927 allowed national banks to set up branches in city limits where the home office was located, if state-chartered banks had the same privilege. Newly admitted state member banks of the Federal Reserve System could continue branches in operation on February 25, 1927, but were forbidden to set up new branches. (5) The 1927 legislation allowed national banks to maintain legally approved branches as well as branches not legally sanctioned if they had been established twenty-five years or more. (6) The Banking Acts of 1933 and 1935 allow national banks to establish state-wide branches if the local state law permitted such branch banking to state-chartered institutions. National banks can organize branches only to the same extent as the state banks. Generally speaking, national and state member banks must have at least $500,000 capital to establish branches outside the home-office city. The capital of these banks and their branches must at least equal the capital required if each branch and home office were an independent entity. (7) The Board of Governors of the Federal Reserve System must approve new branches of state member banks outside their home cities and the maintenance of branches set up after February 25, 1927, beyond the home city. Similarly, nonmember banks must obtain the approval of the Federal Deposit Insurance Corporation to establish new branches or change their location. (8) State law usually provides for branches if a community is not already served by adequate banking facilities. (9) The Federal Reserve Act of 1913 authorized foreign branches for national banks with a capital and surplus of at least $1,000,000. In 1916, national banks were allowed to invest up to 10 per cent of their capital and surplus in foreign banking subsidiaries. They are regulated by the Board of Governors of the Federal Reserve System.

ARGUMENTS PRO AND CON BRANCH BANKING. These advantages can be listed in favor of branch banking: (1) The growing size of American business requires the services of large, soundly managed banks. (2) Banking facilities are more plentiful and accessible. (3) The larger the bank, the more numerous its services. (4) A strong banking system is promoted by a diversity of loans and investments. (5) Small-town personal favoritism and antagonisms are minimized, since large loan applications are usually passed on by the home office. (6) Superior management, characteristic of an organization capable of attracting superior personnel, is reflected in numerous internal economies. Routine operations are not duplicated.

These are the disadvantages of branch banking: (1) Bank failures mean large bank failures. Business is more adversely affected than in the case of small bank failures. (2) Home-office control over loan and investment policy delays bank credit grants and penalizes smaller communities which must wait upon the pleasure of the central office. (3) Small-town funds are shifted to the large urban centers where money-market operations offer more opportunities for a diversified portfolio, to the disadvantage of the small town customer. Furthermore (4), present-day federal and state supervision, coupled with deposit insurance protection, minimizes the dangers of failures; therefore an independent bank should be about as safe as a branch bank.

Group and Chain Banking. Group banking is holding company control of several legally independent banks. Chain banking is individual, family, or associate control of a number of banks.

PROS AND CONS OF GROUP AND CHAIN BANKING. Group and chain banking have these advantages: (1) Large loans may be granted jointly by several banks. No one of them alone could handle the large transactions. (2) The group's funds are concentrated in the hands of the major bank located usually in a large center and able to put money to work easily. (3) As in branch banking, operating economies are feasible. (4) The limitations of branch banking as to the area it may cover are overcome. (5) The holding company may diversify its portfolio through control of corporations other than banks. Then it is not subject exclusively to the fluctuations of the banking business.

There are these disadvantages: (1) Dominant interests in group and chain systems may misuse the resources of the individual banks for their own personal gain through heavy loans to officers, unwarranted dividends, and risky speculative undertakings. (2) The controlling group or holding company can shift sound assets from a weakly controlled to a strongly held subsidiary unit. (3) A diversified portfolio can result in heavy losses in nonbanking fields. Since 1934, investment banking subsidiaries have been prohibited to group holding companies.

REGULATION OF GROUP BANKING. Before a holding company can vote the stock of any federal reserve member bank subsidiary, it must obtain a permit from the Board of Governors of the Federal Reserve System. This permit is granted only if the holding company and its subsidiaries open their books to examination by the Federal Reserve System, if it is not connected with an investment banking organization, if it establishes an adequate reserve and limits dividend payments to its net earnings, and if it publishes required individual and consolidated statements of affiliated banks.

Most states forbid commercial banks to purchase financial interests of 50 per cent or more in other banks. Some states examine holding companies, limit their financial transactions with subsidiaries, and generally discourage holding company control of commercial banks.

Little regulation of chain banking has occurred.

BANK FAILURES

Although not a problem in recent years, bank failures plagued the United States in the past. For example, between 1921 and 1933, about sixteen thousand banks suspended operations. Today there are about fourteen thousand active commercial banks.

Causes. The major causes of bank failures were: (1) weak organization, management, and supervision, especially of unit state-chartered banks (branch banking advocates argued, therefore, for its extension); (2) depression conditions in any one economic activity, especially in the agricultural field, which weak management could not combat successfully; (3) the dual banking system which forced national banks to follow the weak banking practices of the state banks, especially as regards the types of loans the banks would grant and the weak capitalization encouraged by state regulation; and (4) fraudulent and illegal banking practices.

Reconstruction Finance Corporation Aid to Banks. The government organized the Reconstruction Finance Corporation in 1932 to aid the weakened banking structure (and debt-embarrassed railroads) after the National Credit Corporation, a privately financed banking organization set up in 1931, had proved inadequate. The Reconstruction Finance Corporation could issue securities to the Treasury and lend the proceeds to hard pressed banks, railroads, and farmers. However, its efforts also were inadequate, and the bank holiday of March, 1933, followed.

The banks reopened shortly under Treasury or state licenses, generally if they had sufficient assets to borrow at the federal reserve banks to pay off depositors' claims. The problem of strengthening the American banking structure was dealt with by: (1) encouraging banks to sell preferred stock, capital notes, or debentures to the Reconstruction Finance Corporation; (2) reopening closed banks by issuing new stock, assessing old stockholders, voluntary waiving of claims by depositors, or by a combination of these techniques; (3) liquidating a failed bank if it could not be reorganized.

REVIEW QUESTIONS

1. Describe the organization procedure for a national bank.
2. Why are national banks required to have a paid-in surplus? How does it serve as a substitute for double liability?
3. Who are a bank's officers? What are their duties?
4. Distinguish among unit, branch, group, and chain banking. What are their respective advantages?
5. What branch banking powers does a national bank now have?
6. What were the major causes of bank failures between 1921 and 1933?

☒

Bank Deposits and Checks

A commercial bank has four functions: (1) acceptance and protection of depositors' funds; (2) paying off depositors' passbook claims, their checks, and their drafts; (3) lending to business for working and fixed capital purposes; (4) lending to governments, a relatively new role typical of bank credit operations since the early 1930's.

DEPOSITS

Origin. Deposits result from: (1) cash placed in banks by depositors; (2) claims to money, like checks, placed in depositors' accounts (these checks are collected by depository banks from debtor banks through clearing agencies); (3) bank loans and investments which increase debtors' bank-deposit balances.

Types. Deposits may be classified as primary, resulting from cash and claims to money placed in depositors' accounts, or derivative, resulting from bank loan and investment operations. When individual businessmen, corporations, or governments borrow, the bank sets up deposit credits against which they can draw. In other words, it "monetizes" their credit by substituting its widely accepted promises to pay, called "checks," for their unacceptable or limited promises to pay.

If the depositor is a private citizen or a business firm, the deposit is called private. If the depositor is a government, the deposit is termed a public deposit.

Deposits are subject to payment on demand or after due notice. Time deposits, when kept in a savings bank or the thrift division of a commercial bank, are called savings or thrift deposits and require notice, usually thirty days, before withdrawal. Special types of time deposits are Christmas Club and Vacation Club accounts. All these time deposits are recorded in depositors' passbooks. Other time deposits are evidenced by certificates of deposit, payable after sixty days, and ordinarily used for investment purposes. Still other savings deposits are placed with the government post office. Demand deposits, usually drawn upon by check, are subject to call at the depositor's discretion. On a few occasions demand certifi-. cates of deposit are used to transfer funds.

Deposits are insured or uninsured. Since 1934, most individual deposit accounts have been fully protected by the governmental organization, the Federal Deposit Insurance Corporation. Accounts up to $5,000 are fully insured; individual deposits above this figure are not protected by the FDIC.

There are secured and unsecured deposits. Thus, governments deposit funds in banks pledging as collateral protection specifically required securities.

Interest Rates. Since 1933, federal reserve member banks and others joining the federal deposit insurance system have been prohibited from paying interest on demand deposits because: (1) bank management would be discouraged from investing in slow moving assets which endanger a bank's ability to repay demand deposits; (2) demand depositors already receive interest in the form of banking services; (3) interest payments reduce bank reserves and special funds set up to meet emergencies.

Maximum interest rates on time deposits are fixed by the Board of Governors of the Federal Reserve System and the Federal Deposit Insurance Corporation for banks under their jurisdictions. Interest payments are believed justified since: (1) legal reserve requirements—cash reserves in federal reserve banks against member bank deposits—are smaller than for demand deposits, enabling the accumulation of more bank earning assets; (2) bank management can invest these funds for a relatively long period of time at a relatively high rate of interest; (3) check transactions do not result from these deposits, and overhead expenses are reduced since little clerical work is involved.

State supervisory agencies, individual banks, and clearinghouses also determine interest rates and may fix them at a lower point than the maximum established by the two federal organizations mentioned above.

Service Charges on Demand Deposit Accounts. These charges are imposed to handle and invest demand deposits when the earnings from these funds are insufficient to cover the cost of administration. For example, each depositor may be required to pay a fixed price for checks drawn above a stipulated number, or a bank may survey its income from each account and impose charges in accordance with this income and the expenses involved in earning it.

DEPOSIT CURRENCY AND CHECKS

Importance of Deposit Currency. (1) Deposit currency, against which checks and drafts may be drawn, dwarfs the amount of money in circulation in the United States. In the early part of 1950, demand deposits totalled $94,000,000,000, time deposits, $56,000,000,000, and money in circulation only $25,000,000,000. (2) It expands and contracts with business requirements. When trade grows, banks can finance a greater business volume if they have the necessary reserves. A business downturn is usually accompanied by called loans, or credit contraction, and a reduction of outstanding deposit currency.

The American businessman settles his obligations by check; individual checking accounts are steadily growing in importance.

Checks. A check is a depositor's written order on a commercial bank to pay a stated sum of money on demand to the order of the bearer or a specific party. Figure I presents a typical check used in everyday business operations.

FIGURE I: A Typical Check

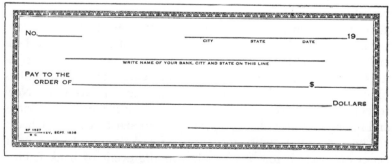

CLASSES OF CHECKS. (1) A personal check is drawn by an individual or business organization against a demand deposit account. (2) A certified check is drawn by a depositor on a bank which indicates on the face of the check that it holds an amount of the drawer's funds adequate to meet the claim of the party to whose order it is payable. The bank sets aside the specified sum to meet this obligation. (3) A cashier's check is a claim on a bank drawn by a bank official. Such a check is issued to accommodate thrift or time depositors lacking checking accounts, and is also used by banks to discharge their own obligations. (4) A bank draft is a check drawn by one bank against an account it holds with another institution. Interior banks hold large deposits with New York City banks against which they draw for their own purposes or to facilitate customer business deals.

NEGOTIABILITY OF CHECKS. A check may pass through many hands after issuance. If drawn payable to the bearer, it may be negotiated by mere delivery. Indorsement is not necessary. When drawn payable to the order of a specific party, it is negotiable by indorsement—writing the drawee's name on the back of the check. Subsequent negotiations may take place by each holder indorsing the check.

LIABILITY FOR PAYMENT OF A CHECK. The drawer is primarily obligated. If he fails to satisfy his obligations, indorsers are liable. An indorser may write the words "without recourse" after his signature. These words put all subsequent holders on notice that he believes the check valid, but relieve him of personal liability.

An unqualified indorsement is required by banks, for it enables them to sue and collect from the indorser if the maker of an instrument defaults.

ADVANTAGES OF CHECKS. (1) They are negotiable and easily passed from hand to hand. (2) They possess the same buying power as coins and paper money, for today most banks pay the full face value of checks drawn against demand deposits. Prior to the Federal Reserve System's organization, many banks charged for remittances on checks drawn upon them. Federal reserve authorities campaigned for check par collection or payment at face value. Now federal reserve banks offer their clearing services only to par banks and refuse to collect checks drawn upon nonpar banks. (3) Checks are safe in sound commercial banks, for depositors have a prior claim on assets before stockholders in the event of bank failure. Legal cash reserves either in their own vaults or with other institutions—for example, the federal reserve banks—plus the deposit insurance system, give depositors further protection. Public deposits are protected by special collateral. (4) Checks increase the community's means of payment. (5) Banks need relatively little cash to meet check obligations, for an efficient system of check clearance minimizes interbank demands for cash payment. For the most part, check credits and debits offset one another. (6) Large payments can be made by checks, virtually at a moment's notice, thereby avoiding the use of currency, the danger of robbery, and delay in payment. (7) Drawers can stop payment on checks and thus protect themselves against robbery, carelessness, or incorrectly drawn checks. (8) Forged checks, honored by a bank, do not result in losses to the depositor, for the bank is responsible. (9) Checks, deposited and collected on by creditors, are debt payment receipts.

DISADVANTAGES OF CHECKS. (1) Checks are not accepted as readily as money, especially if a debtor's credit standing is unknown or uncertain, indorsers are unfamiliar, or the bank's credit position is unknown to a creditor. (2) Service charges are imposed on many types of checks. (3) Checks can be forged and their terms changed if carelessly written out.

CHECK CLEARANCE

American businessmen operate on both a local and national scale. They receive checks on local and distant banks. The clearance system: (1) enables a quick determination of the soundness of the checks received; (2) shifts funds from debtor to creditor banks.

Local Clearance. It is a method of settling local interbank debts growing out of checks and bank drafts drawn on local banks and deposited in other local banks. The procedure follows: (1) The clearinghouse division of a bank receives and prepares checks against other local institutions for the local clearinghouse by computing the value of the claims it holds against other local clearinghouse members. (2) Each local clearinghouse member prepares a clearinghouse settlement sheet showing its claims against other local banks. Clerks from the various banks arrive at the clearinghouse at a designated hour for adjustment of their mutual obligations. (3) The clearinghouse manager is advised by the bank clerks of the claims their banks hold against other banks. (4) The delivery clerk from each institution turns over the checks his bank holds against its neighbors to their settling clerks. (5) Each institution is now aware of its check obligations to other local banks as well as the claims it holds against these banks. (6) The clearinghouse manager is advised of the net debits or credits each clearinghouse bank holds against the other member banks. (7) The debit or credit of each bank is settled by (a) the clearinghouse manager drawing against the balances left with him by debtor banks and crediting them to the account of the creditor banks, or (b) the clearinghouse manager notifying the federal reserve bank of the district in which the local institutions are situated to increase or decrease their reserve accounts by the amount of their indebtedness or credits, or (c) small-town banks paying off their creditors by checks drawn on city correspondents holding their deposit balances for this purpose. (8) In large cities clearance takes place daily. (9) Banks in communities lacking a clearinghouse use messengers to settle interbank claims.

NONCLEARING FUNCTIONS OF CLEARINGHOUSES. Clearinghouses have expanded their functions to other activities aimed at strengthening local banks. These functions include: (1) regular examination of all member banks to determine their solvency and liquidity; (2) regulation of interest rates and charges for services like checking accounts, safe deposit boxes, and trusteeships; (3) public relations to develop higher standards of banking conduct and local educational activities like household budget advice and income tax guidance; (4) issue of clearinghouse certificates to meet emergency money demands and to maintain public confidence in the banks; (5) interchange of credit information through credit bureaus to improve member loan policies.

Clearance through Correspondents. Checks drawn on out-of-town banks may be sent to debtor banks directly and payment made by bank draft or currency shipment.

This procedure is objected to on these grounds: (1) Small-town country banks resent paying checks drawn on them at par. They often need the revenue from remittance charges. (2) Time is lost in forwarding and collecting on out-of-town credit instruments.

To avoid charges and speed up collection and remittance on out-of-town checks, banks enter into correspondent agreements to pay off their own checks at face value as well as collect at face value all checks drawn on neighboring institutions.

Federal Reserve Collection. Most out-of-town bank checks and other credit instruments are collected through the Federal Reserve System's intradistrict and interdistrict clearance facilities. Nonmember as well as member banks can use these services, if the nonmember banks maintain balances with their federal reserve banks to meet all items in transit held for their accounts.

INTRADISTRICT CLEARANCE. This type of clearance deals with the settlement of a check drawn on an out-of-town bank within the same federal reserve district as the depositor's bank. In settling this check claim: (1) the depositor's bank, after giving deferred credit to him, forwards the check to the local federal reserve bank; (2) this federal reserve bank sends the check to the bank on which it is drawn and reduces its reserve balance; (3) the drawer's bank writes down the drawer's account by the amount of the check and returns the cancelled check to the drawer; (4) the payee, who first received a deferred credit when the check was deposited, is allowed to draw on his account after collection; (5) the payee's bank, first given a deferred credit with its local federal reserve bank when the check was presented for collection, is given an available credit within at least three days.

INTERDISTRICT CLEARANCE. This clearance procedure settles checks drawn on a federal reserve clearing bank in one district but deposited in a clearing bank in another district. Thus: (1) A depositor's bank after giving him deferred credit forwards the check to its federal reserve bank. (2) This federal reserve bank returns the check to the district federal reserve bank of the drawer. (3) The latter federal reserve bank sends the check to the drawer's bank debiting its account. (4) The drawer's bank debits the drawer's account and returns the cancelled check to the drawer. (5) The Interdistrict Settlement Fund, holding at least $1,000,000 of each reserve bank's legal reserves, is notified of the check transaction by the district federal reserve bank of the payee. The fund credits the account of the district federal reserve bank of the payee and reduces the reserve account of the district federal reserve bank of the drawer. (6) The payee can draw on his newly acquired funds when the check is collected, while his bank has an available credit at its federal reserve bank within three days. (7) Daily interdistrict clearance takes place through telegraphic instructions sent by each federal reserve bank and its clearing branches to the Interdistrict Settlement Fund.

The Interdistrict Settlement Fund settles member bank drafts which have been drawn against and have been accepted by the federal reserve banks. Similarly, the federal reserve banks handle the telegraphic transfers (amounting to at least $100) made by the member banks of the various districts.

DISTINCTIONS BETWEEN BANK NOTES AND DEPOSIT CURRENCY

(1) Noteholders do not concern themselves with the credit standing of bank note issues, for governments usually guarantee their soundness; but recipients of checks lacking government protection are concerned with the credit standing of banks on which the checks are drawn and the financial status of the drawers. (2) Bank deposits are transferred by check whereas bank notes are engraved on governmentally supervised paper. (3) Checks will find their way back quickly to the banks on which they are drawn, for the holders wish payment, but bank notes circulate for long periods of time before returning to the issuing banks. (4) A sound deposit currency depends on prompt payment of checks, while bank notes may circulate even though their collateral is impaired. (5) Checks are not legal tender, but most countries have given this power to bank notes.

REVIEW QUESTIONS

1. How do bank deposits originate?
2. Explain four classes of checks.
3. What are the advantages and disadvantages in the use of check currency?
4. Describe a typical local check clearance procedure.
5. What facilities for clearing checks are offered by the Federal Reserve System?
6. Explain the distinctions between bank notes and deposit currency.

☒

Commercial Bank Loans and Investments

When a commercial bank puts its funds to work in earning assets, production and trade are increased.

LOANS AND DISCOUNTS

Definitions. (1) A short-term loan is generally called a discount, since interest is ordinarily deducted at the time the credit is arranged. (2) A long-term loan, such as a real-estate or investment loan, carries an interest charge collected at stated intervals or at maturity, with the borrower having full use of the loan's face amount until maturity. A discount imposes a higher interest cost upon a bank borrower than a loan.

Line of Credit. A large borrower of good credit standing arranges for a line of credit at his local bank. This line is the maximum a bank will lend either unsecured or with security. The total credit at the borrower's disposal may be modified as conditions warrant, and the borrower must maintain a minimum balance.

BASES. To determine whether or not to establish a line of credit for a prospective borrower and to decide what the maximum line will be, a bank rates the prospective borrower on: (1) the trend of his earning power; (2) the increase in his deposit balance; (3) the average deposit balance he maintains (it should equal from 10 to 20 per cent of his desired line of credit); (4) the claim subsidiaries' debts have on parent company earnings; (5) a comparison of the consolidated balance sheet of the parent and subsidiaries over a representative period of business years; (6) the ratio of inventory to net working capital, of net sales to net working capital, of net sales to tangible net worth, of net profits to tangible net worth, and of net profits to net working capital; (7) marketability of a borrower's security portfolio; (8) the ratio of funded debt to net working capital (to determine whether long-term debt is in the proper proportion to the borrower's net working capital);

73

(9) the ratio of fixed assets to tangible net worth (it should not be too large, for it may impair the loan applicant's net working capital); (10) depreciation of the borrower's fixed assets; (11) the borrower's promptness in meeting obligations; (12) his understanding of the current business picture as reflected in an undersized or oversized inventory relative to current demand; (13) the success of a sales and advertising program in reaching the broadest possible market; (14) price policy and the reception it receives from the buying public; (15) credit position reports from business associates, credit agencies, and financial institutions with whom he has dealt; (16) bank officer's report after personal conference with the borrower and examination of his business establishment.

ADVANTAGES. To the customer, the advantages are: (1) assurance that bank accommodation will be available when needed; (2) a loan immediately obtainable up to a specified amount at the time required without the costly delays of prolonged negotiations.

To the bank, the advantages are: (1) the cultivation and maintenance of good risks—bank losses on line-of-credit loans are less than one-half of 1 per cent; (2) prompt repayment of the loans (usually annually).

TYPES OF LOANS

Working-Capital Loans. Businessmen and farmers borrow short-term credit to obtain working capital like raw materials and labor. They expect their loans to be repaid out of the sales proceeds of the goods and services produced. These loans are self-liquidating. Borrowers may require loans to cover the costs of producing goods and services sold but not yet paid for by purchasers or to replenish impaired working capital.

LOAN EVIDENCE.

Single-Name Paper, the Borrower's Short-Term Promissory Note. A borrower buying goods on open account with a large discount for cash payment may be able to borrow on his own unsecured paper to obtain the discount. Again, a seller on credit may discount or borrow on his note to replenish his cash position if buyers do not take advantage of the discounts but pay off at the end of the credit period.

Two-Name Paper. This consists of (a) an indorsed customer's note, (b) an indorsed time or demand trade draft growing out of a sale of goods acknowledged by a debtor accepting a draft drawn against him (a typical draft is presented in Figure II), (c) a credit instrument of a poor individual credit risk made out or indorsed by stronger credit risks. In the case of corporation notes, the accommodating parties may be the enterprise's officers and directors.

COLLATERAL. Secured loans may be protected by the pledge of: (1) bills of lading, warehouse receipts, and trust receipts representing respectively claims on goods in transit, in a warehouse, or released for trade purposes; (2) readily marketable securities; (3) indorsed customers' notes and trade acceptances or borrowers' own notes collateraled by these notes and acceptances; (4) accounts receivable; (5) real-estate mortgages; (6) beginning in 1942, partial or full guaranties by the War and Navy Departments and the Maritime Commission of loans to provide war materials, and in 1943 loans guaranteed to provide working capital for reconversion when war contracts were cancelled but not yet settled.

"Term" Loans. Business organizations borrow on "term"—for more than one year—from a single bank or a group of banks: (1) to acquire or construct new plant; (2) to refinance capitalization; (3) to obtain the funds for acquiring other enterprises; (4) to secure new net working capital.

CAUSES. There were several reasons for the development of "term" loans: (1) short-term bank loans which both borrowers and banks realized would not be paid at maturity even when negotiated; (2) fear of short-term loans being called at maturity even though the banks knew initially that the loans were to be used for long-term purposes; (3) working capital needs during the depression of the 1930's to improve deteriorated plants and equipment; (4) inability to borrow on long term in the stagnant capital market of the 1930's; (5) avoidance of new issue registration costs, especially by medium-sized and small enterprises; (6) refunding high interest-bearing, long-term debt with a low-interest-cost "term" loan; (7) availability of federal reserve loans on any sound asset regardless of maturity under the terms of the Banking Acts of 1933 and 1935; (8) 1938 revision of federal bank examination procedure emphasizing asset soundness rather than short-term maturity.

BASES. Since "term" loans do not mature for some years, banks place prime emphasis on the borrower's long-term prospects. These yardsticks and protective provisions are used to judge his credit merit and safeguard the lender's equity: (1) future estimated earning power over a typical period of years; (2) soundness and con-

tinuity of management; (3) capacity to cope with difficult finan‑
cial problems; (4) competitive position; (5) maintenance of min‑
imum net working capital to assure the lender he will be repaid
before the borrower's operating losses exhaust his liquid assets;
(6) maintenance of a minimum ratio of current assets to current
liabilities; (7) limitations on a borrower's debts; (8) "term" loan
repayment if earnings exceed average income. A default on another
debt automatically constitutes a default on the "term" loan.

EVIDENCE.   It is a note or notes drawn according to the terms
and conditions of a formal agreement between the borrower and
lender.

COLLATERAL.   Over one-half of the dollar amount of "term"
loans are not secured. Where security is taken, it consists of stocks,
bonds, inventory, real estate, and assignment of claims and re‑
ceivables.

Capital Loans.   (1) Like "term" loans, capital loans finance
the purchase of long-term, fixed or investment assets. On occasion,
borrowers ask for repeated renewals of short-term working-capital
loans. These credits can also be classified as long-term loans, al‑
though they are not used to acquire fixed assets. (2) They are paid
off in installments over a period of years. (3) Evidence of the capi‑
tal loan is a note secured by claims on fixed assets like chattel mort‑
gages and marketable securities.

Real-Estate Loans.   (1) Real-estate loans are long-term credits
to finance the purchase of real property and its improvement. (2)
They are discharged by periodic repayment of interest and prin‑
cipal. (3) The mortgagor is indebted to the bank by a bond or
note corresponding to a first mortgage on improved property. The
mortgage is the legal instrument conveying title to the property.

INSURANCE.   The National Housing Act of 1934, creating the
Federal Housing Administration, provides for different types of
real-estate loan insurance by the federal government: (1) Title I
of the act insures commercial banks against losses suffered on loans
granted for the repair and modernization of residential property
occupied by either the owners or lessees whose leases expire only
after the loan has matured. (2) Title I also insures loans for new
construction of small homes and farm buildings. (3) Title II pro‑
vides FHA mortgage loan insurance up to $16,000 or 80 per cent of
the property value, whichever is the smaller, on a four-family house
or less; if an insured loan does not exceed $6,000, it may represent

as much as 95 per cent of the property value. This loan must be amortized and the interest rate charged by the insured lending institutions cannot exceed 4.5 per cent. An insurance premium of 0.5 per cent of the outstanding insured mortgage loan principal is paid into a mutual mortgage insurance fund to meet insured mortgage losses. (4) Title II also authorizes FHA-guaranteed first mortgage loans by private institutions and governmental agencies for apartment housing projects if the insured loans do not exceed $5,000,000 or 80 per cent of a completed development's valuation. The FHA Commissioner must approve the loan maturity, while the mortgagors can be charged up to 4 per cent on a big housing project and 4.5 per cent on small developments. The insured institutions are required to pay yearly insurance premiums of .5 per cent of outstanding loans to discharge defaulted claims. (5) In 1941, the FHA was authorized to provide war-housing insurance for residential construction in important war-production centers. At the same time, loan insurance was arranged to finance the purchase of completed houses and to refinance mortgages. (6) The Servicemen's Readjustment Act of 1944 authorizes the Administrator of Veteran Affairs to insure lenders up to 50 per cent for funds advanced to veterans for home purchase, construction, or repair, or for farm and business acquisition. The guaranty can amount to $4,000 on real-estate loans; on all other loans it may total $2,000.

Investment Loans. (1) Investment banking houses, brokerage firms, and individuals obtain investment credit. Underwriters borrow to purchase new issues, repaying usually when the securities are sold at a profit. Brokers borrow to finance customers wishing to purchase securities or sell short on margin. The margin trader makes partial payment equal to the margin requirement, with the remainder made up of borrowed money. Individuals also borrow from banks to finance security market margin operations. (2) In all three cases, the loans are protected by securities purchased. For adequate protection, the bank cannot lend the full market value of the securities. Margin requirements between January 21, 1946, and January 31, 1947, as prescribed by the Board of Governors of the Federal Reserve System in accordance with the Securities Exchange Act of 1934, amounted to 100 per cent; on February 1, 1947, they were 75 per cent, in 1949, 50 per cent, and currently are 75 per cent. If existing collateral becomes inadequate due to a decline in security prices, banks call for additional collateral, or, if necessary, sell the securities pledged to protect themselves. (3) These loans are evidenced by demand notes enabling borrowers to pay off and banks to call them when desired. Loans to brokers may be evidenced also by time notes up to six months.

Consumption Loans. (1) Recent years have seen a great growth of commercial bank loans for the purchase of durable consumers' goods such as automobiles, radios, and homes. These loans differ from business credits in that they do not provide the means to pay off indebtedness. They finance the purchase of goods and services whose utility will be exhausted in time. Repayment depends upon a borrower's business or investment income and his reliability in discharging debts. (2) Consumer loans, evidenced by borrower promissory notes, frequently with comaker signatures, are made directly or through sales finance companies and small loan organizations. Bank loans to sales and personal finance companies and the purchase of installment obligations from retail dealers also finance consumers. (3) Many loans are secured only by notes. Large amounts are collateraled by chattel mortgages, securities, savings bankbooks, and life insurance policies. Additional protection is afforded by installment payments directly applicable to the loan or accumulated in a savings account pledged as collateral and used to repay the obligation at maturity.

Other Loans. A miscellaneous group representing chiefly interbank secured loans by large city banks to smaller banks.

Overdrafts. Bank customers overdraw their accounts. The banks may honor their checks and so extend credit if they believe them good risks and valuable clients.

LEGAL LIMITATIONS ON BANK LENDING POWER

National bank loan powers are legally restricted to protect bank solvency and liquidity and to serve community needs: (1) Loans to and security investments in one party cannot exceed 20 per cent of a bank's capital and surplus. No restrictions apply to: (a) discounts of business paper, with parties other than bank debtors as principal obligors; (b) discounts of such trade paper as acceptances secured by goods in transit; (c) loans to bank receivers, conservators, and supervisors in exchange for bank assets, subject to the Comptroller of the Currency's approval; (d) discounts of drafts drawn against legitimate business debtors for values rendered. Other exceptions provide that: (e) 25 per cent of a bank's capi-

tal and surplus may be lent on indorsed or guaranteed notes maturing within six months, if they do not represent commercial or
business transactions; (f) 25 per cent may be lent to one party if
his note is secured by United States government obligations, whose
face value equals the loan; (g) 50 per cent of the capital and surplus may be extended on instruments secured by such claims to
readily marketable, nonperishable staples as warehouse receipts if the
goods are fully insured and exceed the principal loan value. (2) On
a loan secured by an amortized mortgage, 60 per cent of the
property's appraised value may be lent for ten years, if 40 per cent
of the loan is paid off in that time. If these requirements are not
met, a mortgage loan up to 50 per cent of the value of the property may be granted for five years. Property reappraisal takes place
whenever these loans are up for renewal. FHA loans under Title II
of the Federal Housing Act are not subject to these limitations;
neither are commitments insured by the Veterans Administration
or real-estate, residential, and farm-building loans maturing within
six months. (3) All bank mortgage loans may not exceed 60 per
cent of time and savings deposits or 100 per cent of capital and
surplus, whichever is the larger. This restriction does not encompass
real-estate bonds, mortgages guaranteed by the FHA, and obligations representing only part of a real-estate claim. (4) Loans to
finance brokers, dealers, and their customers, who purchase securities on margin, must comply with the requirements of the Board
of Governors of the Federal Reserve System. (5) National and state
member banks can lend each officer only $2,500, with each loan
requiring approval of the bank's board of directors. (6) National
banks cannot lend on their own stock as collateral. (7) Federal
reserve member banks can lend on security only 10 per cent of their
capital and surplus to one affiliate and 20 per cent to all. Affiliates
are holding companies with a controlling bank stock ownership in
the commercial bank or other enterprises controlled jointly by
commercial banks and parent companies. (8) Bank employees must
not accept compensation from prospective borrowers for arranging
loans.

COMMERCIAL PAPER

Borrowers. Banks lend to exceptionally good credit risks for
working capital purposes when they buy their notes in the open
market.

Open-market borrowers are: (1) large establishments whose net worth exceeds $500,000; (2) dealers in staple commodities like textiles and foodstuffs.

These firms obtain more funds at lower rates than they do by borrowing directly at commercial banks. Legal limitations on bank lending power, restrictive bank loan policies, and insistence on maintenance of minimum bank balances are avoided through open-market borrowing.

Nature.   Most open-market paper is unsecured, with the greater part of it straight (unindorsed) and the rest indorsed or guaranteed by peoples interested in the business. Notes read "pay to the order of ourselves," are signed and indorsed in blank by the makers so that commercial paper dealers do not need to indorse them, and are ordinarily payable at designated banks to the makers' order. They are traded at a discount. Secured notes are covered by collateral held by a trustee or are notes or trade acceptances indorsed by the sellers of goods. The maturities vary from 90 days to 180 days, with notes varying in amount from $2,500 to $50,000.

Commercial Paper Dealers' Operations.   (1) The paper is usually sold through commercial paper dealers who buy it at a discount and then resell at the same price, or at a price determined by market conditions, or occasionally on consignment, with the proceeds remitted as sales are made. (2) Sales are made through personal contact or solicitation. The commercial paper dealer does not guarantee the paper. However, since he wishes to maintain his outlets, he naturally investigates the open-market borrower's credit standing. Paper-buying banks with the help of their city correspondents, the borrower's own bank, and credit agencies also may examine the borrower's credit standing. (3) The dealer's compensation is a commission varying from one-eighth to one-half of 1 per cent, or the discount accruing while the paper is held, and, perhaps, an advance in sales price over the figure at which he bought the paper.

Since the dealer buys the paper outright, he runs the risk of a frozen asset if investors shy away from it, or an injured reputation if the paper is not paid off at maturity.

Advantages to the Bank.   Buying commercial paper offers several advantages to banks: (1) Commercial paper of prime borrowers is always paid off at maturity and is an excellent liquid loan; (2) earnings compare favorably with the return on comparable risks; (3) bank loans are not confined to the industries or businesses in the immediate locale; (4) outside business contacts may be cultivated through commercial paper purchases.

Decline of Commercial Paper. Recent years have witnessed a sharp decline in outstanding commercial paper because: (1) the growth of business surpluses during the 1920's and the development of a new securities market has made possible internal financing and new issues; (2) large banks in the nation's financial centers have sought business all over the country and have eliminated the need for selling commercial paper to them (they also are prepared to grant direct loans nationally); (3) business has required less current capital since cash sales and improved means of transportation and distribution were introduced, stimulating the flow of business money income; (4) federal reserve credit facilities have expanded the lending and investing power of member banks.

FINANCING FOREIGN TRADE

Foreign trade is financed usually through letters of credit and bankers' acceptances.

Cash Letters of Credit. They expedite international trade when exporters are uncertain of importers' capacity to pay and importers are unwilling to pay their debts until the goods have been shipped. Thus: (1) At the request of an importer, a cash letter of credit is issued by an importer's bank to a third party—the exporter—authorizing the latter to draw drafts on the bank payable on demand. The exporter is now assured the drafts will be paid. (2) The exporter draws a draft on the bank, thus holding a guaranty of payment by a well-known financial institution rather than by a little-known merchant. He can sell it to his bank at a discount and so receive immediate payment. His bank collects on the draft through its correspondent and so builds up its foreign balances. (3) The importer pays his bank for the purchase when he receives papers indicating that the merchandise has been shipped and insured.

Bankers' Acceptances. Time drafts drawn on letters of credit are accepted and the obligations acknowledged when the drawee banks write "accepted" across the faces of the drafts and sign them. Their marketability is immeasurably increased, and they can be sold at a slight discount in the acceptance market.

ADVANTAGES. (1) Banks can commit themselves on future obligations beyond their loanable funds since no immediate payment is required. (2) Foreign trade is increased, since exporters are hesitant to sell unknown individual risks. (3) Creditors can obtain cash for accepted drafts by selling them in the open market. (4) Foreign trade transactions are financed on a time basis. (5) Commissions from letters of credit increase bank earnings.

FIGURE II: A Typical Draft

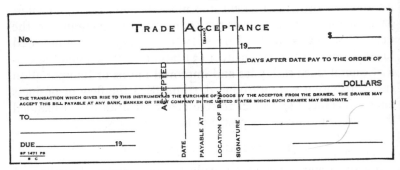

TRADE ACCEPTANCE

NO._____

_____19___

_____DAYS AFTER DATE PAY TO THE ORDER OF

_____DOLLARS

THE TRANSACTION WHICH GIVES RISE TO THIS INSTRUMENT IS THE PURCHASE OF GOODS BY THE ACCEPTOR FROM THE DRAWER. THE DRAWEE MAY ACCEPT THIS BILL PAYABLE AT ANY BANK, BANKER OR TRUST COMPANY IN THE UNITED STATES WHICH SUCH DRAWEE MAY DESIGNATE.

TO_____

DUE_____19___

A Foreign Trade Transaction. In import financing, the following procedure is employed: (1) A duplicate of a letter of credit is mailed or cabled abroad so that the seller is notified of its terms. (2) When the goods are to be shipped, the seller obtains and prepares a consular invoice, a bill of lading, and a commercial invoice, all of which are taken to the seller's bank and a time or sight draft, equal to the selling price of the goods, is drawn. (3) Since the draft is usually sold to the exporter's bank, it is drawn in favor of this institution. (4) The seller's bank sends the draft along with the shipping and other documents to its representative in the importing nation. (5) The bank that issued the letter of credit "accepts" the draft. The accepting bank may credit the seller's bank with the face value of the time draft at maturity, or sell it in the acceptance market with the dollars disposed of according to the exporter's bank's instructions, or return it to the seller's bank. In the case of a sight draft, the bank will pay it immediately and charge the importing customer's account. (6) The accepting bank releases the shipping documents to the importer who is now able to obtain his purchase. (7) The importer discharges his obligation to the accepting bank on or before the maturity date of the acceptance. (8) If the seller draws a draft in terms of the buyer's currency, he runs the risk of losses due to currency fluctuations. He can protect himself by making a future sale to an exchange dealer of the draft on the buyer or his bank. (9) An exporter who needs funds for current obligations, like payrolls, can draw a draft on a home bank secured by the acceptance of the foreigner or his bank. This draft, accepted by the domestic bank, can be sold in the acceptance market. When the foreign importer or bank meets his obligation, the exporter's accepted draft is paid off.

Other Uses of Bankers' Acceptances. (1) Bankers' acceptances can be used to finance domestic purchases and sales, with sellers drawing drafts accepted by purchasers' banks. (2) They can be used to finance the storage of goods, the acceptances being sold in the acceptance market to provide marketers with the necessary funds to hold the goods in warehouses. The stored merchandise is kept off the market, while the bank is protected with the warehouse receipts. (3) Bankers' acceptances can provide time dollar exchange to foreign bankers and businessmen, who, in turn, sell this exchange on a sight basis to their customers owing American dollars. The Board of Governors of the Federal Reserve System must approve such use of American acceptance credit. The accepting institution may require foreign debtors to collateral their loans with securities. This type of acceptance credit may equal 50 per cent of the accepting bank's capital and surplus. (4) They can be used to obtain foreign funds for short-term use. Bankers' acceptances are sold in the open market. The accepting institution is then reimbursed by the sale of short-term assets, like securities, purchased originally with foreign funds.

The Acceptance Market. It is made up of: (1) banks that buy as well as accept drafts drawn upon them (commercial banks purchase both their own bills of exchange and bills accepted by other banks); (2) brokers who for a commission buy and sell claims on banks for commercial banking institutions; (3) commercial bill brokers who deal in bills of exchange resulting from exports (they buy and sell these claims and generally deal in foreign exchange); (4) acceptance dealers who buy and sell time bankers' acceptances; (5) the federal reserve banks that deal in gold and bills of exchange (they rediscount accepted drafts and buy foreign trade paper in the open market); (6) the United States Stabilization Fund, which in carrying out its function to stabilize the dollar's foreign exchange value, bought and sold foreign exchange (the Stabilization Fund's working capital has been allocated largely to the International Monetary Fund); (7) the United States Post Office Department, wire and cable companies, the American Express Company, and travel agencies which deal in foreign exchange in small sums.

Legal Limitations. The legal limitations on acceptance credit, as laid down in the regulations of the Board of Governors of the Federal Reserve System, are: (1) total acceptance credit at any one time may not exceed 50 per cent of a bank's capital and surplus; (2) the acceptance liability may equal a bank's capital and surplus if the bank has a surplus of 20 per cent of its capital and if its liabilities mature in six months; (3) acceptances may equal 150 per cent of a bank's capital and surplus if they are used to provide dollar exchange and if the bills mature in ninety days; (4) acceptances growing out of domestic sales and shipment of goods can be accepted only if shipping documents or warehouse receipts accompany them; (5) acceptances in excess of 10 per cent of a bank's capital and surplus must be secured.

Financing Foreign Travel. The two instruments used in foreign travel are: (1) a traveler's check issued by a bank or travel agency in book form and usable only if countersigned by the traveler (it is issued in domestic or foreign currency; if in the latter, the risk of fluctuations in the price of sight exchange is eliminated); (2) a traveler's letter of credit addressed by a bank to a correspondent abroad directing it to honor drafts drawn on the issuer (if addressed to more than one institution, it is called a circular letter of credit).

INTEREST RATES ON BANK LOANS

National banks are permitted to charge no more than the maximum legal rates stipulated by the states wherein they are located or 1 per cent above the federal reserve discount rate on ninety-day commercial paper, whichever is greater. In the event no legal rate has been set by a state, 7 per cent is the legal rate.

Rates of interest are not uniform for all borrowers. They vary with: (1) a borrower's credit position; (2) the use to which a loan is put; (3) the business outlook; (4) a bank's lending power.

However, credit investigation service charges, among other things, may force the loan rate above the legal rate. If a national bank charges more than it is legally permitted, it forfeits its interest claim; and if interest in excess of the legal rate has been collected, the borrower may recover two times the amount of the interest charges.

COMMERCIAL BANK INVESTMENTS

Decline of the Commercial Loan. Commercial loans have declined relative to total earning assets because: (1) depression conditions during the 1930's reduced both the demand for legitimate business loans and the bank's readiness to grant such loans; (2) changes have occurred in business and banking practices.

Among these changes may be mentioned: (1) the growth of cash sales reducing business reliance on bank credit; (2) a smaller percentage of business losses on credit accounts, due, in part, to improved credit techniques; (3) smaller business inventories during periods of business uncertainty since goods are now rapidly delivered; (4) an increasing trend toward business self-financing with accumulated surpluses; (5) the facility with which security flotations can be arranged (commercial banks with growing and stable time deposits are showing a greater tendency to invest these deposits in long-term securities).

Investments. The net result of these factors has been a growth in unused cash assets which bank management has put into investments. A bank investment is a long-term loan to a government or corporation for capital purposes like construction, evidenced by promissory notes usually called "bonds." Government bonds are ordinarily unsecured as are high grade corporate obligations. In other cases, collateral like a property mortgage is pledged to protect the bondholder.

Securities are purchased because: (1) the issuer is considered a sound risk, due to its strong credit position; (2) the security can be readily sold on security exchanges.

During World War II, the federal government sold billions of dollars of its obligations to the commercial banks until they constituted the bulk of all loans and investments.

The preponderance of bank investments over bank loans is indicated in Chart II on page 86.

REGULATION. The leading federal commercial bank investment regulations are as follows: (1) A federal reserve member bank can invest only 10 per cent of its capital and surplus in the securities of any one company or government. Federal government securities, both direct and guaranteed, and state and municipal government issues are exempt from this limitation. (2) A member bank cannot buy speculative securities. (3) Bank investments are considered primarily from the viewpoint of soundness rather than marketability. Thus, banks may even buy bonds of limited marketability if they mature within ten years and if at least 75 per cent of the issues will be retired before maturity. (4) If securities are purchased at a premium, member banks must amortize this premium before maturity. (5) Member banks may buy only federal reserve bank stock or the stock of subsidiary corporations like safe-deposit affiliates, foreign banking subsidiaries, or the stock of companies owning the buildings in which the banks carry on their work.

CHART II: Total Loans and Investments of All Member Banks *

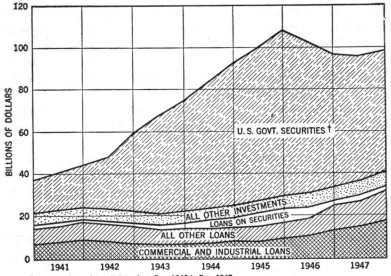

* June and December call dates from Dec. 1940 to Dec. 1947.
† Direct and guaranteed.

Source: *Thirty-third Annual Report of the Federal Reserve Bank of New York, for the Year Ended December 31, 1947,* p. 28.

Advantages of Loans over Investments. Local loans offer advantages over investments and encourage banks to seek loan outlets. These advantages are as follows: (1) Good community relationships are developed, thus encouraging local patronage and yielding income. (2) Loans result in the creation of deposit balances in favor of borrowers, while investments usually result in the immediate withdrawal of funds. Thus, loans give banks a broader cash basis on which to operate. (3) Small-town unit banks are poor bond buyers and are much better judges of local loan risks. (4) Business disturbances cause "runs" on banks, frequently leading to simultaneous bond portfolio liquidation by many banks and depressing below their real worth the market value of security holdings. The capital position of bond-holding banks is thereby threatened. (5) Banks suffer a "money risk" as well as a "credit risk" on their long-term bonds. These securities carry a fixed rate of interest, and as market rates of interest increase bondholders seek these higher rates by liquidating their current bond holdings and purchasing the newer securities which promise them a higher rate of return. The "credit risk" refers to the credit standing of the borrower and the danger of a default due to business difficulties.

BANK EARNINGS

About one-half of all bank gross income is derived from interest on securities (chiefly United States government obligations), about one-third from interest on loans, and the remainder from service charges and other income. A little more than one-third of gross income remains as operating earnings after deducting expenses— largely salaries, wages, directors' fees, other operating expenses, interest on deposits, and income taxes.

CAPITAL TO DEPOSIT RATIO

Sound bank management should restrict its outstanding deposit obligations if capital, surplus, profits, and reserves for contingencies decline much below 10 per cent of total deposits. Capital accounts may be impaired by heavy loan and investment losses endangering depositors' funds.

Bankers object to legalizing a specific deposit ratio since it would: (1) reduce their profit opportunities; (2) adversely affect the sale of government bonds, vital to a government with an unbalanced budget; (3) force interest rates up as compensation for the shrinkage in the earning assets, loans, and investments, which create deposits. Within recent years the Federal Deposit Insurance Corporation has acquiesced in bank departure from the 1 to 10 ratio since bank assets are made up in good part of federal government obligations and cash providing greater assurance than formerly of bank capacity to meet depositor withdrawals.

Another yardstick of bank management soundness is the ratio of capital accounts to all assets less United States government securi-

A GRAPHIC EXPLANATION OF

Cash on hand, amounts with federal reserve, and deposits with other banks. Proportions of deposits that must be kept in reserve with the federal reserve are less for country banks and on time deposits.

Treasury bills, certificates of indebtedness, notes, and bonds. Fully guaranteed obligations of United States agencies may be included, with the title so specifying. If purchase price is above par, stated value must each year be reduced (amortized) so that the book value stands at par at maturity or first call date. Many banks voluntarily reduce the stated value more rapidly. The figure is not adjusted upward if the market rises.

At present, state and municipal bonds, mostly short-term, make up the major part.

Not a marketable item but thoroughly sound in the improbable event of liquidation.

Discounts represent loans upon which interest has been paid in advance or which have been purchased below face value. Loans include ordinary commercial loans (maturing in less than one year); term industrial loans (usually payable in installments over more than one year); and personal and installment purchase loans. Mortgages are often carried separately. Doubtful loans are usually shown net after reserve or write-downs.

Part of building may be rented to outside tenants.

Mainly property taken over in foreclosure of mortgages or loans.

Interest accrued but not yet due on securities and loans in good standing.

TYPICAL STATEMENT

RESOURCES

Cash and Due from Banks	$22,000,000
United States Government Obligations . . .	57,000,000
Other Securities	4,100,000
Stock in Federal Reserve .	135,000
Loans and Discounts . .	15,000,000
Bank Premises	1,000,000
Other Real Estate . . .	515,000
Acceptances	100,000
Accrued Interest, etc. . .	50,000
Miscellaneous Assets . .	100,000
	$100,000,000

Drafts or bills of exchange accepted by the bank for payment, in effect a guarantee of payment. Generally used by customers for carrying goods through transportation or a short process. This item is the customer's liability to the bank. On the liability side, as a rule, will be found a comparable amount representing the bank's liability.

RESOURCES AND LIABILITIES *

OF CONDITION

LIABILITIES

Capital	$1,600,000
Surplus	2,100,000
Undivided Profits . . .	900,000
Reserve for Contingencies	400,000
Reserve for Losses . . .	100,000
Reserve for Taxes . . .	·100,000
Liability on Acceptances .	60,000
Unearned Discount . . .	20,000
Miscellaneous Debt . .	10,000
Dividend Payable . . .	50,000
Time Deposits	9,560,000
Demand Deposits . . .	85,100,000
	$100,000,000

For example, 80,000 capital shares of $20 par each. (If a national bank the par would be at least $100.)

Capital funds beyond par value of stock; generally derived from earnings and every few years moved out of less permanent "undivided profits" classification. They may represent a "contributed" amount included in cost of shares to original stockholder.

Profits after reserves are regularly taken into this account before payment of dividends.

This item does not refer to any known or possible losses to be taken, except in a very small minority of cases. Variously termed "general," "capital," "unallocated," or "free valuation" reserves. This item is now justifiably included with capital, surplus, and undivided profits in obtaining an accurate measure of capital funds and book value.

This may be considered a genuine liability, reflecting the best judgment of the management on specific assets. This item may not appear in liabilities but may be deducted directly from assets, which are accordingly shown net (less this reserve).

Income taxes not yet due but accrued on earnings to date.

The bank's liability on payments guaranteed.

Discount interest received in advance.

Salaries accrued, unpaid bills for work on premises, etc.

Dividends declared but not yet paid.

Part are deposits of the "savings" type. Bank can compel advance notice of withdrawal. Some interest paid.

These can be withdrawn without notice. Interest cannot be paid.

* From *Banks — 1945*, pp. 14–15, Merrill Lynch, Pierce, Fenner & Beane.

ties and cash. The danger to capital accounts of losses on other loans and investments, the real risk elements in bank portfolios, can then be judged.

Sound management—not an automatic ratio—is the best protection for depositors. This implies that management, aided by proper organization and expert personnel, will determine the amount of its investments on the basis of probable *liquidity* needs and an appropriate degree of *solvency* protection; that it will diversify its investments so as to avoid burdensome losses should one security go bad; that it will plan for relatively continuous maturities; that it will seek to maintain a high standard of quality (over and above the standard enforced by supervisory authorities, for there are "best buys" among the legal investments); and that it will continuously review its holdings so as to keep pace with the changing times.

THE ECONOMIC ROLE OF THE BANK

Banks can help or hinder economic progress in granting loans and making investments: (1) they can make full or only partial use of the community's idle savings; (2) they determine which enterprises and governments shall obtain credit and which shall not; (3) they put the depositors' and stockholders' funds either to productive or unproductive use.

TYPICAL BANK STATEMENT OF CONDITION

An explanation of individual items on the asset and liability sides of a commercial bank balance sheet is presented in the statement of condition on pages 88 and 89.

The outstanding item on the asset side is the large portfolio of United States obligations, a reflection of the reliance of the federal government on commercial banks for financial aid, a reliance which sharply increased bank deposit liabilities.

REVIEW QUESTIONS

1. Distinguish between a loan and a discount. What is a self-liquidating loan?
2. What credit yardsticks would you apply to a bank credit applicant?
3. What is a line of credit? Distinguish between a "term" loan and a capital loan.
4. List four outstanding legal limitations on bank loans.

5. How do commercial paper dealers operate?
6. Describe the financing of a typical foreign trade transaction.
7. Why do United States government bonds play so large a role in commercial bank operations today?
8. What are the advantages of loans over investments?

⌸

Bank Management, Supervision, and Deposit Insurance

OBJECTIVES OF BANK MANAGEMENT

A commercial bank's responsibility to its depositors and stockholders can be discharged successfully if: (1) deposits are protected through wise loans and investments; (2) depositors' claims are met upon demand, for ready repayment assures their use in transactions many times their money value; (3) bank funds are put to such productive use as yield stockholders dividends and increase the bank's surplus account, cushioning it against losses.

How are deposits protected and ready repayment assured?

PRIMARY RESERVES

Definition. Primary reserves are a bank's first line of defense when depositors withdraw funds. They consist of: (1) cash on hand; (2) deposits held in other banking institutions, callable on demand; (3) legal reserves held with the federal reserve bank.

Causes of Growth and Decline. There are five causes of the growth and decline of primary reserves: (1) gold imports which increase bank reserves and gold exports which decrease them; (2) Treasury money issue which finds its way to commercial banks; (3) Treasury income from taxpayers and security buyers which usually is deposited with the government's fiscal agent, the federal reserve banks, and which, when cleared, reduces primary reserves; (4) a variation in such federal reserve items as capital and surplus which also vary member bank subscriptions to federal reserve bank stock and either decrease or increase primary reserves; (5) federal reserve credit operations.

Determinants. The determinants of a federal reserve member bank's legal reserves are: (1) the type of deposit, time or demand, for larger reserves are required against demand deposits because of their greater activity; (2) the location of the bank, since rural area banks are called upon for smaller demand deposit reserves (their deposits will be used less frequently than demand deposits held by large city institutions); (3) general business conditions, for banks in large cities holding interior bank deposits are subject to heavy withdrawals in difficult times.

Banks keep cash on hand to meet customer withdrawals. However, vault cash need not be large because: (1) the check-clearing process assures banks that their obligations will be offset, in part at least, by claims against other banks; (2) the federal reserve banks can lend to supplement a member bank's vault cash.

Funds are kept with correspondent banks: (1) to facilitate payment of customers' out-of-town bills; (2) to take advantage of investment and money-market opportunities in New York and Chicago; (3) to gain the services and advice of metropolitan banks.

Amount. The size of bank primary reserves is determined by: (1) the length of time depositors keep their funds in the bank (some time deposit accounts are active and warrant a large primary reserve even though called time deposits); (2) the amount of deposits that may be quickly withdrawn and the likely disparity between withdrawals and new deposits; (3) liquidity and marketability of bank loans and securities to replenish dwindling primary reserves; (4) the existence of a central bank or correspondent bank providing a ready source of cash to meet depositors' claims; (5) legal reserves with the federal reserve bank.

The unit banking system of the United States means that each institution is pretty much on its own, except for recourse to the Federal Reserve System and correspondent banks. A branch banking system would make more likely the shifting of idle funds from an area where business has declined to a section where seasonal business activity is increasing.

PRIMARY RESERVES AND PYRAMIDING OF BANK CREDIT

A bank lends its free funds above its primary reserves. But the total amount of credit available to borrowers is far greater than the amount of these free, loanable funds. Why?

Expansion of the Banking System's Demand Deposits. Assume that bank X holds $10,000 of primary reserves above the cash resources it maintains with a federal reserve bank, correspondent banks, and in its own vault. This $10,000 is available for loans and investments. If bank X lends the $10,000, its debtors receive equivalent deposit balances against which they can draw checks to meet their obligations. Let us assume the checks do not find their way back to bank X, but are deposited in bank Y which clears these checks and collects the $10,000 excess primary reserve of bank X.

When bank Y's cash reserve expands, bank Y will increase its excess reserves according to legal requirements and its own needs for cash on hand and with correspondent banks. Then it will seek new customers for its new excess reserves. New loans will be granted, and its deposits will expand by both the $10,000 plus new derivative deposits. Its clients will now draw against their new deposit balances, pay over their checks to their creditors who deposit them with their banks. These institutions will collect on the checks and then find their primary reserves expanded by the amount of the checks. They, in turn, can relend their excess primary reserves which originated in bank X. This process can go on until there are no longer any excess primary reserves.

On the basis of a $10,000 excess primary reserve, bank deposits can be created many times the excess reserve. If the nation's banks established a 10 per cent primary reserve against every dollar of deposits, a $10,000 new excess primary reserve would permit credit extensions of $100,000 for the banking system as a whole according to the law of infinite geometric progression.

Credit Expansion by an Individual Bank.   In the case of an individual bank, loans and investments can exceed only slightly its surplus primary reserves because: (1) individual borrowers withdraw their demand deposit claims within a short time; (2) most checks drawn will be deposited in other institutions and represent a clearinghouse claim against it. However, since borrowers are expected to maintain balances with the lending banks and since some of the checks will be redeposited in the lending bank, an excess primary reserve permits credit extensions slightly above this reserve.

Contraction of the Banking System's Demand Deposits.   The banking system is forced to reduce its total credit grants when any one institution loses a part of its excess primary reserve necessitating the calling of loans or their payment at maturity.

Thus, if more than $10,000 of bank X's primary reserves are withdrawn, total primary reserves remaining will be inadequate to protect the bank against further deposit losses. Hence, the management will call in outstanding loans or fail to renew such loans, and a credit contraction will set in. People whose loans are called will demand that their debtors pay off their obligations, which in turn, will force withdrawals of primary reserves from other banks which will also be forced to curtail their credit operations.

SECONDARY RESERVES

Definition. Secondary reserves are loans and securities readily convertible into cash without serious loss.

Determinants. The factors determining the size of bank secondary reserves are: (1) deposit stability (if small deposits are greater than large deposits, if time accounts exceed demand claims, and the deposit turnover is relatively slow, as in the case of a rural bank, secondary reserves can be smaller than if a bank holds chiefly large demand deposits used frequently); (2) the ratio of capital to deposits (the smaller this ratio, the larger the secondary reserves required to protect deposits and prevent capital impairment); (3) liquidity and marketability of the loans and investments included in secondary reserves; (4) business fluctuations (during depressions, secondary reserves should increase, for the public will withdraw deposits, while bond investments and loans generally will decrease in marketability and liquidity; when a business revival occurs, such asset holdings will permit the acquisition of cash to finance riskier commitments).

Characteristics of Secondary Reserve Assets. Secondary reserve assets are characterized by: (1) liquidity; (2) marketability; (3) earning power. Bank management must meet depositors' claims, satisfy time depositors expecting interest, and stockholders desiring dividends.

Marketable assets, like securities, are not considered as suitable secondary reserves as liquid loans, for their price rapidly declines when all banks are selling them. Liquid assets, like self-liquidating loans, can become frozen loans in a depression, but a well-diversified loan portfolio, with paper maturing at different times, is not likely to become frozen.

Types of Secondary Reserves. There are six types of secondary reserves: (1) self-liquidating, short-term working capital loans that will not be extended at the borrowers' insistence due to the latters' new business commitments or because they cannot repay at maturity; (2) bankers' acceptances readily marketable because banks are primarily liable for their payment (this market is assured since the federal reserve banks purchase these acceptances at a very low rediscount and are even ready to buy them under repurchase agreements permitting banks and dealers to take them back within ninety days); (3) commercial paper ordinarily paid off at maturity on which banks borrow at the federal reserve banks if the paper matures within ninety days of the loan date and complies with all other laws and regulations (commercial paper houses occasionally repurchase the paper they sell, thereby bolstering the selling bank's cash position); (4) impersonal stock market "call" loans to brokers, negotiated through the New York Stock Exchange money desk or through a money broker, and callable the day after arranged (brokers also borrow some money on time loans; such loans cannot be called until maturity, but additional collateral is asked if the amount pledged proves inadequate); (5) short-term government securities maturing within five years whose marketability and market value are well maintained by the government's strong credit position and by their availability as collateral for federal reserve bank loans to member banks (they include Treasury bills, maturing in ninety-one days and sold at a discount rate, depending upon the prices bid for them when they are offered for sale, certificates of indebtedness bearing a fixed rate of interest and maturing in from six months to a year, and fixed-interest-bearing Treasury notes maturing within three to five years); (6) prime corporate, state, and local government bond issues enjoying a broad market.

Secondary Reserve Management. (1) Sound management assures a constant flow of cash into primary reserves. Depositors and new borrowers can then be accommodated without resort to the sale of securities or refusal of essential credit to worthwhile business risks whose patronage would be alienated. (2) Bank management must recognize the money risk in long-term bond purchases and arrange secondary reserves to avoid losses on security sales when security prices are depressed. Cash resources should be sufficient to meet customers' needs until bonds adversely affected by money rate changes are retired.

Criticisms of Investment Policy. Investment portfolio management has been criticized on these grounds: (1) Securities are bought in dull business periods when interest rates are low and bond prices at their peak, only to be liquidated at a loss when the loan demand grows and their interest rates advance. (2) Bank runs bring forced sales and heavy losses. (3) Small-town banks, managed by officers with inadequate investment knowledge, have been particularly guilty of purchasing worthless bonds. A few losses and a bank's capital may be threatened as reserves are eaten away.

GOVERNMENT SUPERVISION

Internal bank management is supervised by governmental agencies to assure wise and effective use of a bank's loan and investment capacity and to protect depositors' funds.

Justification for Regulation. Bank supervision is believed desirable since: (1) through loan and investment operations, banks create deposit currency and provide the nation with its most important medium of exchange; (2) the country's economic development can be helped or hindered by an intelligent credit policy; (3) banks are important agencies of government finance and can aid or obstruct the spreading philosophy of centralized monetary management; (4) the state in its growing role as a regulator of economic life should oversee the credit operations of the banking system.

Arguments Pro and Con Federal Regulation. (1) Although the Constitution vests Congress with the sole authority to coin money, the major medium of exchange, deposit currency, is created by banks and serves as money. (2) Notwithstanding our dual banking structure, banks do an interstate business and so should be subject to federal control. (3) The dual banking system has led to supervisory weaknesses as both state and national authorities have vied for members.

Opponents of national supervision argue that differing economic situations in different sections of the United States require the special understanding of local officials.

Supervisory Structure. (1) The Comptroller of the Currency, the Federal Deposit Insurance Corporation, the Federal Reserve System, the Treasury, and the Reconstruction Finance Corporation are federal supervisory agencies, overlapping considerably in their work. (2) State banking departments supervise the organization and operation of state-chartered banks.

Supervisory Functions. These functions are indicated in the following listing of supervisory powers of the Comptroller of the Currency, top national bank supervisory official: (1) chartering national banks; (2) examining them and supervising their reports; (3) controlling establishment of branches and the merger of a national bank with another bank; (4) interpreting disputed and unclear points of the National Bank Act; (5) supervisory control of all commercial banks and trust companies in the District of Columbia; (6) appointing receivers for insolvent national banks; (7) making an annual report to Congress on the state of the national banks and recommending legislative changes governing their organization and operation; (8) prior to 1935, controlling the issue of national bank notes, since retired.

PURPOSES OF BANK EXAMINATION. Bank examination is designed: (1) to supervise bank liquidity and solvency; (2) to determine whether banks are following legal practices; (3) to determine whether a bank is insolvent and requires liquidation or whether it can be kept open by reorganization and recapitalization.

FEDERAL AND STATE INTERAGENCY CO-OPERATION. (1) The Comptroller of the Currency must examine national banks at least twice a year and may conduct other examinations if he thinks it advisable. (2) While federal reserve banks may examine national banks, they ordinarily accept the reports of the Comptroller of the Currency and so avoid duplicatory work. But federal reserve banks may conduct independent investigations especially if they suspect a national bank of using federal reserve credit for speculative purposes. (3) Duplicatory examinations of state member banks are usually avoided since state banking superintendents accept federal reserve reports or co-operate in examinations. (4) The Federal Deposit Insurance Corporation may examine insured state nonmember banks, usually in co-operation with the state banking departments. (5) The Federal Deposit Insurance Corporation may examine both state member banks and national banks with the approval of the state superintendents of banks and the Comptroller of the Currency respectively. (6) The Reconstruction Finance Corporation may examine banks whose preferred stock, capital notes, and debentures it has purchased, with the approval of the United States Treasury. Examination is made prior to purchase of special issues and following thereafter to determine whether the Reconstruction Finance Corporation's rights are being protected. (7) State banking boards work with state bank superintendents to prevent unwise banking practices and to close insolvent institutions.

INTERNAL BANK SUPERVISION. Each bank carefully supervises its internal affairs through an auditor and through public accountants who advise the board of directors of the bank's position. On the basis of their recommendations, plus the recommendations contained in the reports of governmental supervisory agencies, the board of directors may modify internal operating practices.

BANK REPORTS. (1) Supervisory officials call upon the banks under their jurisdictions for reports of their condition—statements of assets and liabilities and capital accounts. (2) All federal reserve member banks turn in at least three reports each year, while insured nonmember banks are called upon for at least two annual statements.

Co-ordination of Supervisory Practices. In 1938, federal supervisors revised their classification of bank assets to emphasize soundness. In place of the expressions "slow," "doubtful," and "loss," loans and investments are now classified in three groups: Group I, those certain of repayment and investment in nature; Group II, risky loans or investments below the four highest ratings of the investment services; Group III, loans likely to result in considerable loss or investments in default; Group IV, loans which should be charged off as losses or stock investments. Greater reserves for contingencies are required to assure adequate coverage of loan and investment losses on unsound credits.

The National Association of Supervisors of State Banks agreed to this revision.

The revision offers two advantages over the previous classification: (1) it avoids the danger of marked "write-downs" in asset values in a depression and a subsequent need for bank loan liquidation with adverse pressure on the business community; (2) it avoids the danger inherent in increased marketability and liquidity of bank loans and investments in good times which encourage further credit extensions and add fuel to inflationary tendencies.

DEPOSIT INSURANCE

Bank failures were frequent disasters to business and depositors before the Great Depression. The flood of bank closings in 1932–1933 created a demand for governmental deposit protection. The Banking Act of 1933 established the Federal Deposit Insurance Corporation.

State Experience. Western and southern states pioneered in deposit insurance schemes. Oklahoma established the first such plan in 1908, but, like the others established subsequently in Nebraska, Texas, South Dakota, North Dakota, Washington, and

Mississippi, it collapsed as a result of bank failures during the agricultural depression of the 1920's.

THE FEDERAL DEPOSIT INSURANCE CORPORATION

FDIC Capital. The Federal Deposit Insurance Corporation's
funds were obtained originally by: (1) the federal government's
purchase of $150,000,000 of the corporation's capital stock; (2)
the federal reserve banks' capital subscription of one-half of their
surplus accounts on January 1, 1933. Neither of these two stockholders have voting power, nor do they receive dividends. The
corporation may supplement these contributions by the sale of
obligations of $3,000,000,000 to the Treasury.

Insured Banks; Assessment. Insured banks include: (1) national banks and state bank members of the Federal Reserve System
that must join; (2) state bank nonmembers such as commercial
banks, mutual savings banks, trust companies, industrial banks, and
all others receiving deposits which may join if their capitalization,
community financial services, earning power, management, and history warrant admission according to the corporation's standards.
Insured nonmember banks, among other things, cannot pay interest on demand deposits, must abide by the FDIC regulations
fixing interest rates on savings and time deposits, and cannot merge
or consolidate with a noninsured bank without the FDIC's approval.

Each insured bank pays an annual premium of one-twelfth of
1 per cent of its average daily deposit balances. The FDIC uses
this sum to cover its operating expenses and to provide for possible
losses from bank failures; it then puts 40 per cent of the remainder
in its surplus account (which is invested in United States Government securities) and assigns the remaining 60 per cent to the
insured banks which can use it as a contribution to the subsequent
year's assessment.

Expulsion and Withdrawal. Insured banks can quit the system voluntarily and may even be expelled because of illegal and
unsafe practices. Whether expelled or withdrawing voluntarily, deposits at the time of expulsion or withdrawal are insured for two
years, during which period the bank must continue assessment payments. Deposits received after the date of expulsion or withdrawal
are not protected.

A federal reserve member bank which withdraws or is expelled loses its federal reserve membership status, while a national bank must surrender its federal charter.

FDIC Management and Procedures. The corporation is managed by a board of three directors—the Comptroller of the Currency and two presidential appointees approved by the Senate and serving six-year terms; none of the three may serve as a bank officer, director, or stockholder while an FDIC official. The FDIC is concerned primarily with the prevention of bank failures rather than with paying off depositors.

Bank stability is sought by: (1) bank examination and analysis of bank reports; (2) controlling combinations of insured and non-insured banks as well as the assumption of noninsured bank deposit liabilities by insured institutions and vice versa; (3) assisting the mergers of weak, insured institutions with well-established, insured banks through loans and the purchase of assets of unstable banks to make the arrangements attractive to the absorbing institutions; (4) buying the assets of, or granting loans to, closed insured banks.

In the event of an insured bank's failure, the FDIC: (1) serves automatically as receiver for national banks, and for state banks when named by state banking authorities; (2) pays off individual depositor accounts up to $10,000 each directly by check, or through the establishment of accounts for depositors in going institutions, or by organizing a deposit-insured national bank; (3) accepts depositors' rights against failed banks when their individual claims up to $10,000 are paid off. If a depositor's account exceeds $10,000, he holds a claim for the balance against the failed bank's assets.

The total claims of any depositor against the FDIC cannot exceed $10,000, no matter how many separate accounts he maintains with a bank.

Benefits. The community gains since: (1) depositors no longer fear bank failures due to unsound management characteristic of our unit banking system prior to 1933; (2) most deposits, by far, are insured deposits of middle income and low income earners who can ill afford bank failures with their attendant losses.

Criticism. (1) Large banks claim many of their depositors are only partly protected since their accounts exceed $10,000. (2) Under the assessment system, large banks contribute to the FDIC a disproportionate share of all bank assessments since they hold such a high percentage of all bank deposits. (3) Large banks claim they do not require deposit insurance because they usually do not fail,

Therefore, deposit insurance penalizes sound management. However, large banks do suffer from small-town failures. Bank panic spreads quickly, and interbank deposits owed small interior institutions are subject during a critical period to hasty withdrawals which may have the effect of embarrassing large banks in big cities.

REVIEW QUESTIONS

1. What is a primary reserve? What factors influence its size?
2. How can excess primary reserves be the basis of a multiple-bank credit expansion for the whole banking system?
3. What is a secondary reserve? What factors determine its size?
4. List five secondary reserve assets. Why are they considered suitable secondary reserve assets?
5. Name three major supervisory functions of the Comptroller of the Currency. How do federal and state supervisory agencies cooperate in their work?
6. Describe the purpose, organization, and membership of the Federal Deposit Insurance Corporation.

CHAPTER ELEVEN

The Federal Reserve System

The American banking system's capacity to finance business has increased since the organization of the nation's central banks, called federal reserve banks.

FUNCTIONS OF THE FEDERAL RESERVE BANKS

Bankers' Banks. (1) Federal reserve banks hold the legal cash reserves of federal reserve member banks. Cash reserves held in excess of legal reserves are termed *excess reserves*. (2) They increase and decrease bank primary reserves and lending power through loans to member banks and their repayment, by open-market purchases and sales of United States government securities and bankers' acceptances, by changes in reserve and margin requirements, and by direct action. Under unusual conditions, nonmember banks are eligible for loans.

Direct Lenders to Industry and Individuals. They lend directly to individuals in emergencies if banking accommodations are not available elsewhere, and can lend directly or join with other banks in five-year working capital loans to established industrial and commercial enterprises under similar circumstances.

Note Issuers. They issue federal reserve notes to member banks requiring money to satisfy depositors and borrowers. The issue of notes results from central bank loans to member banks and/or member bank withdrawals of excess reserve balances.

Reserve Depositories. (1) They hold reserves against outstanding federal reserve notes. At least 25 per cent of these reserves must be in gold certificates; the remainder, in liquid and marketable paper and direct United States government obligations. A 5 per cent gold certificate reserve is also held with the Treasury as a redemption fund for that part of the issue against which assets other than gold certificates serve as backing. (2) A 25 per cent gold certificate reserve must be maintained against deposits. (3) The gold certificate requirement can be suspended for thirty days and for additional periods of fifteen days each if a gold shortage warrants it, with the reserve banks taxed according to their reserve deficiency. This tax is added to the discount rates on loans to member banks.

Business Stabilizers.   Since the 1930's, some authorities, including federal reserve officials, have urged the Federal Reserve System's social obligation to aid in stabilizing business activity.

Fiscal Agents.   Federal reserve banks are: (1) depositories of government funds drawn against by check (many banks are also depositories, but when the government is ready to use its funds, it orders them shifted to the federal reserve banks); (2) transferors of government funds; (3) sales agents receiving subscriptions for federal securities, determining their allocation among those wishing to buy and delivering securities to purchasers; (4) fiscal agents for government corporations like the Reconstruction Finance Corporation; (5) foreign central bank correspondents performing such duties as holding foreign central bank deposits, safekeeping earmarked gold, and investing idle foreign balances in American securities; (6) holders of different moneys needed for business purposes by commercial banks; (7) advisers on government fiscal policies influencing bank primary reserves and business activity.

NEED FOR THE FEDERAL RESERVE SYSTEM

Under the National Banking System, established in 1863, the American economy suffered from various weaknesses: (1) Each commercial bank, holding a small part of the nation's gold reserve, met its problems without assistance from a co-ordinating central bank holding the bulk of the nation's gold reserves. (2) The national bank note issue was not responsive to business requirements. Until 1875, the total issue was fixed by law and could not exceed the issuing bank's capital. The bond collateral underlying this money was retired when the government enjoyed a budgetary surplus in prosperity. Government bond prices rose and yields dropped, reducing the incentive for bank investment and forcing a decline in the bank note issue. In a depression, the banks held more bonds and had a growing capacity for issuing bank notes. (3) Uniform high reserve requirements on all deposits of 25 per cent for large banks in central reserve and reserve cities and 15 per cent for country-district banks forced a slowing down of loan activity when the demand for bank credit was rising. (4) Reserves were centralized in New York, Chicago, and St. Louis, called central reserve cities, since the law permitted banks in other cities, called reserve cities and country districts, to keep one-half and three-fifths respectively of their reserves in these larger centers. Interior bank funds were attracted—especially to New York—by a 2 per cent return paid out of the income from speculative loans available in the large financial centers. When the balances were called in, the big institutions found it difficult to comply since the funds were invested in loans and securities not readily convertible into cash and there was no central bank to whom they could turn as a "lender of last resort," nor could they increase their bank note issue. Therefore, banks hoarded their reserves, called in loans, refused new credits, and forced such liquidation of securities and commodities as to create a "money panic." (5) The maldistribution of bank reserves resulted in high interest charges in those sections with little loanable cash on hand and a low money cost in the big-city centers, especially New York. (6) The lack of an acceptance market deprived banks of an outlet for surplus funds while foreign trade financing was forced into foreign markets because national banks could not accept drafts drawn upon them under letters of credit. (7) National banks objected to the stronger competitive position of state-chartered banks which could underwrite securities, receive savings deposits, and conduct a trust business. (8) The independent treasury system forced a withdrawal of money from circulation and the temporary hoarding of it in banking offices, created high interest rates, and reduced the banking system's capacity to grant credit. When the funds were disbursed, bank reserves rose and interest rates dropped. Even when national banks were occasionally designated as government depositories, political favoritism often determined the depositories. But interest rate fluctuations were minimized, for the liquid resources of the business banks were not as sharply reduced. (9) A clumsy national check-clearing system was marked by remittance charges and a roundabout collection procedure for nonlocal checks.

BANK LEGISLATION, 1908–1913

Immediate Causes. The many years' demand for reform of the American banking system reached a climax during the panic of

1907. The large number of bank failures, the "money panic," and the cessation of gold payments resulted in the Aldrich-Vreeland Act of 1908 and the Federal Reserve Act of 1913.

Aldrich-Vreeland Act. It authorized: (1) a National Monetary Commission to consider the whole issue of bank reform and (2) an emergency bank note issue by "national currency associations" of ten or more national banks with a total combined capital and surplus of $5,000,000 minimum. The Secretary of the Treasury could permit individual banks to issue like notes. All notes issued were secured by municipal and other bonds or commercial paper of a certain quality with the objective of introducing an elastic money issue into the nation's currency system. It further provided that (3) each "currency association" bank was liable in proportion to its capital and surplus, with the government taking a lien on deposited securities and bank assets. When the act was extended in 1914, (4) the top limit of $500,000,000 of these emergency note issues was suspended, with the total issue for any one bank increased from 100 to 125 per cent of capital and surplus and (5) federal reserve member state banks and trust companies also were given the privilege of issuing these emergency notes.

Only when World War I started was money issued under the act; by November, 1915, the notes issued were completely retired.

Federal Reserve Act. A fundamental banking change was effected in 1913 when the Federal Reserve Act became law. Since the Democrats opposed concentration of monetary authority especially in the East, their legislation called for a number of regional central banks. An organization committee, directed to divide the country into from eight to twelve districts with a federal reserve bank in each district, decided upon twelve federal reserve districts.

FEDERAL RESERVE SYSTEM ORGANIZATION

Member Banks. (1) National banks must join. Conversion from a state to a national bank requires membership. (2) State commercial banks, trust companies, and industrial banks can join if they are able to meet membership eligibility requirements. Among these requirements is capitalization equal to that of a national bank. However, state banks with at least $25,000 capital may join if organized before June 16, 1933, or if members of the Federal Deposit Insurance Corporation. (3) Mutual savings banks are eligible. Since they do not issue capital stock, their surplus and undivided profits must equal national bank capital requirements in the same locality.

ADVANTAGES OF FEDERAL RESERVE MEMBERSHIP. (1) Federal reserve banks can increase member bank lending power through loans to them. (2) The interdistrict and intradistrict clearance systems provide nation-wide clearance for checks, notes, and similar obligations. Check-clearance service is offered without charge, while other instruments are handled at little or no cost. (3) Currency in any denomination is obtainable from the reserve banks which absorb the cost of shipping money to member banks. (4) Reserve banks provide advisory services.

DETERRENTS TO MEMBERSHIP. In 1952, there were about 14,000 insured commercial banks, only about 7,000 of which were federal reserve members granting more than 70 per cent of all bank loans and making the bulk of all bank investments. The nonmembers, chiefly small banks, have not joined because of: (1) the large capital requirements; (2) loan and investment supervision eliminating profitable credit opportunities; (3) the incurring of both federal and state supervision which federal reserve membership entails; (4) reserve requirements higher than for nonmember banks resulting in increased unprofitable idle reserves; (5) the federal reserve par collection system; (6) the availability of federal reserve clearance and collection facilities without membership, provided that funds are kept on deposit and remittances made at par; (7) the ability to apply for loans from reserve banks under special circumstances and from their correspondent institutions at all times; (8) the belief that the Federal Reserve System encourages branch banking, to which small banks are opposed; (9) opposition to increasing federal business and banking controls; (10) lack of need for such services as rediscounting and collection (for example, in trust companies and mutual savings banks).

EXPULSION AND WITHDRAWAL. (1) State member banks may be expelled if the Board of Governors, the system's top ruling and co-ordinating agency, finds that they have violated pertinent federal banking laws or Board regulations. (2) State member banks may quit the system voluntarily upon six months' notice, which may be waived by the Board of Governors. Whatever the circumstances of withdrawal, a member bank turns in its stock purchased at the time of joining the system, and is paid off at par, plus accrued dividends of one-half of 1 per cent per month, if earned.

Federal Reserve Banks. (1) There are twelve such banks, each one in an important city of the federal reserve district whose credit activities it oversees. (2) Member banks in each district subscribe up to 6 per cent of their capital and surplus to their reserve bank's capital stock, one-half subject to call. (3) A federal reserve bank must have a minimum subscribed capital of $4,000,000. (4) An increase in a member bank's capital and surplus obligates it to subscribe to additional federal reserve bank stock; a reduction in its capital and surplus means that it must surrender an equivalent proportion of its federal reserve bank stock. (5) Member banks may receive a cumulative dividend of 6 per cent upon their paid-in stock subscriptions. Earnings above 6 per cent are retained by the federal reserve banks.

MANAGEMENT. Each federal reserve bank is managed by a board of nine directors chosen for three-year terms. There are: (1) three Class A directors, representing the banking interests of the district, with the large, intermediate-size, and small banks choosing one such director every three years; (2) three Class B directors representing the business and agricultural interests of the district, with one such director also selected every third year by the member banks in the large, intermediate, and small categories (these directors cannot be officers, directors, or employees of other banking organizations); (3) three Class C directors selected by the Board of Governors. Class C directors cannot have any other banking affiliation during their terms of office, and to assure familiarity with the district's problems, they must reside therein for at least two years prior to appointment.

OFFICERS. The chief officers of a federal reserve bank are: (1) the president, chosen for five years by the board of directors, subject to approval by the Board of Governors; (2) the chairman of the bank's board of directors, selected by the Board of Governors from the Class C directors. He serves also as federal reserve agent, supervising the federal reserve note issue and holding the collateral security for it. Another Class C director acts as deputy chairman.

BRANCHES AND AGENCIES. Twenty-four branches are in operation to speed up and smooth the system's work like collections and other services. In addition, they smooth over local resentment against the reserve bank cities. Each branch is managed by its own board of directors consisting of at least three and not more than seven members. The parent federal reserve bank chooses a majority of the directors, and the others are named by the Board of Governors.

Federal reserve agencies were established in Cuba and Savannah for the performance of routine duties. They no longer are operating.

FEDERAL RESERVE BANK OF NEW YORK. It is the most important unit of the twelve federal reserve banks because: (1) it has the largest capitalization, approximating $65,000,000; (2) its location permits it to oversee the financial activities of New York City —the world's leading financial center; (3) most of the system's open-market transactions are effected in the New York market; (4) it handles the greater part of the system's foreign business.

Board of Governors of the Federal Reserve System. (1) This is the top supervisory agency of the Federal Reserve System, composed of seven persons appointed by the President with the advice and consent of the Senate for fourteen-year terms, so arranged that a new member is appointed every two years. (2) No member can be reappointed after serving his full fourteen-year term. (3) In making appointments, the President must assure fair representation to the country's financial, industrial, commercial, and agricultural interests, and only one member may come from any single federal reserve district. (4) During their terms of office, members cannot hold a position in a member bank or be a stockholder, director, or officer of a nonmember bank. These limitations also apply for two years after a governor resigns from the board prior to the end of his appointed term.

POWERS.

Over Organization. The Board of Governors can influence the system's organization by: (1) fixing the boundaries of the twelve federal reserve districts and classifying cities as central reserve, reserve, or country-bank cities; (2) providing for the clearance of checks and other credit instruments through the Interdistrict Settlement Fund; (3) assessing the twelve federal reserve banks to administer the system.

Over Member Banks. The Board of Governors: (1) examines state member banks and requires reports of condition; (2) supervises the opening and closing of state member bank branches and changes in member bank capitalization; (3) removes officers and directors for unsound and illegal practices; (4) authorizes trust departments in national banks; (5) fixes margin requirements on loans for buying and carrying securities registered on national security exchanges; (6) fixes member bank reserve requirements; (7) directs action against member banks using their credit power and federal reserve credit to finance speculative loans unduly; (8) fixes maximum interest rates on time and savings deposits; (9) authorizes holding companies to vote the stock of member bank subsidiaries.

Over Federal Reserve Banks. Board powers over federal reserve banks include: (1) supervision of federal reserve bank credit policy; (2) examination at regular intervals and inspection of financial statements (assets deemed worthless by the Board of Governors must be written off); (3) suspension of reserve bank operations if legal violations occur (similarly, directors, officers, and employees may be suspended if circumstances warrant); (4) supervision of federal reserve note issue; (5) passing on a reserve bank's application to establish a branch or agency in a foreign country, or a possession outside the United States, or to appoint correspondents there; (6) regulation of the reserve system's clearance procedure and the charges imposed by member banks for the collection and payment of checks and other credit instruments.

Federal Open Market Committee. This committee, made up of the seven members of the Board of Governors and five representatives elected by the twelve federal reserve banks, determines open-market operations—federal reserve bank purchase and sale of United States government securities and bankers' acceptances.

Federal Advisory Council. This council consists of twelve representatives, with each federal reserve bank's board of directors choosing a member. It advises the Board of Governors of the Federal Reserve System on federal reserve bank policies and operations and general economic conditions. Its advice and recommendations are not binding on the Board of Governors.

The organization of the Federal Reserve System is pictured in the diagram on the opposite page.

CREDIT CONTROL POWERS

Federal reserve banks are essentially bankers' banks. They can expand or contract member bank resources available to the business and financial communities in different ways.

Rediscounts and Advances. Federal reserve credit is obtainable through either rediscounts or advances for a period of fifteen days

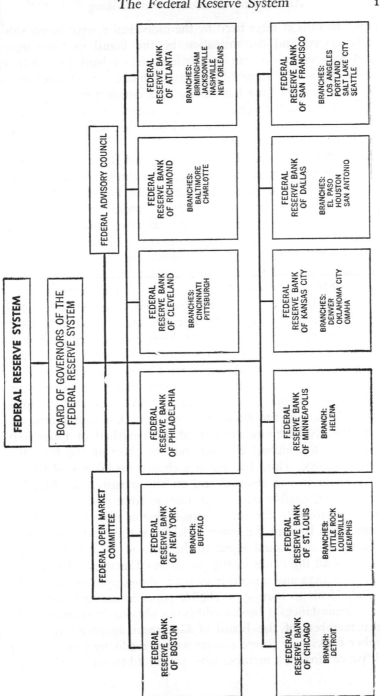

FEDERAL RESERVE SYSTEM

BOARD OF GOVERNORS OF THE FEDERAL RESERVE SYSTEM

FEDERAL ADVISORY COUNCIL

FEDERAL OPEN MARKET COMMITTEE

FEDERAL RESERVE BANK OF BOSTON

FEDERAL RESERVE BANK OF NEW YORK
BRANCH: BUFFALO

FEDERAL RESERVE BANK OF PHILADELPHIA

FEDERAL RESERVE BANK OF CLEVELAND
BRANCHES: CINCINNATI, PITTSBURGH

FEDERAL RESERVE BANK OF RICHMOND
BRANCHES: BALTIMORE, CHARLOTTE

FEDERAL RESERVE BANK OF ATLANTA
BRANCHES: BIRMINGHAM, JACKSONVILLE, NASHVILLE, NEW ORLEANS

FEDERAL RESERVE BANK OF CHICAGO
BRANCH: DETROIT

FEDERAL RESERVE BANK OF ST. LOUIS
BRANCHES: LITTLE ROCK, LOUISVILLE, MEMPHIS

FEDERAL RESERVE BANK OF MINNEAPOLIS
BRANCH: HELENA

FEDERAL RESERVE BANK OF KANSAS CITY
BRANCHES: DENVER, OKLAHOMA CITY, OMAHA

FEDERAL RESERVE BANK OF DALLAS
BRANCHES: EL PASO, HOUSTON, SAN ANTONIO

FEDERAL RESERVE BANK OF SAN FRANCISCO
BRANCHES: LOS ANGELES, PORTLAND, SALT LAKE CITY, SEATTLE

Source: *United States Government Manual*, 1952–1953, p. 583.

to nine months at rates fixed by the individual reserve banks subject to review and determination by the Board of Governors. (1) A rediscount is a loan by a federal reserve bank to a district member bank on a negotiable instrument like a promissory note which the member bank has previously discounted for a customer. Since the member bank indorses its customer's note, it is secondarily liable. (2) An advance is a loan based on the promissory note of the borrowing bank.

ELIGIBLE PAPER.   (1) The original Federal Reserve Act permitted rediscounts only of business paper maturing in ninety days and agricultural paper maturing within nine months if the business or agricultural paper resulted from productive operations or their proceeds were to be used for productive purposes like the producing, purchasing, carrying, or marketing of goods.

Subsequent amendments have modified the type of eligible discountable paper and the uses to which the loan proceeds can be put. (2) Member banks may borrow up to ninety days on their own notes collateraled by federal obligations, or up to fifteen days on notes secured by federal intermediate credit bank debentures due in six months, and Federal Farm Mortgage Corporation bonds, and Home Owners' Loan Corporation bonds when guaranteed as to both principal and interest by the United States government. These advances are renewable. (3) The Banking Act of 1935 authorized reserve banks to grant advances subject only to the rules and regulations of the Board of Governors. On four-month advances the discount rate must be at least one-half of 1 per cent higher than the highest discount rate in effect at the time the advance is made. Thus, the way was cleared for the use of federal reserve credit in any channel and on any security. (4) Member banks lacking eligible paper may borrow from reserve banks on suitable collateral by forming groups of five or more banking institutions. Each bank in the group is liable for the funds jointly borrowed up to an amount equal to the ratio of its deposits to the deposits of all the banks in the group. (5) Emergency legislation, adopted in 1932 and amended in 1935, allows nonmember banks and individuals to borrow on eligible paper in unusual and emergency circumstances if bank credit is not obtainable elsewhere and if five members of the Board of Governors approve. (6) Nonmember banks may secure federal reserve credit by rediscounting their paper through a member bank permitted to act in this capacity by the Board of Governors. (7) The Emergency Banking Act of March 9, 1933, permits ninety-day advances to nonmember banks, individuals, partnerships, and corporations if secured by direct obligations of the United States government.

ACCEPTABLE PAPER. Even though a member bank may have eligible paper, a reserve bank can rule such paper unacceptable because it is considered unsafe or because rediscounting it will overextend the bank.

REPURCHASE AGREEMENTS. Reserve banks buy member bank acceptances and Treasury bills at a discount, which the commercial banks can repurchase before maturity at the sale price plus the discount.

Direct Loans to Industry. (1) A departure from their function as bankers' banks was permitted by 1932, 1933, and 1934 legislation noted above. (2) The Loans to Industries Act of June, 1934, enables federal reserve banks to lend directly and to join with other banking institutions in lending for working-capital purposes to established industrial and commercial enterprises for a five-year maximum period. Such loans are permitted only in exceptional circumstances and if borrowers cannot be financed by regular banking channels at reasonable rates. A joint loan may call for a reserve bank to participate on certain terms, discount the borrower's paper, lend to a participating bank on the security of the borrower's promise, or buy the borrower's obligation from the lending bank. The reserve bank can suffer at most a loss of 80 per cent of the loan, for, according to the law, the lending bank must either extend 20 per cent of the loan or be liable for 20 per cent of the losses suffered by a reserve bank.

Open-Market Operations. (1) Bank primary reserves and lending power are increased or decreased by the open-market purchase or sale of United States government securities, chiefly, and of bankers' acceptances; bills of exchange; cable transfers eligible for rediscount; tax-anticipation, state and local government securities maturing within six months of their purchase date; Federal Farm Mortgage Corporation and Home Owners' Loan Corporation bonds maturing within six months; and federal intermediate credit bank acceptances. (2) Under the Second War Powers Act of 1942, reserve banks may also buy and sell government securities directly from and to the Treasury. But only $5,000,000,000 of such investments can be held at any one time.

NONBANKING PURPOSES. (1) Open-market operations may be employed to support the market prices of government securities. (2) Since government security holdings have been the reserve banks' major source of income in recent years, they may be bought to build up the central banks' income.

Reserve Requirements. (1) Member banks are required to maintain reserves against deposits with the federal reserve bank of the district in which they are located. (2) The Federal Reserve Act of 1913 reduced member bank reserve requirements under those of the National Bank Act and classified demand and time deposits separately. (3) A 1917 amendment to the Federal Reserve Act fixed the central reserve city (New York and Chicago) member bank reserve requirements against demand deposits at 13 per cent, the reserve city (other leading cities) member bank demand deposit reserves at 10 per cent, and the country-bank reserves at 7 per cent. Time deposit reserves for all banks, regardless of location, were fixed at 3 per cent. (4) The Banking Act of 1935 gave the Board of Governors power to boost, by as much as twice, these reserve requirements of any and all bank classifications if approved by four members. Reserve requirements cannot be reduced below the 1917 limits. (5) If a member bank fails to maintain required reserves, a tax penalty is imposed on the daily deficiency at a rate 2 per cent above the ninety-day commercial paper rediscount rate. The Board of Governors may tax more heavily if it sees fit. Banks can avoid a reserve deficiency by borrowing from those institutions with a surplus reserve at their federal reserve banks. Loans are arranged on a daily basis in the "federal funds" market. (6) The Board of Governors can suspend for thirty days and for additional fifteen-day periods any and all reserve requirements.

The Board of Governors can affect the reserve requirements of member banks by modifying the reserve requirements for any and all classifications of banks.

Margin Requirements. The Securities Exchange Act of 1934 gave the Board of Governors power to fix margin requirements on loans granted for buying and carrying securities registered on national security exchanges. The margin rules of the Board of Governors apply to all commercial banks and all brokers and dealers who do business through national security exchanges.

Direct Action. Direct action is taken by the Board of Governors against those member banks whose loan and investment policies are considered unsound: (1) The Banking Act of 1933 authorizes the Board of Governors to suspend the borrowing privileges of member banks making undue use of federal reserve credit for speculative purposes or using it to create unsound credit conditions. (2) The board can prohibit a member bank from increasing security market loans for one year. Failure to comply means denial of rediscount privileges. (3) Advances on a bank's own note secured by government bonds may be suspended if the bank continues to increase its security market collateral loans after due warning. Previous federal reserve bank advances can be declared due immediately. (4) The board may fix the ratio of member bank capital and surplus which can be lent for loans on stock and bond collateral. (5) Officers and directors of member banks can be removed if held guilty of unsafe and unsound banking practices.

Regulation of Consumption Credit. A presidential executive order in 1941 directed the Board of Governors to establish rules minimizing the use of credit facilities for the purchase of consumers' goods. On November 1, 1947, Regulation W, under which consumer credit was controlled, was eased. Subsequently installment-buying curbs were removed.

CONTROVERSY WITH THE TREASURY

During the Second World War the public debt of the federal government mounted sharply. While the debt was on the rise, the Treasury considered it important to maintain a low level of interest rates on government paper. This could be accomplished by holding up the prices of government paper and keeping the yield thereon at a low level. The Federal Reserve System complied with this Treasury policy, although reluctantly. See Chapter 21 for a full treatment of the Treasury-Federal Reserve controversy and current policy.

REVIEW QUESTIONS

1. Describe the major functions of the federal reserve banks.
2. In what ways did the National Banking System fail to meet the money and credit requirements of the United States? How does the Federal Reserve System seek to satisfy these needs?
3. What is a member bank? What are the qualifications of a member bank? Why are there so many nonmember banks? What are the advantages of federal reserve membership?

4. How can the Federal Reserve System make money "tight"? How can it make money "easy"? Explain.
5. What is the purpose of the Loans to Industries Act of 1934?
6. What powers does the Board of Governors exercise over the member banks? Over the federal reserve banks?

田

Federal Reserve Credit Operations and Treasury Monetary Policy

How does the Federal Reserve System use its credit power instruments to influence money and credit conditions?

QUANTITATIVE CONTROL POLICY

Rediscount Rates. Rediscount rates are adjusted to the business situation. For example: (1) Rediscount-rate increases force banks borrowing at reserve banks to raise their rates to customers if they wish to maintain earnings. A rediscount-rate rise could be a deterrent to business when its profits are eaten into by higher bank charges. (2) A rediscount-rate reduction is aimed at stimulating business by encouraging bank loans at lower rates which would increase profit opportunities.

While the discount rates are set by the individual federal reserve banks, the Board of Governors can reject rate changes and establish rates it deems more suitable.

EFFECTIVENESS. The availability of rediscounts does not insure their use: (1) Member banks do not like to be indebted to the federal reserve banks. (2) Low rediscount rates do not encourage member banks to lend more liberally to their customers, since the cost of borrowed money is only one factor determining the profitability of a business enterprise. During the 1930's, negligible borrowing occurred in spite of drastically reduced rediscount rates. (3) High discount rates do not deter businessmen from expanding operations if the net profit is attractive.

Open-Market Operations. (1) When federal reserve banks buy government securities, they pay the seller—a bank, an individual, or an investing institution—by check. A selling member bank can present the check for payment to its federal reserve bank which will credit the seller's reserve account and increase its reserve balances and primary reserves. If a selling bank demands cash, holds it, or deposits it with correspondent banks, the net effect is also a primary reserve increase. Individuals and nonbanking institutions selling their securities to reserve banks will also be paid off by check and deposit the proceeds in local banking institutions, thereby increasing bank primary reserves and loanable funds. The growth of bank primary reserves serves to effect a more lenient bank credit policy with a possible greater flow of loanable funds into business. (2) When federal reserve banks sell open-market paper, they receive check payments settled by reductions of member bank reserve balances with the federal reserve banks, drafts upon correspondent banks, or cash payments which decrease the bank reserve position and reduce its lending power and willingness to lend.

EFFECTIVENESS. The effectiveness of open-market operations depends upon: (1) the general business situation; (2) bank willingness to grant credit when reserves are increased or to curtail credit when reserves are depleted; (3) the size of bank excess reserves.

Heavy purchases of government securities during the early 1930's, aimed at increasing bank loans and business investments, did not encourage the flow of bank credit for the business outlook was bleak. Open-market paper sales in the late 1930's would not have absorbed the large excess bank reserves completely. These excess reserves in a healthy business situation would have led to a flow of bank credit into business channels.

Co-ordination of Open-Market and Rediscount Rate Policy. (1) During the 1920's, the Federal Reserve System used its open-market powers to make rediscount-rate policy effective. When rates were raised, federal reserve banks sold securities to decrease bank reserves and force member bank rediscounting at the higher rates, which would, in turn, be passed on to bank customers and perhaps discourage business borrowing. (2) When federal reserve bank rates were lowered, the reserve banks bought securities and so encouraged a low member bank customers' loan rate. (3) During the 1930's, when the government was engaged in its pump-priming campaign, federal reserve banks maintained low rediscount rates and bought federal securities or avoided their sale to facilitate the government's program of borrowing at low interest rates. This program indicates a deviation from the original purpose of the Federal Reserve Act—financing business—to using credit control instruments to supplement the government's direct efforts at stimulating business activity. (4) During World War II, when the government was intent on the success of low interest rate bond sales, federal reserve open-market policy was directed toward support of the government bond market and catering to the Treasury's needs. This support was especially pronounced when new issues of federal securities were marketed. It also was evident when the commercial banks' reserve positions required bolstering to avoid selling their government holdings and to insure a good response to new offerings. (5) After the war, the federal reserve banks were active government bond buyers to protect the member banks' reserve position faced by a growing volume of nonwar loan accounts requiring reserves.

Reserve Requirement Policy. Reserve requirements are determinants of bank excess reserves and bank ability to expand outstanding credit: (1) A large excess reserve permits a greater bank credit expansion than does a smaller excess reserve. (2) Since excess reserves are not distributed equally, some banks are embarrassed by higher reserve requirements while others can meet the new requirements easily. Therefore, reserve requirement changes force some banks to curtail loans and investments but do not affect other bank portfolios. (3) Reserve requirements should not be changed too often unless imperative. The fear of increases discourages bank loans and investments and hampers business activity.

HISTORY. (1) The Board of Governors, vested with authority to increase reserve requirements by the Banking Act of 1935, took its first action in 1936 when it increased required reserves by 50 per cent. It believed that the growing volume of bank credit could be controlled only by supplementing rediscount rate and open-market operations by increasing required reserves. Reserve requirements were increased further in 1937 and reached the legal maximum. (2) The 1938 recession induced a slight cut, but the maximum was restored in 1941 to combat inflation. (3) In August, 1942, New York City and Chicago required reserves against demand deposits were reduced slightly, for New York City bank reserves had been depleted as both they and their customers, purchasing federal securities, drew on bank liquid resources to pay for their purchases. (4) Reserve requirements for all federal reserve member bank demand deposits were sharply raised, after World War II, to curb inflationary bank credit.

QUALITATIVE CONTROL POLICY

The Federal Reserve System seeks to control the uses to which its credit is put as well as the quantity used.

Margin Requirements. (1) The initial margin requirement—the difference between the market value of a security and its maximum loan value—was first placed upon brokers' and dealers' loans to customers in 1934 through Regulations T and U. (2) In 1936, commercial bank loans granted to buy and carry registered securities were made subject to this margin requirement. (3) Short sale margin regulation was initiated in 1937. (4) In 1945, margin requirements for brokers' and dealers' loans on listed securities, for short sales, and for bank loans were increased to 75 per cent, and in 1946, security buyers were required to put up 100 per cent of the market value of securities. This margin requirement increase was considered necessary because of the sharp stock market price advance and the Board of Governors' fear that stock market loans would also increase sharply, diverting productive credit into speculative channels. (5) All margin requirements were reduced to 75 per cent in 1947.

Direct Action. (1) The most noteworthy illustration of direct action against member bank credit policies was taken during the 1929 stock market boom. The Board of Governors warned member banks that if they had a big portfolio of speculative loans, they would not enjoy the rediscount privilege. (2) During World War II, bank financing of consumers' good purchases was discouraged by Regulation W of the Board of Governors.

THE 100 PER CENT RESERVE PLAN

Justification. The 100 per cent reserve plan is advocated by those believing that a partial reserve against deposits encourages bank credit expansion and feeds a business and inflationary boom to society's detriment. For a boom is followed by a severe deflation causing widespread suffering and economic loss.

The Plan. (1) Commercial banks, holding only demand deposits, would not be able to lend or invest these funds, for against these deposits a 100 per cent dollar reserve would be maintained either in the banks' vaults or with the federal reserve banks.

(2) Business loan and investment operations would be financed by specialized banking institutions, perhaps affiliated with demand deposit organizations. The funds to carry on such activities would be obtained from the sale of capital stock and certificates of indebtedness and the receipt of time deposits. (3) Against time deposits little or no reserves would be required, but a 100 per cent reserve would be needed to meet the demands for all sums lent or invested, especially if the commitments were transferred to demand deposit organizations. (4) Since the time deposits could be withdrawn only after due notice, while the certificates would also have a strictly enforced maturity date, they could not become mediums of exchange. (5) The means of payment would be stabilized for, as demand depositors drew upon their checking accounts, the amount of money outside demand deposit departments or institutions would increase; conversely, an increase in demand deposit checking accounts would be offset by a decline in the amount of money outside these departments. (6) The plan could be introduced by giving the Board of Governors of the Federal Reserve System the power to raise member bank reserve requirements against demand deposits to 100 per cent. All commercial banks with checking accounts would be required to join the Federal Reserve System and their reserves could be built up to 100 per cent by the exchange of their government security investments for member bank reserves. (7) The income loss to demand deposit institutions due to abandonment of their loan and investment operations would be made up out of increased service charges on accounts handled or through government subsidization aimed at minimizing such service charges.

ARGUMENTS FOR THE PLAN. (1) It will eliminate banking panics and the unhealthy effects of cyclical demand deposit expansion and contraction. (2) Deposit insurance will be unnecessary. (3) Since the central bank or some like institution referred to as a "monetary authority" would acquire a good part of commercial-bank-owned government securities, the cost of the public debt would be reduced.

CRITICISMS. (1) Time deposit departments would still be under heavy pressure in depression when loans and investments might be frozen. (2) Credit contraction would reduce the supply of money as demand deposits were used to pay off time deposit institutions. (3) Time deposit departments could not control demand deposit circulation velocity nor could they necessarily follow a loan and investment policy that would put all their available funds to work. (4) The plan is not an all inclusive system of credit control, for installment and commercial financing institutions not subject to the central governing board authority would flourish, while large business enterprises could finance their own and other business organizations' needs. (5) A higher level of service charges for demand deposit accounts would discourage their use, and government subsidy to minimize this service charge would penalize the efficient as against the inefficient demand deposit organization.

TREASURY MONETARY POLICY

The Treasury can also influence monetary policy in the hope of stabilizing the economy.

Gold Policy. The Treasury can influence the United States gold reserve by: (1) licensing and restricting gold exports and controlling the movement of monetary gold reserves into industrial and artistic channels; (2) sterilizing gold imports and preventing their use as primary reserves by selling securities in the open market to obtain funds to pay for the gold, instead of drawing upon governmental deposits with the federal reserve banks and issuing gold certificates based on the new gold acquisitions (the effect of this securities sale is to shift an equivalent amount of commercial bank primary reserves to the Treasury's accounts with the federal reserve banks. From 1936 to 1938 when member bank excess reserves, due largely to heavy gold imports, were an inflationary threat, a gold sterilization policy was followed); (3) gold dollar devaluation yielding a profit to the government, which, if spent, increases bank primary reserves (an upward valuation of the gold dollar would decrease the dollar value of the gold certificate holdings of the federal reserve banks and force the Treasury to borrow to recompense the federal reserve banks).

Silver Policy. Silver purchases influence bank primary reserves: mining companies deposit Treasury checks with local banking institutions whose balances with the federal reserve banks and lending power are increased.

Silver legislation in 1946 called upon the Treasury to buy all newly mined domestic silver offered to it at 90.5 cents per fine ounce. The Treasury determines the price and amount of foreign silver it will purchase and the terms of sale of its silver hoard.

Paper Money Policy. Paper money in circulation and commercial bank primary reserves can also be increased if Congress legalizes the issuance of new paper money. This paper money would be deposited to the Treasury's account with the federal reserve banks and would find its way into bank primary reserves as the Treasury drew upon the federal reserve banks to meet its obligations. Treasury retirement of money in circulation reduces bank primary reserves because the funds for the operation are obtained by tax increases or the sale of government bonds which shift bank resources to Treasury accounts in federal reserve banks.

Cash Balance Policy. Bank primary reserves can be increased by shifting Treasury funds from federal reserve banks, or from the Treasury's own vaults, to the commercial banks. They can be reduced by shifting funds back to the reserve banks or the Treasury's vaults.

Budgetary Policy. (1) If tax receipts exceed expenditures, bank demand deposits and primary reserves decline by the amount of the surplus. (2) Heavy taxation may force the tax-paying public to borrow at commercial banks with a resultant increase in bank demand deposits and a shift of excess reserves to required reserves. (3) Government borrowing from commercial banks increases deposit currency and necessitates larger required reserves, reducing excess reserves and contracting bank lending power. Between 1929 and 1939, the demand deposit structure was inflated 50 per cent by federal deficit financing at commercial banks. (4) During World War II, the sale of government obligations direct to the federal reserve banks also increased bank primary reserves. (5) Fiscal policy, however, aimed at minimizing bank deposits and primary reserves by selling savings bonds directly to the general public. These "baby bonds" could not be used as collateral for commercial bank loans, nor were they purchasable by these institutions. (6) Still another technique for minimizing commercial bank primary reserves during the war years was the sale of certain government bond issues only to nonbanking institutions like insurance companies and wealthy people. Commercial banks cannot buy these "tap issues" for ten years after their issue. (7) Again, bank subscriptions to new issues during the war were limited, while tax savings notes were sold to attract the funds of individuals and nonbanking institutions. These notes could not be purchased by commercial banks for purposes other than tax payments. (8) Retirement of public debt held by banks and individuals affects the reserve position in different ways. If the redeemed bonds are held by banks, they exchange their bond holdings for new primary reserves while their demand deposits and required reserves shrink since individuals have drawn upon their deposit accounts to meet their obligations. If the redeemed bonds are held by individuals, the net effect is to keep unchanged both primary reserves and bank deposits. Taxpayers first draw on their bank accounts when they discharge their tax obligations and then rebuild them when the government pays out the money to redeem the bonds. If federal reserve banks hold the redeemed government bonds, a reduction of both reserve bank federal bond holdings and of a corresponding amount of deposit liabilities owing to the government occurs.

REVIEW QUESTIONS

1. Under what conditions are the federal reserve rediscount rate, open-market, and reserve requirement credit controls effective?
2. What is qualitative credit control? How and when is it used?
3. What is the 100 per cent reserve plan? Why is it urged? What are its weaknesses?
4. Explain gold sterilization. Under what circumstances was it employed in the United States?
5. Explain five different ways government cash balance and budgetary policies affect bank primary reserves.

H

History of United States Commercial Banking

The history of commercial banking in the United States can be divided into five periods: (1) the years prior to the organization of the first Bank of the United States; (2) the period during which commercial banking was dominated by the first and second Bank of the United States; (3) the state bank era; (4) the period characterized by the development of a federally supervised banking system under the National Bank Act of 1863; (5) the period from 1913 to date, which has been distinguished by the organization and important role of the Federal Reserve System.

PRE-FIRST BANK OF THE UNITED STATES

Organization and Ownership. (1) Special bank charters were issued by colonial and state legislatures to men of established financial reputation. Since these banks were considered state agents, they were usually partially owned by the chartering states. (2) They could be opened before their entire capital was paid in. (3) Their capital consisted of small specie contributions, government bonds, and funds borrowed by subscribing stockholders on the bank's own stocks from the banks they organized.

Loans. (1) These banks financed the movement of goods to market and were repaid shortly out of sales proceeds. (2) Borrowers received bank paper-money issues typical of all early chartered banks in the United States.

ADVANTAGES OF PAPER-MONEY ISSUE. Bank notes were more advantageous than deposit currency because: (1) transportation and communication were so undeveloped that speedy presentment and payment of credit instruments like checks were impossible; (2) the credit soundness of checks could not be verified. Therefore, people preferred to receive bank notes payable to bearer.

Other Activities. The banks: (1) accepted deposits; (2) engaged in foreign exchange dealings; (3) bought and sold gold and silver bullion and federal government bonds.

Early Banks. (1) The Bank of North America was chartered by Congress in 1781, with capital subscribed in part by the government. Shortly thereafter, the bank secured charters from several states since it doubted the ability of Congress to authorize a bank under the Articles of Confederation. (2) The Bank of Massachusetts was chartered in 1784, and the Bank of New York and Fifth Avenue Bank was organized by New York financiers in the same year. (3) While not officially organized as banks, various individuals and business enterprises did a banking business since they accepted deposits, lent money, and engaged in foreign exchange operations.

FIRST BANK OF THE UNITED STATES

Functions. This institution, inspired by Alexander Hamilton's ideas and chartered for twenty years, 1791–1811, serviced the community and government: (1) It issued nonlegal-tender paper money, acceptable for all debts due the federal government, redeemable in gold and silver, and therefore enjoying a nation-wide reputation and circulation. The Constitution forbade the states to issue paper money and did not vest the central government with such authority. Since states could still charter note-issuing banks, there was grave danger of a flood of nondescript paper moneys. To forestall or minimize this danger, Hamilton urged that the Bank of the United States be empowered to issue a sound nation-wide paper currency. The state banks' paper was controlled by forcing its redemption in specie or rejecting it at the Treasury. (2) It extended credit by discounting the business community's notes. (3) It lent to the federal government. (4) It was a depository for the temporarily idle funds of the people and the government, thus serving as a national fiscal agent. (5) It offered domestic and foreign exchange services.

Capitalization. (1) The capitalization was set at $10,000,000, with the federal government subscribing $2,000,000 (subsequently resold at a profit to pay off debts owed by the bank) and the general public, $8,000,000. (2) The government subscription was paid for with a promissory note, while private subscribers could pay three-fourths of their commitment in United States government securities and one-fourth in specie. The lack of specie in the country complicated the bank's organization.

Management. (1) The governing board consisted of twenty-five directors, all United States citizens. (2) Although the shares were largely held abroad, American control was assured by a prohibition on foreign shareholder proxy votes. (3) The Secretary of the Treasury could call for reports and examine the bank's operations, but he rarely did so.

Branches. Branches were established in New York, Boston, Baltimore, Washington, Norfolk, Charleston, New Orleans, and Savannah to assure nation-wide services to the entire business community. Thus, the United States seemed launched toward a branch banking system and a limited number of independent banks along Continental lines.

Note Issue. It could not exceed outstanding capital stock. The management restricted the issue so that at its peak it totaled about $5,000,000.

Termination. The opposition of state-chartered and private banks, the general fear of a money trust in a democratic country, the dislike of foreign ownership of the greater number of shares, and the claim of unconstitutionality seemed to argue for the end of the bank in 1811—one year before the War of 1812 when its services could have been used to advantage.

PRIVATE BANKS

The assets of the first Bank of the United States were purchased by Stephen Girard, the first important private banker in the United States.

Origin. Early private banks flourished when unsound note issues and unsatisfactory or inadequately chartered banking facilities in the midst of a growing business economy offered the private banker the opportunity to meet the community's needs for sound money and banking facilities. In the order of origin, they can be classified in two groups: (1) frontier merchants who accepted deposits, granted credits, and helped finance local projects like canals; (2) mercantile houses that specialized in foreign exchange and the sale of American securities abroad.

Functions. They: (1) accepted deposits; (2) dealt in domestic currency and exchange, buying up notes of chartered banks at a discount and presenting them to the issuers for redemption;

(3) issued paper money, at times doing so by issuing bills of ex‹ change or drafts in convenient denominations—redeemable at the issuing merchant's shop; (4) sold bills of exchange and letters of credit on foreign correspondents; (5) sold gold and silver at a premium when banks suspended specie payments and the metals were in great demand; (6) acted as loan brokers; (7) granted short-term loans.

Effect of National Bank Act.   Profit opportunities were reduced when the National Bank Act provided a sound, national currency and a well-supervised banking system. Many private banks became national banks to secure the advantages of the note-issue power monopolized by these banks.

Private Banks Today.   They specialize as investment banks, foreign exchange dealers, security brokerage firms, and commercial paper houses. J. P. Morgan and Company, Inc., is a private deposit bank.

STATE BANKS

State Bank Ownership.   (1) Private ownership frequently was combined with local governmental ownership for the states wanted to share bank profits and participate in local bank management. (2) The states believed they could fill the need for money capital in the rural areas to which private capital was hesitant to lend since they, rather than private borrowers, could obtain the necessary funds. (3) State-owned or partially state-owned banks first appeared in the older and more highly developed states and then spread to the South and West. The movement was given impetus when various states established their own banks out of a part of the federal government's surplus revenue for 1837 distributed among the states. (4) They enjoyed some success only when supervised by bankers. But there was strong opposition to these successful institutions by debtors who resented pressure for repayment of obligations.

Currency Disorganization.   (1) Worthless state bank note issues flourished as state banks increased from 88 to 208 between 1811 and 1815 and their issue mounted from $23,000,000 to $110,000,000. Since the first Bank of the United States' control over local note issue ended with its life, and banks outside New England issued a large quantity of irredeemable notes, the currency system was badly muddled and seriously hampered trade.

(2) The government, now using state banks as its fiscal agents, found its funds tied up in paper-printing institutions whose notes could not readily be transferred from one section of the country to another. (3) The difficulty of distinguishing good notes from bad facilitated counterfeiting, thereby further disorganizing the money system. (4) So bad was state bank supervision and state note-issue control that failed state banks' notes often circulated for years after the closing of the issuers.

SECOND BANK OF THE UNITED STATES

Reasons for Establishment. A general suspension of specie payments in 1814, save for New England, was caused by: (1) the excessive issues of state bank notes too often of doubtful value; (2) the exportation of about $7,000,000 of specie to pay off stockholders of the first bank; (3) the obvious weaknesses of the banking system especially during the War of 1812.

The second Bank of the United States was organized in 1816. Its functions were identical with those of the first bank.

Capitalization. Its capitalization was $35,000,000, with the federal government subscribing 20 per cent payable in specie or in promissory notes. Actually the government paid in promissory notes, liquidating them completely in 1831.

Service to the Government. The bank paid the government $1,500,000 for its charter. The bank was obligated to arrange for the shifting of public funds to any section of the United States without cost to the federal government.

Management. Like its predecessor, the second bank was governed by twenty-five directors, one-fifth appointed by the government. Special congressional committees could examine the bank's affairs.

Branches. Branches were located in the leading cities. Apparently, the United States had again embarked on a sound program of branch banking with the advantages of asset diversification and ready shiftability of surplus funds from one section of the country to another needing additional money.

Note Issues. (1) Notes could be issued in an amount equal to the bank's capital stock. (2) State bank note issues were kept under strict control by the second bank's insistence on specie redemption on demand. Such control aroused the strong opposition of the rural banks.

Termination. (1) Rural and local institutional opposition to the bank as its charter approached expiration in 1836 resulted from the bank's demand that state-chartered institutions maintain their notes at par. (2) Debtors also clamored for the bank's death, convinced that their troubles resulted from the bank's curb on the activities, especially the note-issuing power, of state banks. (3) The opposition of President Jackson, a son of the pioneer community where state banks flourished, sealed the bank's doom. (4) It lost its federal charter, was converted into a state bank, and finally closed in 1841.

"WILDCAT BANKS"

Although both the first and second Bank of the United States had greatly limited unwise state banking practices, state banking flourished. It boomed when the first and second banks were no longer present to exercise a restraining influence.

Definition. A "wildcat bank" was a bank which issued notes beyond its capacity to redeem them. Wildcat banks were usually located in such distant or inaccessible places that presentation of their notes for redemption was almost impossible.

Why Organized. (1) People, especially westerners, looked upon banks as mere paper-issuing institutions regardless of business needs. (2) They considered banks excellent sources of personal profit when money was greatly needed.

State Encouragement. State legislation created the proper atmosphere for the wildcat banks: (1) failure to redeem notes was not penalized; (2) bank capitalization was reduced.

The 1837 panic forced the failure of many of these banks and encouraged state regulation and supervision of local banks.

PROTECTION FROM UNSOUND NOTE ISSUES

Sound banks tried to protect themselves against the issue of worthless money.

Suffolk Banking System. The Suffolk Bank of Boston, acting for the other city banks as well, began in 1825 to accept and redeem out-of-town New England bank notes at par, if the issuers redeemed their own notes in Boston, out of an adequate deposit plus at least $2,000. If a bank did not join this system, its notes were presented for collection at the bank itself.

ADVANTAGE. This arrangement enabled Boston banks to keep their notes in circulation and maintain their profits, dependent largely on the volume of such bank notes in circulation. Previously, New England had been flooded with doubtful bank paper issues which businessmen, but not the banks, accepted. Boston bank notes were used to liquidate bank indebtedness, while out-of-town notes were used in trade where they passed readily from hand to hand.

Safety Fund System. New York State instituted a Safety Fund System in 1829. This system required each bank to contribute to a guaranty fund for discharging the liabilities of insolvent banks a sum equal to 3 per cent of its capital stock. The fund was subjected to a heavy drain during the panic of 1837 and was inadequate to meet all losses since contributions were based on bank capital stock rather than on notes and deposits. Consequently, an 1845 amendment to the original arrangement stipulated that only bank note liabilities were covered by the fund.

THE INDEPENDENT TREASURY SYSTEM

Reason for Establishment. During Jackson's quarrel with the second Bank of the United States, he had shifted the government's deposits to selected state institutions called "pet banks." A "pet bank" was not a "wildcat" institution, for it had to redeem its notes in specie, agree to federal supervision and collateral the government deposits if the government deemed it wise or if government deposits were greater than one-half of its capital. Nevertheless, several of these banks failed and prompted the establishment of the independent treasury system—banking offices in leading cities to handle the government's income and outgo—whereby the government acted as its own fiscal agent.

Disadvantages. (1) Withdrawal of money as taxes were paid and its subsequent reinsertion into the currency stream made the money system responsive to fiscal requirements rather than to business needs. This difficulty became so aggravated during the Civil War that increasingly the government used national banks as depositories following their establishment under the National Bank Act. (2) Political favoritism in the choice of banks and the amount allocated to them became very apparent and affected the amount of money in bank vaults for financing business operations.

THE NATIONAL BANK ACT OF 1863

Purposes. Provisions of the act were designed: (1) to establish a system of national banks that would help finance the Civil War, for the banks were originally required to buy government bonds (to be paid for in specie) up to one-third of their capital stock or $30,000, whichever was the greater and, with the bonds as collateral, to issue a conservative bond-secured currency (the state banks had not aided the Treasury as anticipated, while the issue of unsecured greenbacks had proved inflationary); (2) to minimize the monetary chaos created by the issue of unsound, poorly secured state bank notes.

Few national banks were organized before the Civil War's end so that these banks were of little financial assistance until the postwar years.

TAX ON STATE BANK NOTE ISSUE. In 1865, when the Treasury was convinced that national bank notes could be issued in sufficient volume to meet trade requirements, a prohibitive 10 per cent tax was levied on state bank notes driving them out of circulation and forcing most state banks to seek federal charters to secure the then vital note-issue privilege. An impossible interest rate of 10 per cent would have been required on a loan of state bank notes, destroying their utility.

Comptroller of the Currency. National banks are under the supervision of the Comptroller of the Currency, a Treasury officer appointed by the President with the consent of the Senate for five years. He controls the organization of national banks.

Original National Bank Requirements. The law originally required: (1) reserves against both deposits and notes; (2) stockholders to pay in prior to organization one-half of the capital stock subscription, varying from $50,000 to $200,000 depending upon the bank's location, and the rest in six months; (3) the purchase of a minimum of government bonds; (4) the surplus account to be built up to 20 per cent of capital stock outstanding before any declaration of dividends.

Note Issue. (1) The note issue of a national bank could not exceed its capital. (2) The bank had to maintain a redemption fund with the Treasury equal to 5 per cent of the face value of its outstanding notes. (3) It was required to pay off its notes on presentation and, in addition to these issues having a prior lien on bank assets, they were guaranteed unconditionally by the federal government.

QUALITIES OF A GOOD NOTE ISSUE. A good note issue is characterized by: (1) security—the national bank note issue was limited in amount, secured by bank assets, and guaranteed by the government; (2) parity—the issuing banks were required to redeem their notes, while other national banks had to accept them from the public; (3) uniformity—all the notes were issued by the federal government under identical conditions.

But, the national bank note issue did not expand and contract with business needs as a good note issue should. It showed an inverse elasticity, for the quantity of notes in circulation varied with the Treasury's fiscal position.

REVIVAL OF STATE BANKING

Development of Deposit Banking. The growing use of checks and deposit currency as an accepted medium of exchange gave a new lease of life to state banks whose note-issue power had been taxed out of existence in 1866. In fact, a generation before the passage of the National Bank Act, the use of checks had already equaled or outstripped the use of notes in metropolitan business transactions. The development of cities, the growth of transportation and communication facilities, and the proximity of the business public to banks meant the development of check and check-clearing facilities with all their conveniences.

State Inducements. State banking laws offered bankers special inducements to incorporate under state law: (1) Capital requirements were lower than for federally chartered banks. (2) State banks could organize profitable activities like nonbanking real-estate, trust, and safe-deposit departments. (3) State supervision, examination, and credit restrictions were more lenient than federal controls.

Predominance of State Banks. State banks multiplied in the late nineteenth century until their number exceeded the national banks. At the end of 1946, only 5,007 commercial banks out of a total of 14,044 were operating under the National Bank Act.

Expansion of National Bank Powers. Additions to national bank powers over the years have been aimed at improving their competitive position: (1) In 1900, they were empowered to issue national bank notes up to 100 per cent of the par value of government bonds bearing the circulation privilege as against only 90 per cent originally. (2) Minimum capital requirements in towns of three thousand or less were reduced from $50,000 to $25,000. (3) The Federal Reserve Act of 1913 permitted national banks to engage in trust and mortgage banking, finance foreign trade, and accept savings deposits.

THE FEDERAL RESERVE SYSTEM

Banking difficulties culminating in the crisis of 1907 called the nation's attention to the need for fundamental bank reform. The Aldrich-Vreeland Act of 1908 coupled with the appointment of a National Monetary Commission to study and propose basic banking and currency reforms preceded the passage of the Federal Reserve Act of December 23, 1913.

WEAKNESSES OF THE BANKING SYSTEM

Bank Failures. (1) The Federal Reserve System improved the banking situation but left unsolved the problem of bank failures—a result of poorly managed, undercapitalized, small-town banks. (2) Branch banking, a possible cure for these ills, was limited or entirely forbidden. (3) While a federal reserve bank could lend to its members, many banks could not borrow for they lacked eligible and acceptable paper.

Competitive Bank Regulation. State and national banking systems were engaged in competition for bank membership. Laws were relaxed as first one jurisdiction and then another removed various restrictions. For example, in 1917, federal reserve state member banks were allowed to by-pass certain national laws that would have eliminated their competitive advantage over national banks. The McFadden Act of 1927 increased national bank powers to grant real-estate loans, permitted national banks to engage in city-wide branch banking on a limited scale where state-chartered banks enjoyed such a privilege, and gave official recognition to national bank purchase of investment securities.

Bank Security Affiliates. The First National Bank of New York in 1908 and the National City Bank of New York in 1911 were among the first to establish security-underwriting affiliates. During the 1920's, bond departments and security affiliates were organized on a grand scale. Unfortunately, the desire of security affiliates to sell their securities portfolios led the related commercial banks to urge their customers to purchase these bonds and stocks, frequently to suffer heavy security losses.

The Banking Act of 1933 ordered the divorce of investment affiliates from commercial banks within one year from the date of passage of the act, June 16, 1933. Federal reserve member banks may still underwrite federal, state, and municipal government issues.

THE BANKING CRISIS OF 1933

Causes.   There were several causes of the banking crisis of 1933: (1) the agricultural depression following the First World War, freezing farm bank loans; (2) the dual banking system and the duality of bank organization and management standards; (3) undercapitalized, weakly managed banks without access to the Federal Reserve System and without eligible paper; (4) the business and real-estate depression of 1929–1933 embarrassing many city institutions and creating a national "run" to withdraw bank deposits.

Number of Failures.   Between 1921 and 1932 inclusive, approximately twelve thousand institutions failed, and in 1933 four thousand more closed down.

Relief Legislation.   The Hoover administration attempted to cope with the chaotic banking situation first through the National Credit Corporation and then through the Reconstruction Finance Corporation.

NATIONAL CREDIT CORPORATION.   This organization was a cooperative venture of the banks to help one another: (1) Sound banks were to subscribe 2 per cent of their deposits for the corporation's debentures. It was hoped $1,000,000,000 would be realized. (2) The banks in each federal reserve district organized a loan committee to pass on applications of distressed banks.

However, the plan did not succeed because: (1) little was lent, especially since the banks had to guarantee the loans made; (2) distressed banks did not wish to reveal their true condition, even to their associates.

RECONSTRUCTION FINANCE CORPORATION.   The government then undertook the task of strengthening the banking structure. In January, 1932, it organized the Reconstruction Finance Corporation with $500,000,000 capital and empowered to issue publicly $1,500,-000,000 in bonds. The funds raised were used for loans to banks, insurance companies, railroads, and other needy individuals and organizations. This organization was more successful than its predecessor although the banking collapse was not avoided. The RFC was especially helpful in aiding the banking and economic reorganization of the country following the bank holiday.

GLASS-STEAGALL ACT OF 1932. This act, passed in February, 1932, authorized: (1) federal reserve bank loans to groups of five or more banks at a cost of 1 per cent above the highest discount rate in effect if they lacked eligible paper for rediscount; (2) loans to member banks, capitalized at less than $5,000,000 and in difficult straits, on any acceptable security.

EMERGENCY RELIEF AND CONSTRUCTION ACT OF 1932. The federal reserve Board of Governors could authorize reserve banks to lend to nonbanking organizations and individuals in emergencies on indorsed and otherwise secured eligible paper if adequate credit accommodations were unobtainable from regular banking channels.

The Bank Holiday. On March 4, 1933, the nation's banks were completely closed, and on March 6, 1933, President Roosevelt continued the moratorium for an additional three days. When Congress met on March 9, 1933, it quickly passed the Emergency Banking Act of that date.

EMERGENCY BANKING ACT OF 1933. (1) Federal reserve member banks were prohibited from carrying on any business during the emergency unless authorized by the government. (2) Unsound national banks were placed under the jurisdiction of conservators authorized to strengthen them and ultimately reopen them. Conservators could release funds to depositors and accept new deposits not subject to restrictions if the Comptroller of the Currency approved. (3) A conservator's reorganization plans were effective if approved by the Comptroller, 75 per cent of bank creditors, or two-thirds of its stockholders. (4) The Reconstruction Finance Corporation could provide new capital by purchasing a bank's preferred stock if approved by the Comptroller and the owners of a majority of the outstanding stock.

End of the Bank Holiday. (1) A presidential executive order on March 10, 1933, reopened the banks. (2) The Secretary of the Treasury was authorized to license federal reserve member banks if they could perform their normal functions. (3) State banking authorities were vested with the power to reopen nonmember state institutions.

FUNDAMENTAL BANK REFORM

The government now sought to correct the banking system's basic weaknesses.

Banking Act of 1933. (1) To create public confidence, the Federal Deposit Insurance Corporation was established. It insured each bank account for $2,500 as of January 1, 1934. (2) Mutual savings and industrial banks became eligible for federal reserve membership. (3) New national banks in towns of less than 3,000 population were to have a capitalization of at least $50,000. (4) The branch banking powers of national banks were broadened. (5) The Federal Reserve Board (now the Board of Governors) was to fix member bank interest rates on time deposits. (6) Interest payments on demand deposits were forbidden. (7) Member banks were prohibited from lending to their own executive officers. (8) Investment affiliates were ordered divorced from commercial banks. (9) A holding company was thereafter to secure Federal Reserve Board approval to vote member bank stock and to allow the board supervisory authority over it and its group of banks. In addition, the voting strength of banks in group organizations was limited in electing federal reserve bank directors. (10) The Federal Reserve Board could restrict member bank credit for speculative purposes. (11) Bank stockholders were not to be doubly liable for national bank stock sold after June 16, 1933. (12) A Federal Reserve Open Market Committee was set up to determine federal reserve bank open-market policy.

Banking Act of 1935. This legislation reorganized the Federal Reserve System and gave the system's authorities greater scope and responsibility: (1) The Federal Reserve Board was given a new title, "Board of Governors of the Federal Reserve System," and was to be made up of seven men appointed for fourteen-year terms with the advice and consent of the Senate. The Secretary of the Treasury and Comptroller of the Currency were removed as ex-officio members. (2) The board could modify member bank reserve requirements to twice the basic requirements, below which they cannot fall. (3) The board could review and determine federal reserve bank rediscount rates and require rate changes more often than every two weeks. (4) It was also to determine the nature of ineligible paper acceptable for advances to member banks. (5) The Federal Open Market Committee was reorganized with the Board of Governors dominating its membership. (6) Each federal reserve bank was to be headed by a president and vice president. (7) A permanent plan of deposit insurance was established, each account being guaranteed up to $5,000. The FDIC could forbid insured nonmember banks paying interest on demand deposits and could restrict interest rates on time deposits. (8) Double liability on national bank stock issued prior to June 16, 1933, could be eliminated effective July 1, 1937, by giving due notice. However, where double liability was eliminated, national banks had to acquire a surplus equal to their capital stock account. (9) National bank real-estate loan powers were expanded.

PROPOSALS FOR BANKING REORGANIZATION

The complexity of the American banking structure and the overlapping functions of supervisory agencies have led to a demand for further reforms.

Different groups argue for: (1) unification of the entire banking structure by eliminating state banking jurisdictions and creating one national system (this could be accomplished by turning the task of deposit insurance over to the Federal Reserve System); (2) vesting the FDIC with authority for regulating and supervising all banks (at the end of 1946, 13,354 commercial banks out of 14,585 were members of this guaranteeing corporation); (3) nation-wide branch banking under national authority to simplify and unify American bank management and supervision with the definite goal of improved management in mind (the failure record of the unit banking system would seem to argue for this proposal); (4) nationalization of the commercial banking system. The large holdings of government bonds in bank investment portfolios indicates the currently strong relationship between the government and the banks. Guaranteed loans are another symptom of governmental influence in commercial bank credit operations which perhaps might better be carried on by the government directly. Opponents of nationalization fear political control of loan and investment policies which should be dominated by business and economic considerations. Again, it is claimed that the record to date of governmental supervision does not augur well for governmental ownership of the banking system.

REVIEW QUESTIONS

1. Why were bank notes the typical bank loan media of pre-Civil War days?
2. What were the functions of the first and second Bank of the United States?
3. Explain these terms: (a) "wildcat bank," (b) "pet bank," (c) Suffolk Banking System, (d) Safety Fund System, (e) independent treasury system, (f) bank security affiliate.
4. What are the qualities of a good note issue?
5. Why are most banks in the United States organized under state law?
6. Explain five ways the Banking Acts of 1933 and 1935 strengthened the American banking system.

H

Money, Bank Credit, Prices, National Income

Money and credit are buying power. What factors determine their purchasing power? Why does the value of money change and how does this affect the national income of the economy?

PRICE CHANGES

Recent History. During the past twenty-year period prices have fluctuated to the benefit or injury of one social group or another: (1) Between 1929 and 1933, when wholesale prices generally declined, farm products dropped most drastically, while commodities other than food and farm products slumped only moderately. These differing declines sharply reduced farm purchasing power. (2) The rural community's financial predicament aggravated the already prevalent demand for farm relief legislation. (3) Between 1933 and 1939, the farmer's position improved slightly as wholesale agricultural prices advanced more rapidly than wholesale industrial prices. (4) During World War II and the early postwar years to the beginning of 1948, wholesale farm prices skyrocketed sharply, while industrial products increased relatively little so that the farmer was in the economic saddle. His buying power relative to the price of industrial products had advanced by leaps and bounds. Price fluctuations since World War I are presented in Chart III (pages 142–143).

Effects of Changing Prices on Different Economic Groups. Rising prices aid: (1) debtors who now earn more money and are better able to repay their debts; (2) stockholders whose dividends rise as corporate money income increases; (3) businessmen whose earnings advance with higher prices and a larger business volume.

Advancing prices injure: (1) fixed-income receivers, like bondholders, whose dollar income is stationary; (2) wage earners and salaried workers whose money income lags behind the price advance.

The gainers and losers reverse positions in falling price periods.

Rising prices do carry compensations to creditors and employees: (1) bond interest and principal payments are more certain than dividend payments; (2) wage earners are surer of continued employment than in a period of declining prices, business losses, and general unemployment, even though the amount of buying power of their dollar income is shrinking.

Falling prices and slumping business lead to wage slashes and business retrenchment.

MEASUREMENT OF PRICE CHANGES

How can price changes be measured and their effects on money purchasing power be determined?

The Index Number. A selected group of goods and services, representative of commodity price changes, can be used to construct an index number or measure of change in money value. The prices of the selected items are averaged from time to time and their changes are indicative of the general price trend.

TYPES. There are these types of index numbers: (1) index of wholesale staple commodity prices; (2) index of both commodity and noncommodity prices, known as a composite index number and advocated by Dr. Carl Snyder; (3) index of retail prices; (4) index of security prices; (5) measure of wage changes.

CONSTRUCTION. Index numbers are constructed in various ways: (1) The simple aggregate is determined by adding the prices of the items in the selected group and comparing the totals for one period with the totals of another period. (2) The weighted aggregate of prices is determined by adding the items and then weighing them (giving them their proper relative statistical importance) according to the quantity of goods sold in the period. It is superior to the simple aggregate because it is not a total of goods sold in different units like bushels and tons, but is an index number of the amounts of money spent on goods at different times. (3) The relative index is found by reducing the items in the index number to relative prices by comparing prices in various years with the prices in a base year, all of which are assumed to equal 100. (4) The relative index number can be weighted by the amount of goods sold in the base period. This weighted relative is superior to the simple relative because it emphasizes the importance of goods according to the amount of goods sold. (5) Geometric and harmonic means of price relatives have also been constructed.

Business, governmental, and statistical organizations like the United States Bureau of Labor Statistics, the Federal Reserve Bank

CHART III: Wholesale Prices

Bureau of Labor Statistics Indexes, 1926 = 100

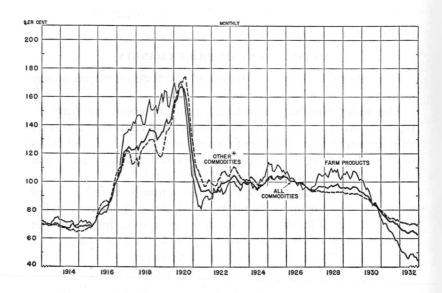

Source: Board of Governors of the Federal Reserve System, *Federal Reserve*

of New York, Dun and Bradstreet, and the Harvard University Bureau of Business Research compile a variety of index numbers readily available to the public.

FACTORS DETERMINING PRICES

The layman is puzzled by price changes. He attributes them to politics, commodity and security speculation, deliberate scarcity programs of both capital and labor, unemployment, or weather influences.

Economists have different explanations of price level variations.

Cash-Transactions Approach. This approach seeks to explain how the value of money is determined during a period of time. During this time, the market for goods is supplied with a quantity of goods, services, and property rights like securities which are seeking buyers and therefore are creating a demand for money. On

CHART III: Wholesale Prices

(continued)

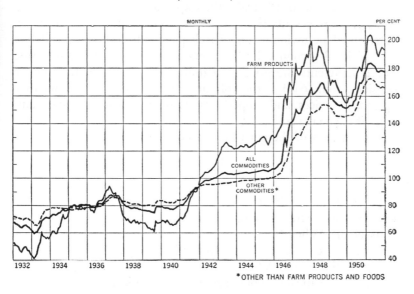

*OTHER THAN FARM PRODUCTS AND FOODS

Charts on Bank Credit, Money Rates, and Business, March, 1950, pp. 100–101, and February, 1952, p. 75.

the other hand, the market is supplied with a quantity of money and bank deposits subject to check—deposits which will be used to create a demand for, and to purchase, the goods, services, and property rights. The physical quantity of monetary and credit buying power can be increased many times during a period of time by the frequency with which it is used to purchase goods, services, and property rights. This latter factor is called the velocity of money and bank deposits.

EQUATION OF EXCHANGE. Professor Irving Fisher's equation of exchange explains mathematically price level determination. The equation reads MV + M'V' = PT. Its terms are defined thus: (1) M represents the amount of money in circulation, exclusive of bank reserves and money in the Treasury. (2) V represents the velocity of circulation of money, determined by dividing total money payments in a given period by the number of pieces of money in circulation. (3) M' represents bank deposits subject to check, exclusive of interbank deposits. Time deposits are not included because they are usually converted into cash or demand deposits before being spent and so will make their appearance either under M or M'. (4) V' represents the velocity of circulation of bank deposits, determined by dividing total check payments, called bank debits to individual accounts, by the average number of dollar deposits. (5) P represents the price level during the period of time under consideration. (6) T is the volume of transactions or the quantity of goods, services, and property rights for which money and bank deposit payments are made.

If both sides of the equation are divided by T, then

$$P = \frac{MV + M'V'}{T}.$$

SUMMARY. (1) In its most elementary form, the quantity theory of money stresses only the physical quantity of money and bank credit. When this quantity increases, prices rise; and when it declines, prices fall. (2) Other things being equal, an up- or downswing in the V and V' factors causes similar changes in P. But (3) variations in the supply of money and bank credit can be offset by changes in the velocity of the circulating medium. Thus, an increase or decrease in the number of money and bank credit units can be negated by a decline or rise in the velocity or turnover of these units. (4) Also, a rising or falling volume of transactions can counterbalance an increase or decrease in the community's media of exchange.

FACTORS DETERMINING M, M', V, V', AND T. The amount of money and bank credit in circulation is influenced by: (1) a nation's gold reserves; (2) government issuance or retirement of money in circulation; (3) reserve requirements governing the central bank and commercial banks; (4) the central bank's monetary and credit policy; (5) commercial bank loan and investment policy.

The velocity of money and bank credit is influenced by: (1) a nation's spending and saving habits; (2) the availability of credit accommodations and the frequency with which they are used; (3) debt contraction and repayment; (4) the business outlook and its effect on the spending habits of the people.

The volume of a nation's goods, services, and property rights is influenced by: (1) productive power; (2) foreign trade; (3) industrial organization and the sale to investors of property rights like securities.

Cash-Balance Equation. This equation is like the cash-transactions expression, but emphasizes the relationship of supply and demand at a moment of time. J. M. Keynes and D. H. Robertson both developed cash-balance formulas expressing how prices are determined. (1) According to Robertson, the price level is determined by (a) the available quantity of money, called M; by (b) the year's volume of trade in commodity units, called T; and by (c) the year's volume of trade in proportion to which people hold cash balances, K, equal to a certain fraction of buying power sufficient to take goods off the market. (2) The more money people hold in K, the cash balances, other factors remaining the same, the lower the price level. (3) On the other hand, the smaller the volume of money which people hold in cash balances in relation to the quantity of goods on the market, the higher the price level. (4) Money is spent in accordance with the public's desire to take goods off the market. When more money is spent, the price level rises, for smaller cash balances are being maintained. Expressed mathematically,

$$P = \frac{M}{KT}.$$

SIMILARITY TO FISHER EQUATION. The K of the Robertson expression is the reciprocal of the V factors in the Fisher equation of exchange. Assuming the quantity of money and bank credit totals $100,000, while the velocity amounts to 12, and the volume of trade aggregates 1,200,000 units, P, the price level, equals 1. If we assume the same price level, the same quantity of money and bank credit in circulation as well as the same number of commodity units for sale, K in the cash-balance equation must equal $\frac{1}{12}$ by simple mathematical calculation.

ARGUMENTS FOR CASH-BALANCE EQUATION. Even though the results obtained by the cash-transactions approach and the cash-balance equation are alike, advocates of the latter favor the cash-balance equation because: (1) it emphasizes the importance of the buyer's desire to have his supply of money represent a certain amount of purchasing power; (2) the cash-transactions equation is unrealistic in that it holds the demand for money to be the equivalent of all the goods, services, and property rights offered for the money supply.

INCOME THEORY OF MONEY VALUE

This theory, unlike the classical approach, seeks to explain why prices change in terms of profit expectations, saving, investment, money income, hoarding and dishoarding of money, etc.

Classical Concept of the Interest Rate Function.   The classicists held that: (1) the market rate of interest would always tend to balance savings and the demand for these savings for investment. (Saving is the accumulation of money income out of current income during the time period in which it is earned. Investment is the putting to work of these savings in an ensuing time period for the purchase of new capital goods.) (2) Savings, considered the sole reservoir of lending power, would automatically be invested for the going interest rate, be it high or low. (3) This interest rate, which would equilibrate savings and investment, was called the "natural" rate. No thought was given to the possibility that savings might not move into investment but be hoarded or that if savings were offered at very modest interest rates, they would find no takers. (4) Savings could always be put to work productively if idle labor and capital were available. (5) The existence of idle factors of production were supposed to increase interest rates because it was believed that entrepreneurs need only to employ the idle factors to step up their profits. (6) On the other hand a paucity of idle factors meant a drop in the interest rate, thus discouraging savings. In either case, the variations in the "natural" rate of interest would balance savings and investment.

Income Theory and the Interest Rate.   But the income theorists contend that savings are not the only source of loan funds. In fact, loan funds can be hoarded and destroyed or dishoarded and created chiefly through the destruction and creation of bank credit. Therefore, the market rate of interest determined by the supply of and demand for loanable funds can and does deviate from the "natural" rate which the classicists claim always brings savings and investment into equilibrium.

Determinants of Prices. The income theorists claim that prices are determined by: (1) the period of production, or the length of time productive operations take until goods are offered on the market; (2) the quantity of goods, services, and property values offered for sale; (3) the size of the community's money income; (4) what income receivers do with their money income—spend, save, invest, hoard, or destroy it; (5) income velocity, or speed with which the money income enters the money stream and creates a demand for goods, services, and property values (it is determined by [a] entrepreneur money payments to the factors of production, [b] the volume of added production enjoyed in a subsequent period and resulting in additional money payments, and [c] the profit outlook); (6) the amount of borrowing for consumptive or productive operations.

HAWTREY'S VIEW. (1) Price changes occur because businessmen can borrow at profitable rates at commercial banks. (2) Their outlays increase consumer buying power as the money and credit reach the public in the form of wages, interest, rents, and profits. (3) The consumer can spend his income on consumers' goods or he can invest his money and affect the price of capital goods through its influence on security prices. (4) Increased consumption forces up prices if productive capacity is fully used, or if capacity is not operating at maximum, it reduces inventory and stimulates a greater use of plant and equipment with little or no effect on prices. (5) As bank loans rise to finance the greater volume of business, the number of dollars in consumers' hands increases and businessmen's outlay, consumers' income, and consumers' outlay probably will rise more than proportionally to the growth of bank credit. (6) A sharp increase in the velocity of money follows while the unspent margin, or cash balances in producers' and consumers' hands, does not increase at the same rate. A rising price level intensifies this trend, for, in periods of price upswing, cash assets are unattractive to the businessman or consumer. A contraction of business bank loans reduces businessmen's and consumers' outlay and shrinks consumers' income whereas falling prices increase the desire to hold on to cash. (7) The decline in bank reserves resulting from an increase in the volume of money in circulation leads to an increase in short-term interest rates. This increase particularly affects the wholesaler whose profit margin is small and who is operating principally with borrowed funds. As his costs rise, due to the rising interest rate, his profits decline, leading to a reduction in operations which, in turn, affects the manufacturer's rate of operations and his requirements for bank credit. (8) A sharp increase in discount rates, even during a period of rising prices, will curtail wholesaler operations. The middleman must then hold inventory longer than usual to benefit from rising prices and so increases his cost of operation. If the speculative price advance does not materialize, he will lose and therefore he may not assume the greater risk.

KEYNES'S VIEW.   The Keynes analysis of price changes revolves around the relationship between saving and investment: (1) Saving is the failure to spend money income on consumption goods during the period when the money is earned or received. (2) Investment is the purchase of new capital equipment, like machinery in a time period subsequent to that in which the income is received. (3) Investment does not reduce the community's money income, for capital goods purchases enable the producers of these goods to meet all their costs of production, and earn a profit. (4) However, savings, if not invested, withdraw money from circulation in the following period and thereby reduce the buying power necessary to take the production of the preceding period off the market. Price change is explainable in terms of the uses to which money income is put.

Determinants of Savings and Investment.   Savings are determined by: (1) the interest rate offered for loanable funds (a low interest rate will not offset the public's "propensity to consume" or its "liquidity preference"; as interest rates rise, these latter two factors are overshadowed by the attractiveness of the rates at which money can be lent or invested); (2) the volume of income out of which savings are effected (as money income rises, consumption does not rise by the same amount, and the volume of savings grows).

Investment is determined by: (1) entrepreneurs' profit expectations from current investments relative to the interest rates paid on borrowed capital; (2) interest rates on short-term bank loans causing corresponding, if perhaps smaller, changes in long-term interest rates, and, in turn, influencing the rates at which productive income is capitalized (a rising discount rate means a rising long-term interest charge and a decline in the capitalized value of income-producing assets; the net result of a drop in the value of capital goods discourages their purchase and slows down business activity); (3) a rise in estimated earnings during a period of advancing prices offsetting a discouraging discount-rate rise; (4) new security issues during periods of high earnings and low interest rates stimulating the flow of savings into investment and business activity (investment bankers are reluctant to underwrite new capital issues when security prices fall as interest rates rise and production declines); (5) rising prices while costs lag (this increases investment because increasing earnings attract investment; a period of falling prices and lagging costs dissipates earning prospects and discourages new capital investment; new investment halts when the anticipated marginal yield on new capital investment just equals the rate of interest on borrowed or invested funds).

WHEN SAVINGS EQUAL INVESTMENT. When savings equal investment, prices, income, and output remain stable because: (1) entrepreneur money payments like wages, rents, and interest as well as owners' profits in one period return to businessmen in the next period for purchase of their production; (2) savings are promptly invested in capital goods and paid out to the factors of production engaged in producing capital goods; (3) entrepreneurs receiving income for their inventories quickly replace them. The money income they receive is quickly passed on to the producers of consumer goods.

WHEN INVESTMENT EXCEEDS SAVINGS. As the business outlook improves, investment expands. The sources of new money investment are: (1) a release or dishoarding of idle money balances; (2) the sale of securities to people and institutions, like banks, hoarding idle cash resources; (3) bank credit expansion as businessmen borrow from and sell securities to banks.

Effects—Boom and Depression. (1) The effects of new investment are felt initially in the capital goods industries that first increase their production and then their prices as productive capacity is used to the full. The increased volume of money flowing into the capital goods industries raises the money incomes of people employed in these industries and of people who provide the raw materials for these industries. (2) All these people spend more for consumers' goods and stimulate their production. (3) The improved business profit situation creates business optimism and leads to investment expansion in all industrial sectors. Bank credit in circulation mounts as the financial system makes new loans and investments. A business boom is well under way.

What brings the boom to an end? (4) As new business organizations are created and their production reaches the market, the price advance slows down and finally ceases since the flow of consumers' goods has caught up with the demand for it. (5) In addition, costs of production which boomed during the business expansion begin to weigh heavily on many entrepreneurs who find their inventories moving into the consumer markets more slowly than they anticipated. (6) Furthermore, new bank credit, readily available at low rates in the early stages of the prosperity period, is no longer easily obtainable or cheap as the banking system's cash reserves decline. (7) The net result of all these influences is a decline in new investment to the point where investment no longer exceeds savings and the price and business uptrend halt. (8) Business prospects are gloomy so that investment drops sharply while savings continue. The maladjustment between these two factors causes a depression.

WHEN SAVINGS EXCEED INVESTMENT. (1) Savings are hoarded as idle cash and used to liquidate outstanding bank loans. (2) Since the savings are not used in business, the factors of production find their incomes contracted by the amount of the savings. (3) Prices fall, and losses are suffered as business costs do not decline immediately. The business outlook appears gloomy, and new investment is discouraged by the deflation. (4) A further investment contraction follows, accentuating the downward business trend. (5) Money and bank credit pile up in idle hoards or savings in the community. (6) Business concerns seeking to reduce expenses and eliminate losses only cause a further drop in consumer income and in the prices of consumer goods. (7) The general business decline is felt in the capital goods industries whose output and prices fall under the pressure of the general slump in buying power.

THE MULTIPLIER; THE ACCELERATION PRINCIPLE; PUMP PRIMING

The Multiplier.   How much new income will be created by new investment in excess of savings in any one period and how much existing income will be destroyed by a deficiency of investment relative to savings? This is determined by the "multiplier" or the multiple effect of an excess or deficiency of investment over savings throughout several periods exercised through an increase or decrease in consumption. During the early stages of an excess of investment, money income will be spent more rapidly than in the latter stages when it moves into the hands of businessmen and professional people and the price level rises. A growing volume of investment increases money incomes, while a declining volume, less than savings, decreases the community's money income by some multiple of the deficiency of new investment.

The forces determining the size of the multiplier are: (1) the spending habits of the people benefiting from new investment (workers are likely to spend new incomes more liberally than professional groups); (2) the income velocity of money; (3) "leakages" which cut down the effect of new investment on income (for example, new consumer money income may be siphoned off into cash balances and so reduce expenditures on current production; again, new income may be used to pay off debts, reducing general buying power).

The Acceleration Principle. According to the proponents of this principle, the tempo of new investment based on the demand for goods determines the level of business activity: (1) As consumption rises, industry must not only maintain its productive equipment but add to its stock of capital goods to keep pace with the demand for its output. (2) The rising volume of industrial activity resulting therefrom will naturally stimulate business as investment in new plants and equipment mounts. (3) Merely to maintain the newly achieved level of new investment requires a constantly growing rate of consumption. (4) Any decline in the rate of consumption results in a decline in the newly achieved rate of new investment and a depressing influence on industrial orders. (5) Both on the upswing and the downswing the volume of consumption of goods accelerates new investment and disinvestment.

Pump Priming. Public works are urged by deficit financiers to pour hoarded bank credit and money into the economy and so stimulate stagnant buying power. In other words, new income is created by public investment in excess of savings during poor private business periods. Pump priming is based on the multiplier principle.

REVIEW QUESTIONS

1. Which economic groups gain from rising prices? Why? Who gains from falling prices?
2. What is an index number? Explain how any one leading wholesale price index is constructed.

3. Explain the Fisher equation of exchange. What factors influence the amount and velocity of money and bank credit?
4. Explain the Keynes income theory of money value.
5. Why do prices decline when savings exceed investment? Why do prices advance when investment exceeds savings?
6. What is the multiplier? The acceleration principle?

⊞

Savings Banks

Savings institutions, like savings banks and life insurance companies, receive people's money savings, invest them, and pay the savers a return called interest or dividends.

MUTUAL SAVINGS BANK

History. (1) The mutual savings bank developed during the Industrial Revolution. It was often sponsored by the church and owned by depositors, generally wage earners. (2) The first mutual savings bank was started in Scotland in 1810. (3) In 1817, the British parliament instituted regulation to prevent and eliminate malpractices. (4) The United States first enjoyed the services of a mutual savings bank in 1816. Philadelphia was the location of the pioneer organization and Boston actually incorporated such a bank. (5) Shortly thereafter, mutual savings banks dotted the northeast. These institutions have never flourished outside the New England and Middle Atlantic areas.

Conditions Essential for Development. There are two conditions essential for the development of a mutual savings bank: (1) industrialization with its concentration of small wage earners seeking an outlet and safe place for their small savings; (2) civic-minded bankers and businessmen willing to assume the task of investing and supervising the use of these funds.

State Control. (1) Mutual savings banks are organized and operated under special state banking legislation. (2) This legislation has strictly confined the mutual savings banks' activities, for its objective is financial strength and safety.

Trustees. A mutual savings bank is managed by a board of trustees, originally composed of the organizers or people selected by them. Upon the death, retirement, or removal of a trustee, the remaining members choose a new trustee so that the board is a self-perpetuating group not directly compensated.

ADVANTAGES OF TRUSTEESHIP. But there often are indirect compensations for trustees: (1) Investment bankers may sell new securities to savings banks more readily. (2) Lawyers may secure the legal business of the banks. (3) Commercial bankers may offer their services to attract more readily the cash deposits of mutual savings banks. (4) Insurance men may find trusteeship advantageous since savings banks often sell life insurance.

TRUSTEE LIABILITY. Trustees are liable to depositors only for gross negligence and for violation of the banking laws.

Officers. The actual operation of a savings bank is conducted by its officers chosen by the board of trustees. (1) The officers of a large savings bank usually are the president, several vice-presidents, a secretary, a treasurer, and a legal counsel, all assisted by junior executives and staff. (2) A small savings bank's affairs are largely under the supervision of a secretary-treasurer. The post of president and vice-president are honorary positions.

Deposits. (1) State laws regulate deposits in the interest of the small depositor and to minimize difficulties arising from heavy withdrawals by large depositors. New York State limits the deposits of any one saver in any one savings bank to $7,500. However, this provision does not prevent a depositor from opening up accounts in more than one savings bank or in the name of other members of his family. (2) A new account is noted in a passbook containing the terms of the contract between the depositor and his bank. (3) Terms of the contract usually require a depositor to give thirty to sixty days' notice before withdrawing his funds, but in practice this rule is usually waived. (4) Withdrawals are made by submission of the passbook accompanied by a withdrawal slip stating the amount. The bank records proper entries in the passbook and the depositor receives the money requested. (5) Savings depositors generally do not use checks or drafts, although some banks permit a limited number of such withdrawals.

Types of Depositors. Savings bank depositors are: (1) those who save for a "rainy day"; (2) those who save for some immediate purpose, usually indicated in the name of the account—for example, vacation club, Christmas club, savings plan for home purchase, school savings, etc.

Dividends. (1) A mutual savings bank does not issue stock. Its depositor-owners receive dividends compounded semiannually. (2) Dividends are dependent upon bank income, managerial policy, and the rulings of supervisory authorities. (3) The Board of Governors of the Federal Reserve System limits the dividend rates of federal reserve members. Nonmember insured banks' maximum dividends are established by the Federal Deposit Insurance Corporation. State banking departments, clearinghouse associations, and individual banks may fix even lower maximum rates.

SMALL DIVIDENDS ARE THE RULE. Small dividends are a result of two influences: (1) state law limits these banks to low interest-bearing, high-grade securities; (2) savings bank management builds up large surpluses. Earnings above dividend declarations are paid into bank surplus accounts. In some states, if this account reaches a certain percentage of bank deposits, bank management must declare additional dividends.

Management may dip into surplus to maintain dividends in periods of poor earnings.

Investments. They can put their funds to work only in securities and assets on the "legal list," prepared by the home state or by its bank supervisory agency. The conservative character of the list is indicated by a few examples: (1) United States government obligations; (2) state and municipal securities of the chartering state or a state of excellent credit standing; (3) corporate securities whose fixed charges have been earned adequately for a period of years; (4) mortgages and real estate; (5) loans secured by real estate and such sound collateral as savings bank passbooks and securities in which a savings bank may invest directly; (6) bankers' acceptances and bills of exchange eligible for purchase by federal reserve banks. The New York State Banking Board may authorize investment in formerly ineligible corporate securities, if at least twenty mutual savings banks or the Savings Banks Trust Company petition their availability. The Banking Board may remove such securities from the legal list at its discretion.*

CRITICISM OF THE LEGAL LIST. There are two principal criticisms: (1) the yield on fixed-income-bearing securities is lower than the return on noneligible investments; (2) investment conditions change so that the legal list lags behind savings bank needs. The second defect gave rise to the aforementioned power of the New York State Banking Board to permit the purchase of formerly ineligible securities.

* Recently savings banks were authorized to invest up to 5 per cent in equities or 50 per cent of their surplus and undivided profits in such securities.

INVESTMENT POLICY. (1) Sound investments with a broad market are vital since savings banks are not required to hold any particular cash reserve. (2) Prior to the 1930's, savings banks invested chiefly in high-yielding real-estate mortgages. (3) The banking collapse of the '30's drew savings bankers' attention to the need for ready convertibility of assets into cash and the desirability of investment in essentially sound assets as United States government securities.

Savings Banks Trust Company and Institutional Securities Corporation. These organizations, established in 1933, were designed to provide a central bank for New York State savings banks: (1) The Savings Banks Trust Company lends against collateral for at most six months out of a pool of loanable funds held in readily marketable securities. If a savings bank cannot repay a loan within six months, it can sell mortgages to the Institutional Securities Corporation for cash and participating debentures; it can also pledge assets with any lender to meet sudden, temporary changes in cash positions. (2) The capital and surplus of the Trust Company, amounting to $5,000,000, was supplied by New York State savings banks. In addition, capital debentures of over $27,000,000 were sold to savings banks and paid for in government bonds or mortgages. But, the major source of the Trust Company's funds are the demand and time deposits of the savings banks and the United States government totaling $248,000,000 at the close of 1946. Additional funds can be obtained by borrowing from federal reserve and government sources. (3) The Institutional Securities Corporation is also owned by the savings banks. Its capital resources may be supplemented by borrowings from commercial banks, the Federal Reserve Bank of New York, and the Reconstruction Finance Corporation.

SERVICES. The Savings Banks Trust Company: (1) acts as investment counselor for mutual savings bank bond portfolios; (2) provides mortgage and real-estate information; (3) serves as custodian of savings bank securities upon a bank's request; (4) subscribes to United States government security issues for constituent members; (5) manages savings banks declared unsafe by the Superintendent of Banks, with an eye to improving their position, effecting a merger with another bank, or liquidating them without loss to depositors; (6) acts as agent or trustee for savings banks in proceedings under the Federal Bankruptcy Act, as amended, to secure the readjustment of defaulted and other nonlegal securities; (7) operates a housing agency to correlate housing activities, like planning and construction, for New York State savings banks; (8) serves as trustee of the Mutual Savings Banks Fund, established in 1934 to protect the deposits of savings banks that withdrew from the FDIC. The fund was discontinued in 1943, and New York State mutual savings banks rejoined the FDIC.

The Institutional Securities Corporation is also more than a rescue organization. It: (1) advises on mortgage loans and services mortgages; (2) aids savings banks to dispose of acquired properties; (3) buys FHA-insured mortgages on property outside New York State, and enables state mutual banks to gain the advantage of these investments by the purchase of Institutional Securities Corporation bonds. (4) It also advises the Savings Banks Trust Company in its work of re-establishing unsafe banks.

Federal Reserve Membership. By the Banking Act of 1933, a mutual savings bank was permitted to join the Federal Reserve System if it met certain requirements: (1) It must buy the stock of its district federal reserve bank up to .6 of 1 per cent of its deposits. (2) If not permitted legally to own stock, its capital contribution might appear as a deposit with the local federal reserve bank. (3) Its undivided profit and surplus must equal the capital of a national bank in the same city. (4) Like other member banks, a savings bank must keep a reserve with its district bank equivalent to the amount required against commercial-bank time deposits.

LITTLE INTEREST SHOWN. Only a few mutual banks have joined since: (1) advantages of federal reserve membership already had been partially available (government bond holdings and bankers' acceptances could be sold to the reserve banks in the open market); (2) they had been made eligible for membership in the Federal Home Loan Bank System in 1932 and could borrow on their home mortgage portfolio.

Competitive Savings Techniques. Savings banks are faced today with competition for their depositors' funds from alternative outlets offering diverse advantages. These outlets include: (1) the savings departments of commercial banks; (2) private pension plans; (3) social security; (4) direct investment security opportunities; (5) investment institutions like building and loan associations; (6) United States government savings bonds.

Nonsavings-Bank Functions. In the light of this competition, many authorities have questioned the current function of savings banks. They have expanded their activities into the life insurance field, the safe-deposit business, the administration of small trust funds, and the personal loan business in an effort to justify their economic role. However, these services are a far cry from the original objective of the mutual savings bank.

STOCK SAVINGS BANK

(1) The stock savings bank is organized under state law and owned principally by midwestern private capital for private profit. (2) Depositors are promised a definite rate of return. All earnings above operating expenses and interest costs accrue as dividends to stockholders. (3) Deposit withdrawals are permitted only after due notice has been given. (4) These banks hold deposits subject to check and make loans like those of state commercial banks.

GUARANTY SAVINGS BANK

(1) The guaranty savings banks are located in New Hampshire. (2) They hold special deposits, which equal at least 10 per cent of all deposits, and general deposits. (3) The special deposits serve as a guaranty fund for the general deposits, and special depositors can be considered stockholders. (4) Interest is paid general depositors, while net earnings go to special depositors.

SAVINGS DEPARTMENTS OF COMMERCIAL BANKS

Legal Recognition. Commercial banks received savings deposits prior to 1913, but, in that year, the Federal Reserve Act recognized this practice as a legitimate function and permitted national banks to include "savings" in their names. State legislatures were quick to follow suit in order to put their banks on the same competitive basis.

Early Weaknesses. Commercial bank savings depositors originally were not as adequately protected as savings bank depositors: (1) Savings funds were not kept separate from regular commercial bank deposits. (2) There was no legal list of investments governing the use of their assets and assuring some special protection. The bank failure epidemic of the 1920's resulted in heavy losses to commercial bank savings depositors. (3) When a bank run and failure occurred, demand depositors were paid off first out of the most liquid assets, while time or savings depositors were required to give notice of withdrawal and only the worst assets were available for discharge of their claims. Hence, time and savings depositors suffered large losses.

Special Protective Provisions for Savings Depositors. (1) After the panic of 1907, numerous states required segregation of savings deposits and their investment in a restricted list of savings assets— the assets to be used only for paying off savings deposits. (2) Various states restrict savings deposits relative to bank capital and surplus. They may even require a separate capital and surplus for the savings department. (3) They also limit the shifting of assets from commercial to savings departments and back again. (4) The FDIC insures all deposits up to $5,000.

THE POSTAL SAVINGS SYSTEM

Purposes of Organization. Established in 1910 by the United States government, the Postal Savings System was set up to accomplish these ends: (1) stimulate savings among the poor, especially the large immigrant class that distrusted banks or were unhappy with their practices or procedures; (2) minimize exportation of American money to foreign postal savings banks; (3) entice out of hiding large hoarded funds; (4) re-establish confidence in American banking following the panic of 1907 when commercial banks failed and savings banks increased distrust by demanding notice of withdrawal.

Noncompetitive Nature. While American bankers argued that savings bank facilities were adequate, the Postal Savings System's advocates emphasized its noncompetitive nature: (1) the commercial and savings banks could offer higher interest rates; (2) they accepted larger deposits; (3) they were well established in their communities' economic life.

Governing Body. The governing body of the Postal Savings System consists of: (1) the Postmaster General, responsible for the routine details and the designation of post offices as depositories; (2) a board of trustees, consisting of the Postmaster General, the Attorney General, and the Secretary of the Treasury, which supervises the management and investment functions.

Deposits and Depositors. (1) Anyone over ten years of age may open an account. (2) The account is evidenced by non-negotiable and nontransferable certificates in denominations from $1 to $500. (3) The maximum deposit for any one depositor is $2,500 besides the accumulated interest. (4) However, an additional $1,000 drawing no interest may be deposited in the system. (5) Deposits are withdrawable, on sixty days' notice, from the depository office where the money was deposited.

Management of Deposits. (1) Postal savings funds can be invested in United States government securities, or redeposited with local state and national banks that pay 2½ per cent on the money. (2) Since the Postal Savings System pays an annual interest rate of 2 per cent, it earns a net return of one-half of 1 per cent. Compound interest is not permitted. (3) Deposits with local banks above $5,000 are secured by the pledge of governmental securities, while the FDIC protects deposits under $5,000. (4) Five per cent of the postal savings deposits must be held as a reserve with the Treasurer of the United States. (5) If the President of the United States so rules, all or any portion of the postal savings deposits, including the 5 per cent reserve, must be invested in United States government securities.

Present Popularity. (1) The 2 per cent interest rate attracted many depositors when, following 1929, commercial and savings banks reduced their interest and dividend rates, frequently below 2 per cent. (2) A fear of bank failures, as in 1920–1933, would again result in a movement of bank deposits to the Postal Savings System.

Criticisms. Critics of the Postal Savings System maintain that it has outlived its usefulness because: (1) there are adequate safe outlets for savings in well-established banks enjoying public confidence; (2) the FDIC has strengthened confidence in commercial and savings banks; (3) it draws savings away from regular banking channels and results in a loss of funds to many communities and a loss of business to local banks. The latter criticism is especially true since postal savings deposits are not finding their way back into regular banking channels due to the required 2½ per cent interest rate on such deposits.

UNITED STATES SAVINGS BONDS

Before 1935, postal savings depositors were allowed to exchange their deposits for postal savings bonds yielding 2½ per cent interest, convertible into cash in one year, and redeemable after twenty years. The terms of the United States savings bonds are very similar.

History and Terms. (1) In March, 1935, the Treasury conceived the United States savings bond idea. (2) Between 1935 and 1941, the government issued about $4,000,000,000 of series A through D savings obligations. (3) Series E bonds, first issued in 1941, were practically identical to their predecessors. They were sold at a price to yield 2.9 per cent if held to maturity, ten years from the date of issue. Series E bonds, which could be purchased up to a maximum of $10,000 of their maturity value by any one buyer in any one year, were redeemable sixty days after their issue date. As of May 1, 1952, series E bonds were changed to yield 3 per cent compounded semiannually. The interest rate on the old issue and those extended for another ten years was also increased to 3 per cent if the bonds were held to maturity. (4) Series F and G bonds matured in twelve years and were redeemable at less than par before maturity; F originally yielded 2.53 per cent if held to maturity; G carried a 2½ per cent interest rate payable semiannually; and no one person could buy more than $50,000 cost price of either series F or G bonds maturing in any one year. (5) Both the F and G bonds have now been replaced for sale by series J and K which—at 2¾ per cent—yield a higher return than the F and G bonds. J and K bonds can be purchased up to $200,000 in one year. (6) An entirely new "current income" series H bond was saleable June 1, 1952, in denominations from $500 to $10,000 at a return of 3 per cent if held to maturity. However, H bonds are redeemable six months after issue date (on one month's notice) rather than two months after issue date as in the series E bond. (7) The redemption value of all savings bonds increases with the length of time they are held by the buyers. The rising level of interest offered over the years on United States savings bonds shows an attempt to induce greater public purchase and retention of the bonds.

Purposes. The government's objectives in selling savings bonds are as follows: (1) It was thought expedient, during the heyday of New Deal financial experimentation, to spread the government debt as widely as possible outside the usual investment channels. (2) The monetization of the public debt is reduced since the government relies less on commercial banks to absorb its security issues. (3) It gives the small man a financial stake in the government's financial position. (4) When World War II opened, the Treasury's objective was to gain popular financial support for the war effort, reduce the growing volume of buying power in consumer hands, and so help offset the gap between purchasing power and the dwindling supply of consumers' goods.

LIFE INSURANCE

Purposes. Life insurance offers another outlet for the community's savings: (1) It enables individuals to protect their dependents against financial distress in the event of their death, those insured paying annual premiums, usually during their entire lifetime, on a policy for a stated amount. (2) It enables individuals to assure themselves of an annuity in their later years through the purchase of an annual income from an insurance company.

An endowment policy provides the insured with a lump sum at its maturity date, or assures his beneficiaries a cash settlement.

Savings Bank Life Insurance. A number of states, including New York, permit mutual savings banks to sell low cost life insurance: (1) The New York State law, passed in 1938, enables its mutual savings banks to sell insurance policies, directly or as agents, to any individual up to $1,000 per bank. (2) No person can obtain more than $3,000 of such insurance. This limitation minimizes the competition of savings banks with regular life insurance companies, yet brings the value of life insurance to the attention of small income receivers.

TREND OF SAVINGS

The savings of the American people reached a record-breaking total during the post World War II period. The major part of these savings was accumulated in bank time deposits, United States savings bonds, and life insurance company reserves, unpaid dividends, and accumulations.

REVIEW QUESTIONS

1. What is a mutual savings bank? Who manages its affairs? What were the conditions essential for its development?
2. How does a mutual savings bank differ from a stock and a guaranty savings bank?
3. What is the legal list? Give two criticisms of this list.
4. What are five functions of the Savings Banks Trust Company and the Institutional Securities Corporation?
5. How is the commercial bank savings depositor in your state afforded special protection?
6. Who may deposit funds in the Postal Savings System? How much may one person deposit?
7. Why is the Postal Savings System criticized?
8. What are the terms of the series E bonds?

⊞

Investment Banks and the Securities Exchanges; Investment Trusts

Savings can be invested in corporate and government securities. The bonds and stocks purchased are either newly issued, or are already sold and traded on securities exchanges.

THE CAPITAL MARKET

The capital market consists of: (1) the buyers and sellers of securities; (2) the institutions bringing them together—the investment banker, the stock exchange, and brokerage houses. Through these institutions savings flow into the capital market for use by those corporations and by governments that seek funds and are considered good risks.

THE INVESTMENT BANKER

Definition. The investment banker offers securities considered attractive to investing savers and savings institutions, and so channels idle funds into business or governmental activity.

Early History. (1) Medieval financiers lent to feudal lords and cities that wished to carry on wars and pay debts, receiving as collateral tax receipts, rents, or land mortgages. These financiers' activities were broadened when the Church eased its restrictions on interest payments. (2) Modern developments, like industrialism, the expansion of private property ownership under the protection of national laws, and the growth of savings, set the stage for the investment banker of today. At first, he dealt in governmental issues—the Rothschilds helped finance the Napoleonic wars. The full flowering of the industrial system and its demand for capital encouraged the sale of corporate securities.

American Development. (1) Commercial banks not only bought, but also often served as investment banks, selling the secu-

rities of early American banking, insurance, and transportation enterprises to domestic and foreign investors. (2) During the Civil
War, Jay Cooke organized groups of banking houses and salesmen
to sell some $2,000,000,000 of Union securities. This technique was
also followed after the war to expedite the sale of railroad obligations. (3) Toward the end of the nineteenth century, organizations
like J. P. Morgan and Company prospered from the financing
of industrial mergers and the refinancing of insolvent railroads.
(4) When World War I opened, foreign governments borrowed
in the American capital market, and the general public was familiar-
ized with securities through the sale of Liberty bonds. (5) During
the 1920's, investment banking prospered as business expanded and
floated new capital issues. Stock exchange speculation further in-
tensified public interest in investment banking, and commercial
bank investment affiliates flourished. (6) The 1929 security market crash and the deep depression of the '30's brought a halt to
these developments. Federal government supervision of investment
banks and stock exchanges followed. Investment affiliates were
divorced from commercial banks. (7) During the Great Depression and World War II, governmental financing dominated the
capital market. The federal reserve banks are the government's investment bankers.

INVESTMENT BANKING OPERATION

Origination and Underwriting.   A security issuer seeks an investment banker to underwrite or guarantee the sales of its issue
at an agreed upon price. It contacts the banker through the latter's
new business department, a commercial bank, or by direct application.

Investigation.   To determine the proposed issue's investment
quality, a costly investigation follows with the aid of engineers, accountants, lawyers, economists, and business analysts into: (1) the
issuer's corporate powers; (2) its capital structure; (3) earnings and
earnings prospects; (4) the productivity of the uses to which the
proposed financing will be put; (5) the condition and efficiency
of the issuer's plant and equipment; (6) the applicant's detailed
balance sheet position; (7) the issue's legality; (8) the likely re-
ceptivity of the new issues market to the proposed financing;
(9) the issue's terms—the type of security, interest rate (in the
case of a bond) which depends in good part upon the movement

of general money rates, maturity, call features, price to the banker and to the public.

If the issuer seems a good risk and market conditions are suitable, the banker contracts to underwrite the issue.

This investigation is unnecessary when governmental securities, most railroad issues, and public utility corporations subject to the jurisdiction of the Securities and Exchange Commission offer securities for sale. The issuers determine the terms of the issue and investment banking houses combined into syndicates bid for the securities with the highest bidder winning the issue and offering it for sale to the investing public.

Trust Indenture Act of 1939. If a corporation is selling a bond or other debt issue of more than $1,000,000 in interstate commerce, an indenture or contract between the corporation and the trustee appointed to protect the bondholders' interest is prepared setting forth the legal obligations of the issuer.

Registration with the Securities and Exchange Commission. The proposed financing is now registered with the Securities and Exchange Commission in accordance with the terms of the Securities Act of 1933 which was designed to guarantee prospective investors all the data needed to judge the issue.

Underwriting Syndicate. When a large issue is underwritten, the financial strength of more than one investment banking house is usually required to assure the security's sale. Therefore, the originating house invites other investment banks to participate in an underwriting syndicate: (1) Each syndicate member agrees to buy a fixed amount of the issue and pay the issuer its financial share of the underwriting, even if the securities are unsold. (2) Divided responsibility insures more rapid sale since it taps a broader market, and the capital of the investment banking house is turned over more frequently, maximizing its profits.

"Joint Account." Prior to 1933, the "joint account" procedure was more popular than it is today. Under this arrangement, the originator, who alone contracts with the issuer, grants part interest in the business to other investment bankers but serves as manager of the financing to facilitate centralized control of the sale to investors.

Stabilization. To expedite sale of the issue and assure investor confidence in the market price of the issue, the originating house or syndicate manager stabilizes the security's market price by purchasing and selling it, as conditions demand, at about the sale price to investors.

Selling Syndicate. The underwriters broaden their distribution facilities by forming a selling group made up of many retail houses and institutional investors like savings and commercial banks and insurance companies: (1) These organizations reserve the privilege of returning unsold securities to the underwriters. (2) The compensation to a member of the selling group is a discount from the sale price to the general investing public. (3) A prospectus, summarizing the information in the registration statement, is widely distributed to likely buyers.

Members of the selling syndicate on occasion have violated the agreement to retail securities. A few violations are (a) price cutting or retailing the issue at a price below the agreed upon price, (b) "beating the gun" or marketing the securities before the date set by the selling syndicate agreement, (c) attracting customers by accepting payment in bonds and stock evaluated above their fair market price. Houses guilty of these practices have been punished by exclusion from underwriting syndicates and selling groups.

SELLING SECURITIES ON A COMMISSION BASIS. (1) On occasion, bankers do not underwrite a new security but only act as a selling agent compensated on a commission basis. (2) If any securities are unsold, they have no obligation to the issuer. (3) This procedure reduces the issuer's selling costs.

Underwriting Stock Issues of Established Companies. When a going concern offers new stock to its stockholders: (1) it insures the sale by arranging for underwriting of the unsold portion at a stipulated price; (2) underwriters are given a small fee for their services, even if the entire issue is taken by the old stockholders.

Private Placement. Since the passage of the Securities Act of 1933, direct sale of new issues to institutional investors, like savings banks and insurance companies, has grown because of: (1) a surplus of investable funds in investing organizations; (2) a desire (a) to avoid registration costs imposed by the Securities Act of 1933 and (b) to eliminate the banker's profit.

During the 1920's, private placement of speculative securities with wealthy individuals on an investment bankers' preferred customers' list was typical. Large profits often accrued to such buyers as the securities soared in price during the "bull" market of 1928–1929.

Services of the Investment Banker. (1) Business corporations and governments tap the capital market more successfully, since the bankers know investment conditions and have ready accessibility to investable funds. (2) Funds are obtained more cheaply than if issuers sell securities directly. (3) An established banker rela° tionship enables a security issuer to finance future needs more readily. (4) Buyers recognize the investment banker's superior knowledge of securities and investment conditions. (5) Investors know that reputable bankers will maintain a market for the securities they underwrite and sell.

REGULATION OF INVESTMENT BANKING

Private Internal Regulation. Investment bankers have voluntarily sought to regulate their activities through: (1) the Investment Bankers Association of America, organized in 1912 to improve the industry's ethical standards and solve its technical problems; (2) the National Association of Securities Dealers, Inc., aiming at fair practices within the industry; (3) the "Better Business Bureau" working to eliminate fraudulent practices.

State Regulation. Individual states have tried to protect investors through "blue-sky laws" and "antifraud acts": (1) Blue-sky laws, the leading type of state law, provide for the licensing of reliable dealers and/or the sale of legitimate securities approved by a state securities commission. (2) Antifraud acts do not prevent fraud but provide for its prosecution through the state attorney-general's office.

CRITICISM. (1) State regulation is inapplicable to interstate securities sales. (2) Differing state regulations open the way for the sale of speculative and fraudulent securities.

Securities Act of 1933. This legislation resulted from: (1) the 1929 stock market crash and large investors' losses; (2) the realization that investment bankers and security issuers were guilty of unethical practices.

PURPOSES. The Securities Act of 1933 was designed: (1) to provide prospective investors with necessary information to judge the worth of a new issue sold in interstate or foreign commerce or through the mails; (2) to prevent fraud.

THE REGISTRATION STATEMENT. A private corporation or foreign government must file a registration statement for a security offering in interstate or foreign commerce, or through the mails,

with the Securities and Exchange Commission, the law enforcement agency. The statement shows: (1) the names and addresses
of the issuer's directors, principal officers, and underwriters; (2) the
issuer's business and capital structure; (3) ownership of the issuer's
securities by its officers, directors, and underwriters, and the iden-
tity of all people owning 10 per cent of any stock issue of the
issuer; (4) purposes of the security sale, its price to the public and
to the underwriters; (5) the issuer's financial statements, its contract with the underwriters, and legal opinion as to the issue's
legality.

Foreign governmental registration statements vary in detail because of differences in the organization of the issuer.

EXEMPTIONS FROM REGISTRATION. Exempted from registration
are: domestic government issues, bank securities, savings and loan
association securities, issues of carriers subject to the approval of
the Interstate Commerce Commission, intrastate issues, securities
put out as a result of reorganization proceedings under court supervision, securities given in exchange for outstanding issues if no
remuneration is involved in the exchange, short-term paper maturing in not more than six months, private offerings, and issues of
$300,000 or less if waived by the Securities and Exchange Com-
mission.

PROSPECTUS. An issuer must prepare a prospectus for distribution to prospective buyers, summarizing the information in the
registration statement but omitting most of the documents.

SALE DATE. Twenty days after a domestic issue's registration
statement and prospectus are filed and seven days after foreign
papers are filed, securities can be publicly sold. The Securities and
Exchange Commission may reduce the waiting period.

PENALTIES. (1) Civil and criminal penalties may be imposed
upon an issuer's officers, underwriters, and all other people responsible for misinformation on, or for omissions of, material facts in
the registration statement and prospectus. (2) The government may
imprison and fine guilty parties. (3) Investors may recapture the
difference they paid for an issue not exceeding the public offering
price and the amount at which it was resold or its market value
when legal action was taken by them.

RESULTS OF THE LEGISLATION. The legislation has had several
effects: (1) Retailers of securities are better able to judge the merit
of the bonds and stocks they sell—to the advantage of their cus-

tomers and of their own reputation. (2) Investors now enjoy a better information basis upon which to select securities—especially is this true of the small investor with little investment knowledge. (3) Many corporations, especially smaller enterprises, have sold securities privately rather than publicly to avoid the provisions of the law. Large institutional buyers have been willing purchasers of the privately sold securities of nationally known enterprises.

STOCK EXCHANGES

Definition. A stock exchange is a market where investors may sell their security holdings or purchase outstanding issues.

Services. A stock exchange provides for ready marketability of securities. Ready marketability in turn stimulates the development of an investing public. In addition, marketability increases the availability and uses of securities as collateral for business loans, especially at commercial banks. A stock exchange stimulates the growth of an investment banking community, which is encouraged by investors ready to buy marketable issues. As the financial position of issuers changes, investors may sell their unwanted or less desirable stocks and bonds and acquire more desirable securities. Supervision by the exchanges and the Securities and Exchange Commission assure a free market.

Disadvantages. (1) A stock exchange encourages speculation and a misdirection of capital. (2) Price quotations do not always reflect the true investment situation since they may be influenced unduly by excessive speculation. (3) The market is not always free since manipulations like pool operations do occur. (4) Stock exchange members at times have divided allegiance since they may be trading for their own account and yet executing customers' orders. (5) Too often an uninformed and gullible public inflates security prices during prosperity periods.

History. (1) The predecessor of the stock exchange was the medieval fair where goods were traded in terms of securities representing them. (2) Subsequently, the earliest continental exchanges took over government financing, displacing the private financier and then expanding to deal in company securities. (3) The growth of the great trading companies between the sixteenth and eighteenth centuries led to trading in their securities and the development of stock broking. (4) When government debt came into the hands of the general public, it became a trading medium. (5) A coffee house was the location of the first London stock exchange in 1773. By 1802, this exchange had a constitution and an official membership list.

NEW YORK STOCK EXCHANGE

History. (1) The New York Stock Exchange grew out of a gathering of brokers at the close of the eighteenth century under an old buttonwood tree in Wall Street, the brokers gathering to deal chiefly in government and bank stock. (2) The New York Stock and Exchange Board was officially organized in 1817 and in 1869 combined with other security traders to form the New York Stock Exchange. (3) In early trading on the exchange, only one security was dealt in at a time. Under the pressure of the unstable monetary situation after the Civil War trading in all issues at one time was permitted. (4) The ensuing years saw the membership and activities of the exchange grow to include a clearance system for speeding settlement of security dealings and a ticker system to record quotations. (5) The 1929 stock market crash ushered in a period of depressed trading and a demand for government regulation to curb loose practices, the latter culminating in the Securities Exchange Act of 1934.

Organization. (1) Stock exchange members own "seats" giving them the privilege of trading in securities if they are approved by the exchange's Committee on Admissions and Board of Governors. "Seat" owners hold their places personally or as partners in brokerage and banking firms. Neither corporations nor their representatives can own "seats." (2) The ruling body of the exchange is the twenty-five-man Board of Governors, twenty-two of whom must be exchange members. The other three are the president of the exchange who is a nonmember, and two public representatives, selected by the elected governors. (3) The president serves at the board's discretion, the public delegates have one-year terms, and twenty-one of the other twenty-two governors are elected for three-year periods, seven of them annually. The chairman of the board, a "seat" holder, is named for one year. (4) The president, as chief executive officer, carries out board policies. (5) The Board of Governors may suspend, fine, or expel members guilty of violating the exchange's rules. (6) Standing committees, of members selected by the president or chairman and approved by the Board of Governors, supervise such matters as admission of new members, security trading, and business conduct. (7) The Stock Clearing Corporation and the New York Quotation Company are subsidiaries transferring securities and selling security price quotations to buyers like the press services. (8) The organization's income is derived from annual membership dues, admission fees, charges for the listing of securities, rentals for the use of space in its buildings, and dividends from its subsidiaries. It does not aim to make money.

Listing of Securities. (1) An issuer applies for listing privileges to the Committee on Stock List. (2) A successful applicant must publish a balance sheet and income account annually, and must show that its securities are distributed widely enough reasonably to assure a competitive market. (3) Separate registrar and transfer offices must be arranged in New York City proper, while the exchange must be notified of any developments which would affect materially the market action of its listed securities. (4) The Securities and Exchange Commission permits registration of an issue on a national exchange after receipt of the information called for by the Securities Exchange Act of 1934 and approval by the exchange.

Stock Exchange Houses, Brokers, and Dealers. (1) Some brokerage houses accept orders only from a limited group of customers, but most firms offer their services to anyone. (2) "Wire houses" usually situate their head office in New York and establish branches and correspondent relationships in other large American and foreign cities. These are connected with the main office by direct telegraph, telephone wire, or teletype. (3) Commission house brokers execute buying and selling orders for their firms' clients. (4) "Two-dollar" brokers, unaffiliated with stock exchange firms, assist stock exchange firms overburdened with orders. While they originally received a $2 commission from the brokerage firms for whom they acted as agents for each hundred shares executed, today they earn more under the current graduated scale of commissions. (5) Specialists concentrate their activities on a limited group of securities assigned them by the exchange. They may also act for floor brokers in the capacity of $2 brokers and may trade for their own account but not in both roles in the same deal. They take orders from stock exchange houses to buy and sell securities at levels other than the prevailing market price. The specialist records these orders in his "book," and is thus enabled to make some judgment of the market trend and can execute orders given him at the most desirable time. His privilege to act as specialist also places upon him the responsibility of making a satisfactory market in the securities specialized in. (6) Floor traders buy and sell exclusively for themselves in the hope of a small profit and without paying any commission. (7) Odd-lot dealers receive orders to buy and sell in amounts less than the regular trading unit of a hundred shares. These orders are received from member firms. The odd-lot dealer is a jobber and effects these transactions by buying and selling for his own account. (8) Some members are inactive and do not trade. Retired brokers and investment bankers who prefer to carry on their business through active brokers are prominent in this category. (9) Bondholders are exchange members specializing in customer orders to purchase and sell bonds. They can also trade in stocks.

Commissions. Stockbroker commissions depend on: (1) minimum rates established by the stock exchange; (2) the selling prices of the stocks handled. The greater the market value of the securities, the greater the brokers' compensation. Odd-lot dealers receive a differential above the commission paid by buyers and sellers of hundred-share lots. This differential is one-eighth of a point above the price for hundred-share purchases and one-eighth of a point below the cost for full-lot sales.

OTHER STOCK MARKETS

(1) The American Stock Exchange (formerly called the New York Curb Exchange) admits securities to trading privileges by a procedure similar to that of the New York Stock Exchange. Some securities have "unlisted" trading privileges, and others are being "seasoned" prior to listing on the stock exchange. Members of the curb exchange are classified in the same categories as members of the stock exchange; but bond brokers may be specialists. (2) Other leading cities also have stock exchanges whose members deal in both local and national securities. (3) The "over-the-counter" market connotes a market in securities, which, for the most part, are not listed. They include United States government bonds, municipal and state obligations, and a vast variety of unlisted real-estate, bank and insurance company, investment trust, industrial, rail, and utility issues. Dealers and brokers in this market buy securities from sellers and profit from higher resale prices whose markups are fixed by the SEC to prevent gouging. The Commission has ruled that "over-the-counter" dealers and brokers must advise their customers whether they are acting for themselves or as brokers for both buyers

and sellers in the same transactions and also whether they have a special interest in the securities dealt in. These dealer-brokers had to register with the SEC in 1936. The Maloney Act of 1938 permitted self-regulation under the auspices of the SEC. The National Association of Securities Dealers, Inc., has established and enforced a code of business conduct in this security market area.

SPECULATION

Stock market speculators may trade on margin and so increase the volume of their security operations beyond their own capital resources.

Margin Trading. (1) The security operator pays in cash or other securities only a part of the market price of the securities he buys long or sells short. (2) The broker finances the remainder of the margin account principally through a bank loan collateraled by securities and arranged directly or through the money desk on the exchange floor. (3) The loan is either on a time or call basis. All time loans are negotiated directly between the bank and broker as are a part of the call loans. (4) The rate on a new call loan or on a loan arranged on a previous day and still outstanding is fixed by the Stock Clearing Corporation. (5) The size of the margin is established by the Board of Governors of the Federal Reserve System and enforced by the SEC. (6) The Securities Exchange Commission Act also vested the Board of Governors of the Federal Reserve System with authority to fix the maximum credit banks may grant directly to customers for buying and carrying securities. Thus, the banks and brokers are under the same supervisory power as regards stock market loans.

CRITICISM OF BROKERS' LOANS. (1) They accelerate stock market price inflation, as during 1928–1929. (2) They speed the downward plunge in security values as banks demand repayment to protect their own position. (3) They encourage security overissue to be carried with borrowed funds at a time when the capital market is not fully prepared to digest new issues. (4) They divert bank credit from legitimate business and agricultural purposes.

SHORT SELLING. (1) A short seller does not own the security he sells, but sells it in anticipation of a drop in its price. (2) He delivers the sold security to the buyer either by borrowing it from his stockbroker or from another broker holding it in a customer's portfolio with permission to lend it. (3) The lending broker is protected by the receipt of the short sale's proceeds. (4) The short sale is covered when the seller purchases the stock and delivers it to the lender. (5) The profit to the short seller depends upon the gap between the price at which the short sale was made and the price at which the sale was covered less the broker's commission. (6) If the stock rises in price, contrary to the short seller's expectations, he loses on the transaction.

SECURITIES EXCHANGE ACT OF 1934

Objective. The Securities Exchange Act of 1934 established the Securities and Exchange Commission to regulate security trading on organized stock exchanges and to enforce the terms of the act.

Terms. (1) Security exchanges must register with the SEC and comply with its rules and regulations. (2) The SEC may penalize security exchanges that fail to register by refusing them post office and other interstate privileges. (3) A registered exchange must provide the SEC with data as to its organization and operations. (4) The SEC promulgates rules and regulations to eliminate unethical trading practices like pool operations, the spreading of rumors to mislead stock market operators, and the abuse of such market practices as short selling, price pegging, and the activities of corporate officers and leading stockholders in stock market transactions affecting their companies' securities. (5) Corporations whose securities are dealt in on registered exchanges must file registration statements with both the SEC and the stock exchanges containing information similar to that incorporated in a new issue registration statement. (6) Corporations with listings on registered exchanges must publish financial reports annually and distribute them to their stockholders and the SEC. (7) Listed securities may be suspended from trading on a registered exchange if such action is in the public interest.

INVESTMENT TRUSTS

Definition. An investment trust is an incorporated enterprise that accumulates investors' funds through the sale of its securities and reinvests them under expert guidance to secure a larger return than otherwise obtainable and to increase the values of the capital contributions.

History. (1) Great Britain was the home of the investment trust. Companies were organized to secure English funds for foreign investment. (2) During the 1920's, investment trusts were organized in the United States. The growing wealth of the country, the increasing investment-mindedness and speculative interest of the American public, coupled with the stock market boom of the time, provided fertile soil for their development. (3) The 1929 stock market crash discouraged public participation in the security market and so deflated the portfolios of many American trusts that large numbers closed down.

Types of Trusts. (1) A general management trust issues both stocks and bonds and invests in a diversified group of securities chosen by the management. A few of them are also holding companies. Such discretionary management power enables the trust to vary its investments with changing conditions. (2) A fixed trust issues certificates to investors representing title to and interest in property placed with a trustee for their benefit. Shares in the trust are always available for purchase and may be redeemed at their net asset value at the holder's discretion. As new capital is accumulated, the investment portfolio is expanded. Most fixed trusts purchase only the highest grade common stocks, while others specialize in a particular investment category like bonds or bank and insurance company securities. (3) There are variations on fixed and general management trusts. For example, investors pay in money to a mutual trust periodically, receiving certificates with a guaranteed maturity face value in exchange. Other trusts sell their securities to the public continuously at a figure equal to their investment cost plus a "loading" charge. The securities issued may be redeemed at about their asset value, less a penalty.

The Investment Companies Act of 1940. This legislation requires registration of investment companies with the SEC to assure honest management, sound capital structure, better public knowledge of their affairs, and cheaper selling costs.

INVESTMENT COUNSEL

Definition. Investment counsel is advice given investors on investments and on the management of their security holdings. Investment bankers and brokers, financial statistical services, and specialized investment counsel firms whose fees vary with the size of the accounts are prominent in this field.

Investment Advisers Act of 1940. (1) Investment advisers must register with the SEC, which can deny registration if conditions warrant this decision. (2) An investment adviser must reveal his interest in his client's transactions. He cannot act as a principal or as a broker for another party in a deal with his client unless the client knows the situation. (3) The SEC can investigate whenever it deems desirable and revoke an investment counselor's registration.

REVIEW QUESTIONS

1. What is an investment banking, underwriting syndicate? What is its major purpose?
2. Describe the factors determining whether a proposed new issue will be underwritten.
3. Why has private placement of securities increased since 1933?
4. Distinguish between a registration statement and a prospectus.
5. Define (a) margin trading, (b) short sale, (c) "wire house," (d) odd lot.
6. What are the purpose and terms of the Securities Exchange Act of 1934?

Trust Companies

The accumulation of private wealth and American corporate development stimulated the growth of the trust company in the United States.

History. (1) The first trust company in the United States was initially an insurance organization. Incidentally it managed funds placed on deposit. (2) After the Civil War, the trust business expanded as private wealth mounted and required expert care. (3) The corporate trustee business grew as private corporations flourished, issued securities publicly, and needed the services of trust companies to handle the transfer of securities on the security market. (4) Towards the end of the nineteenth century, trust institutions invaded the state commercial banking field, encouraged by the relative freedom in loan and reserve policies as contrasted with the tighter regulations over national banks. The shift of the American economy from a bank note to a deposit currency basis facilitated the assumption of commercial banking powers. (5) Commercial banks, in turn, entered the trust business either by establishing trust departments with the approval of the Federal Reserve Board if state bank regulations permitted, or by organizing trust company affiliates. (6) The McFadden-Pepper Act of 1927, which permitted the granting of indeterminate charters to national banks, enabled them to handle perpetual trusts for educational and religious purposes and long-term business trusts.

Definitions. (1) A trust is a three-party relationship—a person called a trustor turns over property to a trustee (an individual or trust institution) for the benefit of a third party, the beneficiary, with the general objective of preserving the value of the property and deriving an income for the trustor, personal dependents, and/or institutions like schools and hospitals. (2) An agent represents his principal in business dealings with third parties but, unlike the trustee, does not hold title to the property he handles.

Voluntary, Living, and Testamentary Trusts. (1) Voluntary trusts, covering all types of agency and trustee relationships, result from voluntary agreements between living trustors and trust companies. They may be revoked if provision for termination is stipulated, and may become effective during the trustor's life or after his death. (2) If it becomes effective during the trustor's life, the voluntary trust is also a living trust. (3) If a trust becomes effective only after the trustor's death and its terms are provided in his will, it is called a testamentary trust.

Life of a Trust. (1) Personal trusts can only run for a definite period or may be terminated by a specific event. New York State law provides that it cannot extend beyond the lives of two people and the minority of a third person. (2) Public trusts for purposes like education and scientific research may be established in perpetuity.

TRUST AND AGENCY SERVICES TO INDIVIDUALS

Trust companies, appointed by trustors voluntarily or by the courts, perform trustee and agency services for individuals.

Trust Services. (1) An executor is appointed by a will to execute an estate according to the provisions of the will. (2) An administrator is appointed by the probate court to administer according to state inheritance laws the property of a deceased person who died without leaving a will. The deceased is said to have died intestate.

Whether serving as executor or administrator, the trustee has similar duties: receiving the property, paying off the claims against the estate, and dividing the residue among those designated by the will or entitled to it legally. (3) A trust institution may be named in a will as both executor and trustee. (4) A guardian cares for the property of a minor upon court appointment. (5) Similar to the work of a guardian is the task of a conservator who handles the estate of an incompetent, as an insane person or drunkard.

WHY PEOPLE APPOINT TRUST COMPANIES. People appoint trust companies: (1) to have the heirs enjoy the income from an estate, while its management remains with a trust company; (2) to assure the family an income which will not be impaired by the trustor's personal business losses; (3) to care for a trust in which the trustor may be the recipient of the income with other parties named as beneficiaries after the trustor's death; (4) to care for funds where the income is divided among beneficiaries with the principal split among designated parties upon the beneficiaries' deaths; (5) to supervise a life insurance trust consisting of the proceeds of life insurance policies to be paid to beneficiaries according to the trust agreement.

Agency Services. (1) As custodian, a trust company cares for personal assets like securities, receives and disburses income, buys and sells securities upon the written instruction of the principal, and submits detailed accounts of its operations. (2) As managing agent, it serves as investment counselor, custodian, and even real-estate agent. (3) As attorney in fact, it directs a person's business affairs. (4) As escrow depository, it holds property on deposit until certain conditions are fulfilled, or disputes as to title are settled.

LEGAL AND DISCRETIONARY TRUSTS

Whether managing a living or testamentary trust, the trustee may be hedged around with restrictions as to the uses to which the trust fund can be put, or he may be given discretion in its employment.

Legal Trusts. (1) The trustee must confine his investments to those securities declared legal trustee investments by state law. (2) Legal investments generally include first mortgages on real estate, government securities, and high-grade corporate obligations. (3) When no legal list is promulgated by the state, investments must be approved by the surrogate's court.

Discretionary Trusts. (1) Trustee discretion is typical of living trusts especially. (2) The trustee is expected to act prudently in the management of the property.

Common Trust Funds. (1) Small trust accounts are given the benefits of investment diversification through the creation of a common trust fund. (2) A trust institution opens participation in such a fund only to trust accounts under its care. (3) Participations are frequently as small as $10 each. (4) New York State permitted the establishment of common trust funds in 1938. No one trust may invest more than $50,000.

INVESTMENT PRACTICES

Sound investment of trust funds requires: (1) an investment organization; (2) a proper investment procedure.

Investment Organization. (1) The well-organized investment staff usually includes an executive committee, a trust committee, and a trust investment committee, supervising the work of a trust investment officer, and a securities investment analysis division. (2) A big trust company may also establish a trust investment division, employ several trust investment officers, and organize securities analyses units dealing with different types of investments. (3) A small trust company will merge the functions of two or more of these divisions, committees, or officers.

Sources of Investment Information. A trust company should have available specialized sources of investment information like: (1) the services of statistical and investment analysis organizations; (2) corporate and governmental reports; (3) firsthand knowledge of securities considered for purchase; (4) access to investment-counseling organizations.

Investment Procedure. (1) A statistical unit under a trust investment officer considers individual investments and their value to individual trust accounts. The condition and investment standing of an issuer is studied with emphasis on its improving or deteriorating situation and its status relative to the securities of other organizations in the same field. (2) A study of investments in a single trust account stresses the quality of the securities therein, diversification, and taxable losses and gains on securities bought and sold. (3) Many trust companies have approved lists of investments in accord with the legal list, in line with the standards established by trust agreements, or adhering to the "prudent man" rule. These lists are a result of intensive study by their research staffs, officers, and committees, and even boards of directors. (4) The trust investment committee considers the conclusions of the trust investment officer and research staff, and passes on its own decisions to the trust committee, the executive committee, or the board of directors for final decision. (5) The securities service division carries out the investment orders of the trust company. In a small trust bank, the trust investment officer may actually carry the policy into effect. (6) The same procedure outlined above is applied to real estate and real-estate mortgages by a separate department.

PROTECTING TRUST PROPERTY

Trust property is protected by: (1) intelligent managerial investment policies and programs; (2) physical safeguards like vaults and storage places and careful systems of checking on intangible personal properties like securities in bank vaults; (3) property insurance like fire and burglary protection for real property and fidelity insurance against negligence or dishonesty of trust company officers and employees; (4) minimum capitalization, segregation, and deposit of part of a trust company's capital or assets with a state authority to guarantee adherence to trust responsibilities; (5) separation of the trust division from the other parts of a trust institution, careful segregation of trust property from other property, separation of the property of each trust from the property in other trusts, and employment of special trust officers; (6) the law, in many states, that idle trust funds special deposits are not subject to the claims of a trust company's general creditors; (7) special safeguards, calling for securities of equal market value legal for trust investment or bank purchase, for trust funds deposited elsewhere as with the commercial banking division of a trust company; (8) bank supervisory authorities examining the condition of trust accounts (the trust company's auditing department reports on the condition of trust funds to its board of trustees); (9) the requirement of courts supervising trust accounts that trust institutions make reports of accounts entrusted to their care; (10) the internal audit.

Trust Company Liability. (1) Trust institutions are held liable for losses suffered through failure to adhere to the instructions in the trust agreement or to state law regulation. (2) However, a trustee is not a guarantor against loss due to an error in investment judgment. Investment policy must be examined in the light of conditions as of the date it was made effective and not as of some future date when the mistake in policy is apparent.

COMMISSIONS AND FEES

Charges for commissions and fees are established by law: (1) During the life of a trust, the trust company annually receives a percentage of the yearly earned income. (2) Upon its termination, a percentage of the principal is paid to the trust company. (3) These percentages are in inverse ratio to income and principal. (4) Agency fees are privately negotiated.

TRUST COMPANIES VERSUS INDIVIDUAL TRUSTEES

Advantages of the Trust Company. (1) The indeterminate life of a trust company enables greater familiarity with, and superior knowledge of, the trustor's problems. (2) Their financial stability and responsibility is greater since trust company resources are much larger than those of an individual. (3) Trust companies are periodically examined by the government, and the banking law establishes safeguards for trust funds in the care of trust companies. (4) The legal, accounting, investment, and tax experts on the staffs of trust companies guarantee more expert supervision than that which could be given by one person.

Disadvantages of the Trust Company. (1) The impersonal relationship between the parties to a trust frequently makes impossible an understanding of the needs and desires of the trustors. (2) Trust companies are concerned too frequently with avoiding law violations and the establishment of claims against them rather than with meeting the needs of their clients.

SERVICES TO BUSINESS ORGANIZATIONS

Trust companies perform trust and agency services for business corporations, educational, religious, and fraternal bodies.

Trustee under a Corporate Mortgage. (1) A corporation selling debt securities or offering new securities for old exceeding $1,000,000 must turn over title to a part or all of its property to a trustee under a mortgage or indenture agreement conforming to the Trust Indenture Act of 1939 and acceptable to the SEC. (2) The mortgage is payable to a trust company or bank acting as trustee and serving as intermediary between the debtor corporation and its security holders. (3) When a default occurs on a bond issue, the trustee notifies the bondholders within ninety days and forecloses or seizes the property to protect its clients' interest.

TRUSTEE QUALIFICATIONS. (1) The trustee must have a capital and surplus of at least $150,000. (2) It cannot have interests contrary to those of the security holders. (3) If a trustee has aided the debtor corporation by direct loans, it is obligated to advise the bondholders of these loans and cannot secure repayment of its claims if such action is contrary to the bondholders' interests.

Trustee under a Reorganization Plan. (1) In reorganizations of bankrupt corporations, bondholders' committees designate a trust company to serve as a depository for the bondholders' obligations. (2) When an acceptable reorganization plan has been developed, the trust company issues reorganization certificates. (3) The Securities and Exchange Commission advises the United States district courts in reorganization proceedings involving a substantial public interest. (4) Trust companies are depositories in consolidations and under voting trust agreements.

Transfer Agent. (1) A transfer agent cancels a sold stock certificate and issues a new one to the buyer. (2) Trust institutions usually perform this work, but the largest corporations have established their own transfer agencies in New York City. (3) Small corporations handle the transfer of title to securities bought and sold. (4) A transfer agent also handles the exchange of bonds for stock or the refunding of an old issue with a new security.

Registrar. (1) A registrar guards against an overissue of a corporation's securities by checking on the work of the transfer agent. (2) When a transfer agent issues a new stock certificate, the registrar examines the cancelled certificate and the new issue to see whether they are genuine and whether the new certificate is issued for the correct number of shares. Proper entries are made in the registration records, and the new issue, signed by the registrar, is returned to the transfer agent. (3) When a registered bond is transferred, no new registered bond is issued—merely the name of the new owner and the date are noted on the old bond. The trustee under the corporate mortgage usually acts as both registrar and transfer agent.

Paying Agent. (1) A trust company pays off bond interest, dividends, and maturing obligations. (2) It may also keep the account books of, and prepare financial statements for, a corporation.

Liquidating Agent. (1) A trust company may be the assignee for the creditors of a financially embarrassed enterprise. (2) It may act as the receiver or trustee in bankruptcy for a concern in liquidation.

Institutional Agent. A trust company administers funds contributed to hospitals, educational institutions, research foundations, and community trusts to assure their most effective use.

TITLE SEARCH AND MORTGAGE INSURANCE

(1) Trust companies both buy and sell mortgages and act as middlemen in arranging real-estate deals. (2) They search titles and insure them for a fee. (3) Trust companies may guarantee repayment of mortgage loans and the interest charges on such loans. Organizations engaged in these two latter types of work are "title and mortgage insurance companies." National banks are for-

bidden to engage in this business but may act as mortgage brokers and agents for insurance companies.

ECONOMIC VALUE OF TRUST INSTITUTIONS

Trust institutions: (1) protect private property against waste and loss; (2) direct investable funds into productive enterprises and so stimulate the growth of industrial and national development; (3) oversee the transfer of property whether sold in an open market like a stock exchange or handed down from trustor to beneficiary.

REVIEW QUESTIONS

1. Distinguish between an agent and a trustee.
2. Explain three important trust and three important agency services.
3. How does a legal trust differ from a discretionary trust? What is a common trust fund?
4. Describe five methods of protecting trust property. To what extent is a trust company liable for losses?
5. Explain (a) transfer agent, (b) registrar, (c) trustee under a corporate mortgage, (d) paying agent, (e) receiver.
6. What is a title and mortgage insurance company?
7. What factors have been responsible for the growth of trust companies?

✠

CHAPTER EIGHTEEN

Urban Real-Estate Finance

NEED FOR LONG–TERM CREDIT

Long-term credit is necessary to finance real-estate transactions since: (1) business properties only produce sufficient revenue to pay off the credit after a period of years; (2) home finance credit, even if granted originally for as short a time as five years, is usually extended to suit the homeowner's convenience.

MORTGAGES AND MORTGAGE BONDS

Borrower's Obligation. (1) The borrower or mortgagor is obligated to meet debt interest and principal payments, pay taxes and special assessments, insure the property, and maintain it in good condition. (2) If he fails to meet his obligations, the lender or mortgagee may demand payment immediately and foreclose, if necessary, on the property.

First and Second Mortgages. (1) First mortgages are typical, while second mortgages are used only occasionally. (2) Second mortgages provide borrowers with funds above the sums they received from the first mortgages. Their soundness is increased by amortization provisos permitting retirement within a relatively short time. Since their market is comparatively unorganized and inactive, these mortgages are discounted at a heavy rate. (3) Building contractors may receive second mortgages from homeowners. They sell these mortgages to a second-mortgage company at a discount with the latter profiting generously from both the interest and discount and being repaid as the amortization and interest payments fall due.

Determinants of Mortgage Value. There are five determinants of mortgage value: (1) the property's earning power; (2) credit standing of the mortgagor or debtor; (3) tax assessment value;

(4) the location of the property; (5) urban real-estate prospects of the neighborhood.

Mortgage Bonds. (1) A large sum is accumulated to finance a large project like a hotel or office building through the sale of mortgage bonds exceeding 50 per cent of the property's appraised value determined from the project's net estimated income. (2) The bonds are generally first-mortgage claims. Second mortgages and leasehold bonds have been used on occasion.

STOCK AND "LAND–TRUST CERTIFICATES"

Preferred and Common Stock. Equities have also been used to finance real-estate ventures: (1) The construction company places a first mortgage on 50 per cent of a big building job, selling preferred stock for the remainder of the cost, while one-half of the common stock is given as a bonus to the preferred stockholders and the other half to the financing company. (2) The preferred is retired from earnings before any income distribution to the common shareholders.

"Land-Trust Certificates." (1) "Land-trust certificates" are issued to finance land projects in the Midwest and in Massachusetts. (2) They are secured by land, title to which is held by a trust company, and leased to people agreeing to maintain and improve it and pay rental sufficient for interest payments on the certificates and their retirement.

TYPES OF LENDERS

(1) Private investors put their funds to work in small local mortgages, whose property value can be determined at first hand. These lenders may be mortgage creditors also as a result of the sale of property to people who cannot meet the whole cost at the time of sale. Personal loans to business associates and families for the purchase of homes also result in mortgage claims. (2) Savings banks invest heavily in mortgages attracted by their high yield as against the legal bond investments available to them. Federal Housing Administration mortgage insurance strengthened the flow of loanable funds into real estate following the collapse of land values during the early 1930's. (3) Commercial banks, similarly encouraged by FHA-insured loans and seeking a profitable outlet for their cash assets, have moved into the mortgage field. (4) Insurance com-

panies are active mortgage lenders because of the attractive yield as contrasted with the low return on legal list securities.

MORTGAGE COMPANIES

Mortgage companies enjoyed wide popularity prior to the 1930's.

Functions. (1) A mortgage company purchases first mortgages with its own and/or borrowed funds and then sells the mortgages to investors. (2) It purchases first mortgages, deposits them with trustees, and sells participations therein to mortgage investors. (3) It sells mortgage collateral bonds and collateral trust certificates, investing the cash proceeds in first mortgages which secure the mortgage company's own issues. (4) On occasion, a mortgage company does not buy a claim with its own or borrowed funds but acts only as a broker competing with other brokers.

Services to Investors. (1) Mortgage companies can satisfy investment needs of large and small investors by either selling them entire mortgages or participations. (2) Mortgage company securities give investors claims on a diversified type of mortgage backing. (3) Prior to the 1930's, surety companies affiliated with mortgage enterprises offered apparent protection of principal and interest on mortgages sold or mortgage company securities marketed by guaranteeing the principal and interest payments on these obligations.

Decline. (1) In 1933, New York mortgage companies could not meet their guaranties. (2) Hence, the New York State Superintendent of Insurance suspended the guaranteed obligations and reorganized the surety companies. (3) These companies had little value, and today both they and mortgage companies are of minor importance in real-estate finance.

Income. The income of a mortgage company is obtained from commissions payable at the time loans are made: (1) The charges are justified since mortgage companies investigate real-estate proposals, underwrite mortgages, and market them. (2) Commissions vary from 2 to 3.5 per cent depending upon competitive conditions. On construction loans, they may amount to 5 per cent in view of the additional risks and the servicing of the loans.

A mortgage company's total income depends upon the speed with which it turns over its capital. A real-estate boom stimulates the growth of these enterprises, while a period of declining and frozen land values is characterized by their decline.

Second Mortgages. (1) These mortgages are used to obtain funds in addition to those realized on first mortgages. (2) Since they are secondary claims, these mortgages are riskier than first liens. But, they are of shorter maturity, usually are amortized to increase their safety, and are only temporary claims. (3) The money is borrowed from second-mortgage companies financed by stock subscriptions by builders, banks, and real-estate dealers. (4) Company earnings are interest receipts on mortgage purchases and large discounts on their purchase price. (5) Since 1933, second mortgages have declined greatly in importance, and the proportion of first-mortgage claims to property values has increased considerably. Thus, the danger of second mortgages again bankrupting investors is diminished for they no longer play a vital role in real-estate finance.

STATE SAVINGS AND LOAN ASSOCIATIONS

These associations are local organizations like building and loan associations, mutual loan associations, building societies, and co-operative banks.

Function. A savings and loan association gathers together its members' savings for loans to good credit risk members or non-members wishing to build or purchase a home.

History. (1) This type of home finance organization was imported from Great Britain. The English called it a "building society." (2) The first such organization in the United States was located in 1831 in a Philadelphia suburb. Thereafter, similar institutions were set up in other parts of the country, and by 1900 more than five thousand such associations with over a million and a half members were functioning. (3) They reached their peak in 1927 when over twelve thousand associations were in operation. (4) The economic difficulties of the 1930's caused heavy losses, income curtailment, and sharp withdrawal of funds, resulting in many failures. (5) In 1947, the United States enjoyed the services of about six thousand such organizations.

The Terminating Plan of Operation. (1) People, joined together by neighborhood or social interest, make weekly dues payments on the par value of shares purchased in the association. (2) The funds collected are lent to association members for home purchase or construction. The volume of loans depends upon the amount of money amassed by the shareholders' payments. An association of two hundred members receiving $10 in dues from each member can finance a home costing $2,000 in the first year. Every member would have a home in approximately seventeen years. (3) A member desiring a more expensive home can invest more money than his associates. (4) Members joining after the association has been started must pay in an amount per share equivalent to what the original shares are worth. (5) Each member borrowing funds must subscribe for shares with a par value equal to the loan, and must give the association a first mortgage on his home. (6) Interest on the loan is paid till maturity. This income along with fines for delinquency are the association's earnings split among the members according to the number of shares owned. (7) When a borrower's monthly payments plus earnings equal the par value of the stock purchased, the paid-up shares are turned over to the association, which cancels the loan. (8) The association is dissolved when all members desirous of obtaining a home have accomplished their purpose; at that time the nonborrowing members' shares are paid off in cash.

DEFECTS. This plan is little used today because these associations rarely carried out their purpose fully: (1) Some members did not borrow, and idle capital accumulated, forcing the adoption of a liquidation scheme like requiring members to borrow. (2) Late joiners were discouraged by the large initial payments of accumulated dues and earnings. (3) The temporary nature of the plan did not encourage its use.

The Serial Plan of Operation. (1) It permits a permanent organization since new members are added at various times—for example, at the beginning of each year. (2) Each group's membership ends when they all have acquired homes. (3) The maturity of each series varies with its date of issue, dues paid, and association earnings distributed alike to all shareholders.

CRITICISM. (1) The plan's accounting technique is complicated and costly. (2) It calls for large liquid resources to pay off the constantly maturing shares purchased for investment and not to finance home building and purchase. (3) The savings arrangement is not satisfactory to many savers called on for fixed dues payments.

The Permanent "Dayton" or "Ohio" Plan of Operation. This plan was first used in Dayton, Ohio, in 1870: (1) A member may join at any time and subscribe to as many shares as he wishes. (2) The plan is elastic, since borrowers may liquidate their debts at their convenience. In some cases, permanent plans call for periodic, uniform payments. (3) When shares mature, upon the completion of payment for them, members are encouraged to keep their savings with the association permanently and to buy additional shares. Thus, this type of association is more assured of a regular flow of investable funds than is the serial plan association. (4) Some Dayton plan organizations accept deposits, pay interest thereon, and protect them by shareholder double liability.

Savings Bank Characteristics. (1) Associations accept deposits as though they were savings banks. (2) They may issue investment certificates to those contemplating the purchase of homes and optional savings shares to those buying them for income rather than to satisfy the need for a home. (3) The optional savings share permits the saver to invest such funds as he sees fit at such times as he deems desirable, with the privilege of withdrawing his funds as he desires. (4) All shares yield equal dividends.

Types of Shares Issued. Although savings and loan associations may borrow from banks to meet extraordinary situations, generally their major funds come from the sale of different types of shares issued in denominations from $100 up: (1) installment shares upon which subscribers make uniform payments called "dues" at regular intervals; (2) optional shares calling for such payment as the subscriber can conveniently afford; (3) prepaid shares sold at an estimated present value which, with dividends, make the shares fully paid at maturity; (4) full-paid shares whose par value is paid in a lump sum at the date of purchase with dividends paid in cash and withdrawn when declared.

DIVIDENDS. Higher dividend rates are often paid on installment shares and lower rates on fully-paid shares to encourage savings.

Other Uses of Funds. State savings and loan associations are generally permitted to invest in government and other high-grade securities.

Supervision. The associations are under the control of state banking commissioners and departments that issue charters, conduct examinations, and require reports of condition.

FEDERAL SAVINGS AND LOAN ASSOCIATIONS

History. The Home Owners' Loan Act of 1933 authorized federal savings and loan associations: (1) to provide mutual thrift and savings organizations enjoying public confidence after the banking crisis of 1933 (state savings and loan associations and savings institutions were unable to satisfy the national demand for safety; locally chartered organizations had suffered heavy losses while their portfolios were weighted down with frozen real-estate assets); (2) to stimulate home building and encourage business recovery during the Great Depression; (3) to provide many communities lacking local savings and home-financing organizations with such facilities; (4) to establish modernized associations, for state laws regulating savings and loan associations were outdated.

Capitalization. (1) The Treasury was authorized to invest $50,000,000 in the shares of these associations. (2) The Home Owners' Loan Corporation was authorized in 1935 to buy $300,-000,000 of both federal and state association securities if the state associations were either members of the Federal Home Loan Bank System (a central mortgage banking system), or their shares were insured. (3) The associations could repurchase the government investments, but repurchase was not required for five years nor in any one year need it exceed 10 per cent of the government's entire subscription. (4) They may borrow up to 50 per cent of their share capital, 40 per cent of which must be from federal home loan banks. (5) They cannot accept deposits or issue certificates of indebtedness.

Types of Shares. A federal association can sell: (1) installment thrift shares; (2) optional savings shares; (3) full-paid income shares; (4) prepaid shares. A shareholder may resell his interest to the association, or avoid loss of income by borrowing from the association against his shares up to 90 per cent of their paid-in price if repurchase application has been made less than thirty days before the loan becomes effective.

Loans. Generally loans are made only against first mortgages on improved real estate within fifty miles of the association's home office: (1) A monthly or quarterly amortized loan for the purchase of a home may not exceed 80 per cent of the appraised value of the land and buildings or $20,000, may not run over twenty years, and must be extinguished at maturity. Interest is charged only on the unpaid part. An unamortized loan cannot exceed 50 per cent of the appraised value of the land and buildings or $20,000 in amount. It must expire in five years. (2) A home and business property loan may be negotiated for 60 per cent of the property's appraised value and must be discharged at the end of three years.

(3) An unamortized apartment-house loan cannot be greater than 60 per cent of the property's appraised value or be outstanding longer than two years. An amortized loan on a four- to six-family apartment house cannot exceed 75 per cent of the property's appraised value, must call for monthly amortization payments, and must mature in fifteen years. An amortized loan on a more than six-family apartment house cannot exceed two-thirds of its appraised value and must mature in fifteen years. (4) A loan on income-yielding business property may amount to 60 per cent of the appraised value, must be amortized monthly, and must mature in fifteen years. (5) In all, only 15 per cent of an association's assets may be lent on homes, apartment houses, business properties, combinations of home and business properties, other improved real estate and unamortized loans without adherence to the $20,000 ceiling and the fifty-mile limitation on the property's distance from the association's home office. If secured by homes or combination homes and business properties, such loans may not exceed 60 per cent of the properties' appraised value or 50 per cent if collateraled by other improved real estate. (6) Federal associations are eligible to make all kinds of FHA- and VA-insured home loans. (7) Virtually all loans are amortized monthly and require borrowers to pay taxes and insurance. (8) Interest is deducted when loans are made so that the lenders assume less of a risk. (9) Borrowers may liquidate debts more quickly than required by paying in sums above the regular monthly interest and payment installments.

FEDERAL SAVINGS AND LOAN INSURANCE CORPORATION

This corporation was created by the National Housing Act of June, 1934.

Functions. (1) The Federal Savings and Loan Insurance Corporation stimulates investment in both federal and state savings and loan associations. Although state institutions are not required to be members of the insurance corporation, an eligible state institution may become a member at any time if its application is accepted. Upon joining, an insured association must pay an admission fee of one-twenty-fifth of 1 per cent of its liabilities. (2) It supervises insured associations through examinations and required reports of condition. (3) It buys an association's uncertain assets and lends or contributes the money necessary to avoid a default. (4) It acts as conservator or receiver of a defaulting association's assets. (5) It carries on the activities of a defaulter to re-establish its credit position or merge it with a solvent insured association or organize a new association to assume the assets, or liquidate the assets. The corporation takes such action as the best interest of the insured members dictate. (6) In the event of a default, the investor receives either a new insured account in an insured, going association or is paid off in cash and noninterest-bearing obligations of the Savings and Loan Insurance Corporation—10 per cent in cash immediately, 45 per cent of the remainder in one-year debentures, and the balance in three-year corporation debentures.

Capitalization. (1) Capital stock totaling $100,000,000 was bought and paid for by the Home Owners' Loan Corporation in bonds of equal par value. The HOLC receives a dividend equal to the interest on its bonds. (2) The corporation may issue its own obligations and even sell the HOLC bonds to obtain cash funds.

Premiums. (1) Each insured member pays an annual premium of one-eighth of 1 per cent of its insured shareholders' claims and the corporation's outstanding creditor obligations. (2) The premium fund must be built up to 5 per cent of all insured accounts and creditor obligations. The premium must at all times be maintained at this level.

Insurance. Total coverage for an investor in an insured association amounts to $10,000 maximum.

Management. (1) Originally, a board of trustees of five persons directed the corporation. (2) In 1942, the Federal Home Loan Bank Commissioner was appointed to govern its affairs. (3) In July, 1947, a Reorganization Act of Congress established a three-man Home Loan Bank Board to carry on the supervisory task.

HOME OWNERS' LOAN CORPORATION

Function. Established in 1933 and now managed by the Home Loan Bank Board, the Home Owners' Loan Corporation aimed at refinancing home mortgages to ease the financial plight of mortgagors threatened with foreclosure. Although the Federal Home Loan Bank Act of July, 1932, set up a banking system to lend on the security of mortgage loans offered by other institutions, it had not extended relief quickly enough to aid the thousands of homeowners defaulting or already in default on their mortgage obligations.

Capitalization. The Secretary of the Treasury provided $200,-000,000 with the corporation authorized over the years to issue bonds, guaranteed originally as to interest and in 1934 as to principal.

Powers. (1) It refinanced existing mortgages either by paying off mortgage creditors in HOLC bonds, or in cash if such payment was not over 40 per cent of the property's appraised value. (2) It granted cash loans to homeowners saddled with tax liabilities or in need of funds to repair and maintain their property.

Results. (1) Homeowners had their mortgages extended from an average maturity of three to five years to fifteen to eighteen years. (2) Sound amortization arrangements were made for paying off the principal obligations. (3) Interest rates were slashed about 1½ per cent while even principal reductions were made in some cases. (4) Bank creditors and their mortgagees had over $2,000,-000,000 in unsound loans taken out of their portfolios and replaced by sound assets. (5) Local governments received back taxes. (6) Business recovery was encouraged through reconditioning loans which created a demand for labor and materials. (7) Real-estate values were so written down as to minimize panicky selling, thereby protecting the real-estate market.

THE FEDERAL HOME LOAN BANK ADMINISTRATION

The Federal Home Loan Bank Act of July, 1932, organized a system of central home mortgage banks under the jurisdiction of a five-man Federal Home Loan Bank Board (succeeded in 1942 by a Commissioner of the Federal Home Loan Bank and in 1947 by a three-man Home Loan Bank Board) to grant loans on mortgage security offered to other lending institutions.

Purposes. Its purposes were: (1) to stabilize the depressed real-estate market; (2) to stimulate the home construction industry and through it the dark business situation of the early 1930's; (3) to improve housing conditions for low income groups.

National Organization. (1) The United States was divided into twelve districts, in each of which a mortgage rediscount bank was established. At present only eleven banks are in operation. (2) Each district home loan bank is governed by twelve directors, four of whom are chosen by the Home Loan Bank Board for four-year terms and the other eight selected for two-year periods by member mortgage institutions. To insure representation to all size institutions, two Class A directors are elected by the largest members, two Class B by the middle-sized organizations, and two Class C by the smallest member institutions, while the other two are selected by all the member institutions regardless of size. (3) The Home Loan Bank Board dominates the district home loan banks by (a) examining them, (b) determining their loan regulations and loan rates, (c) ruling on their debt issues, (d) modifying district boundaries, and (e) assessing district banks for the administration's costs.

Member Institutions. Member institutions include: (1) all federal savings and loan associations; (2) state-chartered mortgage finance companies if they fulfill the Federal Home Loan Bank Administration's requirements as to management, policies, and financial condition. State members may withdraw voluntarily on six months' notice to the Home Loan Bank Board, but a federal savings and loan association cannot withdraw without surrendering its federal charter. The Home Loan Bank Board supervises member institutions by (a) chartering and supervising federal savings and loan associations, (b) ruling on the admission of state mortgage financiers like mutual savings banks, insurance companies, and state savings and loan associations, (c) examining all member institutions, (d) suspending federal savings and loan associations for law violations and insolvency, and (e) dropping state member organizations for unsound practices and legal infractions.

Capitalization. (1) The Treasury originally subscribed $125,-000,000 for home loan bank stock, subsequently transferred to the Reconstruction Finance Corporation. (2) A member organization must subscribe 1 per cent of its unpaid principal of home mortgage loans to the local federal home loan bank stock issue. If any member of the system legally cannot own stock, it must deposit an equivalent amount. (3) Each home loan bank must allocate semi-annually to its surplus 20 per cent of earnings until the surplus equals the paid-in capital—after which, only 5 per cent of the net income need be thus set aside.

ADDITIONAL SOURCES OF LOAN FUNDS. (1) Additional home loan bank funds are obtained from the issue of consolidated home loan bank bonds, for which all the banks are jointly and severally liable with the interest rate fixed by the Home Loan Bank Board. These issues cannot exceed five times the paid-in home loan bank capital at the time of issue nor be greater than the value of member institution obligations held by the district banks. The United States government does not guarantee these issues, but they enjoy a high investment rating since they are lawful investments, enjoy a high degree of tax exemption, and are acceptable as security for trust and public funds under the control of the United States or its officials. (2) Other home loan bank funds are obtained from deposits of member institutions, of any other home loan bank, or of any United States government agency.

Loan Powers. (1) Ten-year loans are available if protected by residential property mortgages maturing in twenty years or by direct and fully guaranteed United States securities. Borrowing institutions must also pledge their home loan bank stock. (2) Loans are made for 50 per cent of the unpaid principal of home mortgage loans, up to 90 per cent of the unpaid principal of Federal Housing Administration insured mortgages, and equal to the face value of direct and government guaranteed securities. (3) Ten-year loans may be made on FHA-insured mortgages maturing after twenty years, on FHA-insured mortgages more than a half year past due, and on FHA-insured mortgage liens on more than four-family houses. (4) Long-term loans generally are repaid in monthly or quarterly installments during their life. (5) Unsecured loans may be made on member institution's promissory notes due within one year if their liabilities beyond those due the home loan banks are not over 5 per cent of their assets. (6) If a member institution's liabilities exceed this 5 per cent, it may still borrow on its unsecured note for thirty days or less. (7) All short-term unsecured loans must be paid off in cash or converted into secured loans at their maturity.

THE FEDERAL HOUSING ADMINISTRATION

The Federal Housing Administration, supervised by an administrator, was established by the National Housing Act of 1934.

Purposes. Its purposes are: (1) to stimulate house renovation and modernization; (2) to insure privately held mortgages (in these two ways all types of buildings have been maintained and brought up to date without recourse to bank credit that might have been frozen in illiquid real-estate property loans); (3) to encourage employment in the construction and related industries.

Capitalization. (1) The Treasury contributed $10,000,000 to start the organization. (2) Insurance premiums are used to cover expenses and claims. (3) The Reconstruction Finance Corporation can lend to the FHA if necessary to foster its work.

Insured Small Loans. (1) Under Title I of the National Housing Act, there is 10 per cent insurance for eligible lenders like commercial and savings banks, savings and loan associations, and mortgage companies against losses on loans for property modernization and repair or credits for new small dwelling and farm-building construction. (2) Insurance on loans up to $5,000 is available if the loans convert or rehabilitate homes in critical areas for additional living quarters with priority to veterans. (3) Loans up to $2,500 are insured if used to improve existing structures, while loans up to $3,000 are insured if used to build new structures. (4) Insured loans must mature within three to twenty-five years and must be amortized in installments. (5) An insurance premium of three-fourths of 1 per cent of the loan proceeds must be paid the FHA except for new residential construction loan insurance when the premium is only one-half of 1 per cent. The fund accumulated is used to meet the claims of insured lenders on defaulted loans and to cover administrative expenses.

Mutual Mortgage Insurance on Modest Loans. (1) Under Title II of the act, mortgage loans are insured if they are first liens subject to no other claims and are offered by eligible financial organizations. (2) Mortgage insurance is granted only on dwellings mortgaged for not more than $16,000 and suitable for four families or less. (3) Ninety per cent insured mortgage loans are available for homes with an appraised value of less than $6,000; on homes appraised from $6,000 to $10,000 the insurance may be 90 per cent on $6,000 and 80 per cent on any valuation above $6,000. (4) The mortgage may run for four to twenty years, except for properties valued at less than $10,000 which may mature in twenty-five years. (5) Loans must be amortized monthly, with interest, insurance, taxes, and special assessments covered. (6) The insured institution can impose a maximum interest charge on a borrower of no more than 4½ per cent annually. (7) An insurance premium of one-half of 1 per cent of the original principal amount of the mortgage is imposed, may be shifted to the borrower, and is paid into the "Mutual Mortgage Insurance Fund"—a revolving fund to meet claims on insured mortgage defaults.

Housing Insurance. (1) Mortgage loans up to $5,000,000 or 80 per cent of appraised property value for the construction of large rental housing projects and slum clearance developments are also insured under Title II. (2) Loan maturities must be approved by the Federal Housing Commissioner. (3) The rate of interest on mortgage loans must not be over 4 per cent yearly on large housing projects and 4½ per cent on small projects. (4) Yearly insurance premiums of one-half of 1 per cent of outstanding loan principal are gathered together in a "Housing Insurance Fund" to pay off defaulted claims.

Payment under Mortgage Insurance. (1) Three months following default, the insured mortgagee notifies the Federal Housing Commissioner, and after four months starts foreclosure or acquires title to the property. (2) The mortgaged property is transferred to the FHA or all claims against the mortgagor are assigned to it in exchange for FHA debentures and a certificate of claim. (3) The debentures mature three years after the mortgage's due date, are a first lien on the "Mutual Mortgage Insurance Fund," bear interest from 2½ to 3½ per cent annually, and are fully guaranteed by the United States government if issued for property covering mortgages insured before July 1, 1937. (4) The certificate of claim represents a share in the proceeds of the property and related claims. When the property is liquidated, the proceeds of sale are distributed to the "fund," the mortgagee, and the mortgagor, in that order.

War Housing Insurance. Title VI of the National Housing Act, passed in 1941 and 1942, insured war housing. Its provisions did not permit insurance after September, 1945. (1) It insured mortgages, on one- to four-family dwellings for sale or rent if war workers were assured occupancy priority. (2) It authorized $5,-000,000 mortgage insurance on rental housing for war workers. (3) Mortgages were insured up to 90 per cent of appraised property value, for a maximum of twenty-five years, at an interest rate of not over 4½ per cent, and amortized monthly. (4) In the event of a default, the mortgagee is given 2½ per cent debentures covering the unpaid portion of the mortgage and all his expenditures for taxes, insurance, and other such items up to 2 per cent or $75—whichever is the greater. (5) Premiums of one-half of 1 per cent are paid into the "War Housing Insurance Fund." Since World War II many veterans have used this insurance program which was revived for their benefit in May, 1946. Their ability to retain their homes will depend upon the soundness of the nation's economy.

THE FEDERAL PUBLIC HOUSING ADMINISTRATION

Purpose. This organization took over the work of the United States Housing Authority established in 1937. Its primary function is assistance to state and municipal governments to develop low-cost, low-rent housing facilities to eliminate slums.

Financial Procedure. (1) Upon application of a local housing authority which must provide 10 per cent of a project's cost, the FPHA may grant a secured loan up to 90 per cent of cost for as long as sixty years. (2) To keep rents low, the federal agency may subsidize low-cost housing up to $28,000,000 per year. Local housing authorities must provide additional subsidies at least one-fifth as great, either in cash, tax exemptions, or remissions.

THE HOUSING AND HOME FINANCE AGENCY

The numerous federal government housing agencies were brought together under a Reorganization Act of Congress in July, 1947, which created the Housing and Home Finance Agency headed by the Housing and Home Finance Administrator appointed by the President to co-ordinate the various organizations. He takes over the functions of the Federal Loan Administrator and the Federal Works Administrator relative to the Federal Home Loan Bank Board, the HOLC, the FSLIC, the FHA, and the FPHA.

This agency, superseding the National Housing Agency created in 1942 by President Roosevelt, is made up of: (1) the Home Loan Bank Board consisting of three people, appointed by the President with the advice and consent of the Senate for four years, whose function it is to carry on the work of the Federal Home Loan Bank Board, the board of directors of the HOLC, and the board of trustees of the Federal Savings and Loan Insurance Corporation; (2) the Federal Housing Administration, headed by a Federal Housing Commissioner, appointed by the President with Senate concurrence, whose function it is to carry on the work of the Federal Housing Administrator; (3) the Public Housing Administration, headed by a Public Housing Commissioner, which assumes (a) the work of the Administrator of the United States Housing Authority (now known as the Public Housing Administration) and (b) the work of the National Housing Administration for nonfarm housing projects and other properties under its jurisdiction pursuant to certain sections of the Farmer's Home Administration Act of 1946; (4) the National Housing Council, made up of the Housing and Home Finance Administrator as chairman, the Federal Housing Commissioner, the chairman of the Home Loan Bank Board, the Administrator of Veterans' Affairs, the chairman of the board of directors of the RFC, and the Secretary of Agriculture, which must promote the most effective use of housing functions and activities within the agency and other departments and agencies on this council.

The Reorganization Act abolished the Federal Home Loan Bank Board, the Board of Directors of the HOLC, the Board of Trustees of the Federal Savings and Loan Insurance Corporation, the Office of Federal Housing Administrator, and the Office of Administrator of the United States Housing Authority.

VETERANS ADMINISTRATION LOANS

The Servicemen's Readjustment Act of 1944 authorized the Veterans Administration to guarantee private and governmental institutional loans to ex-servicemen in service on or after September 16, 1940, discharged honorably, serving at least ninety days (unless discharged sooner for disability incurred on duty), and applying within ten years from the war's end or their discharge: (1) The loans are granted for home construction and repair, for the purchase of farms and livestock, for farm improvements, and for the purchase of business properties within the United States or its possessions. (2) The guaranty is limited to 50 per cent of the loan or $2,000 for nonreal-estate loans or $4,000 for real-estate loans, whichever is less. (3) If another federal agency has guaranteed or made a loan for the above stated purposes, the VA may guarantee a second loan up to the $2,000 or $4,000 limit.

The loan terms follow: (1) the property must not exceed a fair appraisal value; (2) a junior loan cannot exceed 20 per cent of a property's purchase price; (3) realty loans must mature within thirty-five years, but farm loans may mature in forty years; (4) loans, not secured by real estate, must be paid off in ten years; (5) the highest interest rate is 4 per cent yearly on the unpaid portion of a loan; (6) the VA is required to pay the first year's interest on the part of the loan it has guaranteed.

REVIEW QUESTIONS

1. Explain how private mortgage lenders invest their funds.
2. What are the three different state savings and loan association plans of operation?
3. Why were federal savings and loan associations organized? How do the Federal Savings and Loan Insurance Corporation's operations bolster the financial system?
4. What are the major provisions of the Federal Home Loan Bank Act of 1932?
5. What are the purposes of (a) the "Mutual Mortgage Insurance Fund," (b) the Federal Public Housing Administration, (c) the Housing and Home Finance Agency, (d) the Veterans Administration loans?

ℋ

Farm Credit

Uses. The farmer borrows for long, intermediate, and short-term purposes: (1) Long-term credit is sought to buy land, improve it, and purchase costly agricultural machinery. The antiprimogeniture laws of the United States requiring an equal division of property among the children of a deceased person have stimulated long-term farm credit, the heir remaining on the farm mortgaging it to pay off the other heirs. (2) Intermediate-term credit is used to improve the property and purchase the less expensive farm equipment. (3) Short-term credit is devoted to the production of the current crop and its storage awaiting desirable marketing opportunities.

Intermediate and short-term credits have frequently been converted into long-term obligations or written down to realistic levels when farm prices and farm income have dropped to prevent liquidation of agricultural debt.

Peculiar Nature of Farm Credit. Farm credit has been characterized by discouraging loan terms like high interest rates because of hazards peculiar to the occupation: (1) Weather risks like drought, frosts, and heavy rainfall can destroy a crop and minimize the likelihood of loan repayment. (2) Bumper harvests depress farm prices and reduce debtors' capacity to discharge their obligations. (3) The farmer is a strong individualist, and the success of his activities depends more heavily upon personal capacity and management than in most other occupations. (4) Farm loans are often so large as to give lenders a disproportionate interest in the farms relative to the borrowers' financial stake. (5) The capital turnover in agriculture is much lower than in most manufacturing industries, necessitating longer-term credit than most commercial banks and other lenders willingly grant. (6) Farm loans are often granted on inadequate credit data due to inadequate and obsolete accounting and financial information offered by farm borrowers.

PRIVATE LENDERS

Long-Term Lenders.

WEALTHY RETIRED FARMERS. Through farm mortgage brokers, they lend on mortgages.

FARM LANDOWNERS. They are compensated in part for their sold properties by mortgages on their lands.

PRIVATE MORTGAGE INVESTORS. They purchase claims from mortgage companies, trust companies, and banking institutions or lend directly to borrowers on mortgage security.

MORTGAGE COMPANIES. Mortgage companies operate through branches and local area correspondents that investigate credit applicants and determine whether the mortgage companies should purchase the mortgages for resale. Ordinarily, mortgage bankers assign mortgages to investors. Frequently, the mortgage companies sell their own obligations to investors protected by the deposit of collateral mortgages with a trust company. Since mortgage companies lend usually for five-year periods, the farmers find such credit unsuited to their long-term requirements. Therefore, they must seek mortgage loan extensions (difficult in tight money periods), pay renewal fees, and high interest rates. These factors, coupled with the establishment of government farm credit agencies, have led to a marked decline in the importance of farm mortgage companies.

LIFE INSURANCE COMPANIES. They lend directly to farm borrowers or buy mortgages from brokers and mortgage companies. These loans increasingly include long-term amortization arrangements typical of the federal land banks.

COMMERCIAL BANKS, SAVINGS BANKS, AND TRUST COMPANIES LOCATED IN THE FARM AREA.

Intermediate and Short-Term Lenders.

NATIONAL AND STATE RURAL BANKS. They finance the farmers' working-capital needs. These loans are secured by chattel mortgages on farm assets like livestock and crops. Chattel mortgages on automobiles and household goods protect small loans.

LIVESTOCK LOAN COMPANIES. They lend to cattle breeders on their promissory notes, indorse them, and discount them at commercial banks or at the federal intermediate credit banks. Loans vary from $1,000 to $500,000; maturities from six months for fattening cattle and sheep to three years for breeding these animals. The profit to the livestock loan companies is the difference between the rates on farmers' promissory notes and the discount charges of the institutions buying the paper.

FACTORS AND PRODUCE DEALERS. These men purchase farm crops after financing growing operations protected by liens on the anticipated crops. When the crops are sold to processors, the factors are compensated by interest and commission charges.

MERCHANTS. Merchants provide local farmers, especially southern agriculturists, with store credits for the purchase of farm equipment and supplies. These credits are secured by crop liens and chattel mortgages, and repaid with interest out of the proceeds of crop sales. Merchants have been criticized for the high interest rates and the exorbitant prices for equipment.

LANDLORDS. They allow tenant farmers to use their land and provide them with equipment in exchange for part of the harvested crop.

FARM CREDIT ADMINISTRATION

History. (1) After 1900, a sharp demand arose for agricultural long-term credit reform to assure (a) longer term loans, (b) a more equitable distribution of farm credit in the various sections of the United States, (c) lower interest rates, (d) greater certainty of loan renewals, (e) a broader, well-organized, and even a national market for farm loan securities, (f) fairer treatment for the small farmer and tenant. (2) The result of the agitation was the Federal Farm Loan Act of 1916. (3) But this legislation proved inadequate after World War I as farm prices dropped markedly and banks demanded repayment of loans. (4) A Congressional agricultural inquiry followed. As a result of the investigation the Federal Intermediate Credit System was established. (5) The 1916 and 1923 legislation created (a) twelve federal land banks owned by cooperative, national, farm loan associations, (b) a system of joint-stock land banks and mortgage bond companies organized under federal charters, (c) twelve federal intermediate credit banks. (6) By 1933, agricultural credit needs were provided for through six different farm credit agencies. In addition to the three above-mentioned organizations, crop production and seed loan offices were supervised by the Secretary of Agriculture. The Federal Farm Board granted credit to co-operative associations for marketing purposes, and the RFC offered production credit through regional farm credit corporations. (7) However, farmers not only did not know the location of these various organizations, but were confused as to which organization offered the credit their individual needs required. (8) President Roosevelt's executive order of March, 1933, provided for the Farm Credit Administration to co-ordinate the functions of most federal farm credit organizations through twelve land banks, twelve intermediate credit banks, twelve production credit corporations, and twelve banks for co-operatives, one of each type centered in a leading city of the twelve farm districts. The four organizations in each district are supervised by one farm credit board. (9) The FCA, established in May, 1933, was shifted from the Treasury Department to the Department of Agriculture in 1939.

Federal Land Banks. The Federal Farm Loan Act of 1916 divided the country into twelve districts to achieve a diversified agricultural activity in each district and so minimize the effect of crop failure on any one of the twelve banks.

CAPITAL AND SURPLUS. (1) The United States Treasury largely subscribed the original capital of $750,000 per bank. (2) After local farmer-borrower owned and operated co-operative credit corporations, called national farm loan associations, subscribed $750,000 to each federal land bank's capital stock, one-fourth of any additional subscriptions were applied to the retirement of government-owned stock. (Such stock was completely retired by March, 1934.) (3) In 1932, the Treasury was authorized to strengthen land bank lending power by purchasing $125,000,000 capital stock and providing $189,000,000 of paid-in surplus to be retired like the original stock issue. The fund thus accumulated was used to buy federal land bank stock upon request and with the approval of the Land Bank Commissioner who heads the Federal Land Bank System. (4) War prosperity has facilitated retirement of these capital account items. (5) Federal land bank borrowers must subscribe to their local land banks for stock equal to 5 per cent of their loans. (6) Fifty per cent of a land bank's semiannual earnings must be allocated to a reserve until it equals the face value of outstanding privately held stock. Thereafter, 10 per cent of a land bank's earnings must be allotted to this reserve. (7) Dividends on privately owned stock are determined by the district farm credit board, the central governing agency of all Farm Credit Administration organizations in the district where the federal land bank is created. The action of this board must be approved by the Governor of the FCA, its chief executive. Treasury-owned stock does not receive a dividend.

BONDS. (1) Most loanable funds of the twelve banks are obtained from the sale of consolidated bonds secured by farm mortgages and other collateral. (2) These obligations are not guaranteed by the federal government, but their principal is exempt from state and local property taxes, and the interest, from state income taxes. They are usually eligible for purchase by savings banks and trust companies. (3) The amount and terms of these issues must be approved by the Land Bank Commissioner. (4) Federal land bank debt is limited to twenty times capital and surplus.

LOANS. (1) Loans are made to national farm loan associations, to direct borrowers, and to livestock-raising corporations. (2) Loan proceeds may be used to buy agricultural land and essential farm equipment, to improve farm land and construct farm buildings, to pay off agricultural indebtedness and to discharge loans for non-agricultural purposes contracted before January 1, 1937. (3) Individual borrowers may obtain loans from $1,000 to $50,000; loans above $25,000 require the Land Bank Commissioner's approval. (4) Loans may mature in five years, cannot run beyond forty years, and must be amortized on a semiannual or annual basis. (5) Interest charges cannot exceed by more than 1 per cent the interest rate on federal land bank bonds. Since the banks cannot legally pay more than 5 per cent on their bonds, the maximum interest rate on customer loans cannot exceed 6 per cent.

NEGOTIATION OF LOANS. (1) Most land bank loans are made through national farm loan associations of farm owners and prospective owners seeking mortgage credit. These associations are corporations chartered by the FCA. (2) An association consists of ten or more farmers who wish to borrow in all at least $20,000. (3) Each member of an association must subscribe to a $5 association share for each $100 borrowed. The association in turn purchases a like amount of land bank stock. (4) The purchase of a share gives a participant one vote but he cannot have more than twenty votes in the association. Each association chooses its own officers and the administrative work is usually performed by a secretary-treasurer. (5) A loan application is analyzed by the association's loan committee which may recommend that it be approved. The association's board of directors also passes on the application, and if it approves, forwards the loan request to the district federal land bank which evaluates the property offered as collateral. (6) When a loan is approved, it is granted by the land bank to the association, which, in turn, makes the money available to the loan applicant. (7) When a loan is repaid, land bank stock is retired or cash payment is made to the association if it is not indebted to the bank. Where an association owes a land bank money because of losses suffered on loans granted to the association's members, the bank can apply the proceeds of the stock retirement to the association's obligation. In any circumstance, an association member who has paid off his loan is reimbursed for the par value of his stock if the association is able to do so.

DIRECT LOANS. Farmers may not be able to borrow through an association if one does not exist in their neighborhood or for other reasons. However, they may borrow directly upon the indorsement of another party at an interest rate one-half of 1 per cent above the charge on a loan negotiated through an association.

LAND BANK COMMISSIONER LOANS. (1) The Emergency Farm Mortgage Act of 1933 originally empowered the Land Bank Commissioner to lend $200,000,000, and then $800,000,000, for the same purposes as land banks. The loans were to be directly to farmers unable to secure satisfactory credit accommodations from the land banks. (2) A first- or second-mortgage commissioner loan, plus all other claims on property mortgaged, can total 75 per cent of farm property value or $7,500. (3) The commissioner is permitted to lend to part-time farms (rural and suburban farms which do not cover their expenses and maintain a family), if the borrowers enjoy satisfactory income from other sources. (4) Interest rates on these loans are 1 per cent higher than on loans negotiated through associations. (5) These loans must be amortized and may be outstanding for forty years, although most mature within twenty years. (6) The commissioner acts as an agent of the Federal Farm Mortgage Corporation—his loan activities are financed by it and his mortgage assets are its property.

FEDERAL FARM MORTGAGE CORPORATION. (1) Established in 1934 to finance Land Bank Commissioner loans and help finance the land banks, the Federal Farm Mortgage Corporation has obtained its working capital from the $200,000,000 allotted for Land Bank Commissioner loans and through the sale of bonds guaranteed by the federal government as to principal and interest. (2)

These bonds could find a market when the unguaranteed land bank obligations were not salable in sufficient volume to meet the pressing depression demand for new mortgage loans to refinance unmarketable and defaulted mortgage loans. (3) The corporation provides the land banks with funds by selling its bonds publicly and investing the proceeds in land bank obligations or exchanging its bonds for the consolidated issues of the land bank. (4) The corporation can have outstanding at any one time $2,000,000,000 of bonds. (5) It is managed by the Governor of the FCA, the Land Bank Commissioner, and the Secretary of the Treasury.

Joint-Stock Land Banks. (1) The Federal Farm Loan Act of 1916 also authorized private mortgage bond companies, each capitalized at $250,000 or more, and consisting of at least ten people. They were to lend to individual farmers not members of national farm loan associations sums in excess of $25,000 on real-estate security. (2) Loan provisions were similar to those covering land banks and farm loan associations, but each joint-stock land bank's operations were confined to adjoining states. Total loans could amount to fifteen times capital and surplus. (3) The banks could issue bonds secured by mortgage notes and first mortgages. (4) The Federal Farm Loan Board, supervisory authority, issued eighty-eight charters, but by 1933 unsound loan practices and fraud had forced almost half of the banks to merge or dissolve. (5) The Emergency Farm Mortgage Act of 1933 ordered the survivors to liquidate.

Federal Intermediate Credit Banks. (1) The Agricultural Credit Act of 1923 created twelve institutions to provide intermediate credit for carrying and marketing agricultural produce and livestock especially during hard times. (2) The intermediate credit banks were originally capitalized at $5,000,000 by the federal government; additional government capital subscriptions were authorized in 1934 to meet the needs of eligible farm borrowers. The Governor of the FCA can raise or lower the capital and surplus of any and all twelve intermediate credit banks. (3) Loanable funds are provided chiefly by the issue of short-term (not over five years), joint consolidated debentures of the twelve banks, secured by farm paper. The United States government does not guarantee these issues. The financial responsibility of any one intermediate credit bank for these debentures cannot exceed ten times its capital and paid-in surplus. (4) Additional funds may be obtained by rediscounts at the federal reserve banks, interbank borrowings, and the sale of farm paper in the open market. (5) Loans, usually maturing within one year, are granted for a maximum period of three years at a discount rate no more than 1 per cent above the interest rate on the most recent issue of debentures. (6) Intermediate credit bank loans are rediscounts of eligible paper for national or state banks, trust companies, livestock loan companies, production credit associations, banks for co-operatives and other farm-credit-granting institutions. Eligible paper consists of negotiable farm paper bearing an interest rate of not more than three points above the intermediate credit bank rediscount rate. (7) Other loans may be made to production credit associations and banks for co-operatives on their promissory notes protected by collateral approved by the Governor of the FCA. (8) A third type of loan up to 75 per cent of the crop and livestock value is made to co-operative associations for the production and marketing of farm staples and livestock. (9) The Intermediate Credit Commissioner is responsible for the supervision of this credit system. (10) The national agricultural credit corporations were originally part of the Federal Intermediate Credit System. They were organized by five or more people under fifty-year federal charters to lend on farm paper maturing within nine months from the date of purchase except if based on livestock paper which could mature within three years. Federal reserve member banks could be stockholders up to 10 per cent of their capital and surplus. These corporations could issue collateral trust debentures secured by the farm paper purchased. Their functions were taken over by the production credit corporations and associations.

Production Credit Corporations and Associations. (1) The twelve production credit corporations are owned and capitalized by the federal government at $7,500,000 each. The Governor of the FCA is empowered to modify their capital resources according to needs. (2) The corporations help organize, capitalize, and supervise production credit associations. (3) A corporation purchases nonvoting Class A stock of each local association for 20 per cent of the loans made or likely to be negotiated by the association. (4) Associations are organized by ten or more farmers seeking intermediate and short-term credit. For every $100 or fraction thereof borrowed, a farmer must purchase $5 of his association's voting Class B stock. (5) An association loan committee passes on a loan application. If approved, a short-term loan is usually granted for less than a year but may be renewed for three years. The smallest loan is $50 and the largest cannot exceed 20 per cent of an association's capital and surplus except with the approval of the district production credit corporation. Loans above 50 per cent must be approved by the Production Credit Commissioner who heads the federal production credit corporation and association administration. Loans are secured by chattel mortgages. (6) Associations grant loans out of the proceeds of borrowings from or rediscounts of their customers' notes with the federal intermediate credit banks. (7) An association cannot obtain intermediate credit bank credit in excess of ten times its unimpaired capital and surplus. (8) The loan interest charge is determined by the discount rate of the district intermediate credit bank. It must not exceed this rate by more than 3 per cent. Many loans are repaid in installments and the interest rate is applied only to the unpaid balance. (9) When a borrower repays his loan to an association, he exchanges his Class B stock for Class A stock or transfers his Class B stock to another farm borrower or potential borrower. To insure association control by practicing farmers, an agriculturist who does not borrow from an association for two years must get rid of his Class B stock. (10) The federal government originally put up a $120,000,000 subsidy to aid this farm credit arrangement. The production credit corporations are largely supported by the income from it and the return on their security investments of unused capital. The associations have also benefited considerably from the subsidy. (11) Association capital stock proceeds are invested in approved securities, chiefly federal government obligations—additional protection for the rediscounts and loans from the federal intermediate credit banks. (12) Private commercial bankers are critical of the associations because they are strong competitors for agricultural loans.

The Banks for Co-operatives. (1) The Farm Credit Act of 1933 established twelve federal banks for co-operatives in the twelve farm credit districts to make readily available needed capital for farm co-operative associations. (2) A central bank for co-operatives finances large co-operative organizations operating on a national or interregional basis. It is managed by the Co-operative Bank Commissioner and six other directors appointed by the FCA Governor from a group of candidates nominated by borrowing co-operatives. (3) A Co-operative Bank Commissioner supervises the central bank for co-operatives and the twelve banks for co-operatives. (4) The capital stock of each co-operative bank is deter-

mined by the FCA Governor in accordance with the credit requirements of eligible borrowers in its district. The Governor may subscribe for the capital stock out of the revolving fund established by
the Agricultural Marketing Act of 1929. Minimum capitalization
of each district bank was fixed originally at $5,000,000 and has been
increased in some cases. The central bank for co-operatives was first
capitalized at $50,000,000 and then at $75,000,000. The Governor
of the FCA may call on a district co-operative bank to retire a
portion of its stock out of surplus funds. (5) A co-operative association borrowing from a co-operative bank must subscribe for $100
of the bank's capital stock for each $2,000 or any part thereof of
operating capital and facility loans; $100 of stock must be pur-
chased for every $1,000 in commodity loans. (6) If state law for-
bids a co-operative to subscribe to stock, it can participate in this
financing plan by paying a comparable sum into a guaranty fund.
(7) Co-operative banks grant commodity loans to finance the
preparation of farm products for sale, facility loans to enable co-
operatives to purchase capital equipment essential to their activities,
and operating capital loans for meeting various current operating
costs. (8) Facility loans may be granted for twenty years but usually are extended for ten years and are repayable in installments.
Commodity and operating capital loans are for short-term, seasonal purposes. (9) Practically all loans extended by the banks for
co-operatives are protected by collateral liens on farm produce,
capital equipment, real estate, and other assets. (10) Interest rates
are highest on facility loans and lowest on commodity loans.
(11) When a loan is repaid, the bank's stock issue may be retired
or the co-operative association may hold it as an investment. (12)
District co-operative banks can discount their loans with the
Central Bank for Co-operatives. This central bank can sell bonds
up to five times its paid-in capital and surplus. (13) Both the
central bank and the district banks can rediscount their commodity and working capital loans with the intermediate credit
banks. In addition, the district banks can borrow from national
and state commercial banks. (14) The central bank for co-operatives may grant a joint advance to intraregional co-operatives when
the loan is unusually large, for the district bank cannot lend more
than 10 per cent of its capital and surplus for operating capital and
facility loans or 20 per cent for commodity loans to any one
borrower.

Management of the FCA. (1) A Governor, appointed by the President with the advice and consent of the Senate, supervises the FCA. He is a direct subordinate of the Secretary of Agriculture and oversees all the farm credit agencies within the scope of the FCA. (2) The commissioners of the FCA agencies are appointed by the President and are responsible to the Governor. (3) The district federal land bank, intermediate credit bank, bank for co-operatives, and production credit corporation are all separately capitalized, although under the control of a single farm credit board. (4) The farm credit board consists of seven members appointed for three-year terms. One director is chosen by the district federal land bank borrowers, a second by short-term borrowers from district production credit associations, and a third by borrowers from the district bank for co-operatives; three more directors are named by the Governor of the FCA with another chosen by him from a list of names submitted by the borrowers from the district federal land bank. (5) The four farm banks in each district are headed by individual presidents, while a general agent appointed by the Governor of the FCA works with the district farm credit board to integrate the work of the four district banks.

COMMODITY CREDIT CORPORATION

(1) The Commodity Credit Corporation finances the farmer by withholding excess crops from the market until they can be sold at a fair price. (2) CCC crop loans, secured by chattel mortgages and warehouse receipts, aim to assure farmers a "parity price" or near parity quotation. "Full parity" means that the buying power of the farmer and of the nonfarm group are in the same ratio as for the period August, 1909, to July, 1914. (3) Borrowers can default without further liability, and consider the loan the selling price of their crops, or sell the loan's collateral, repay the CCC and retain any surplus—whichever procedure is to their advantage. (4) Parity loans are also made by banks which then can sell the borrowers' notes to the corporation. (5) Direct CCC loans are granted for six to twelve months at 3 per cent interest annually. Loans granted by banks may yield the banks 1½ per cent. (6) CCC paper losses are made good from public funds, and the corporation is required to turn back any surplus to the government.

THE FARMERS HOME ADMINISTRATION

Successor in 1946 to the Emergency Crop and Feed Loan Division of the FCA and the Farm Security Administration, the Farmers Home Administration has the following aims: (1) to lend $10 to $400 at 4 per cent for the purchase of livestock feed and seed for planting to those borrowers who cannot secure adequate credit elsewhere; (2) to lend to financially pressed farmers for the purchase of supplies and equipment, for subsistence, and for debt refinancing; (3) to lend to qualified farm tenants, farm laborers, and sharecroppers for the purchase of farm property if they can make the first down payment or provide the essential farm equipment and livestock. Under a 1946 amendment to the Bankhead-Jones Farm Tenant Act of 1937, private lenders can make government-insured loans for farm purchase, enlargement, and development: (a) Mortgage principal obligations of $100,000,000 can be insured in any one fiscal year out of a revolving insurance fund. (b) An insured mortgage loan cannot exceed 90 per cent of an applicant's total farm investment and his farm must have a normal earning capacity. (c) Lenders receive a return of 2½ per cent on unpaid principal, while borrowers pay a 1 per cent annual mortgage insurance charge to the Farmers Home Administration. (d) Principal and interest payments are due annually, and a variable payment plan permits borrowers to make payments ahead of schedule in prosperous years to keep their loans in good standing in lean years when they are less able to pay. (e) Loans are repayable in forty years, but must be refinanced when the borrower can obtain an uninsured loan on satisfactory terms at not more than 5 per cent interest. (f) If a borrower defaults for more than thirty days, the Farmers Home Administration immediately pays the lender due and unpaid principal and interest. A default of more than twelve months requires the Farmers Home Administration to assume the insured mortgage and discharge the unpaid principal and interest plus any authorized payments for taxes made by the lender. (g) Insured mortgages are acceptable collateral for federal reserve bank loans.

RURAL ELECTRIFICATION ADMINISTRATION

This organization: (1) grants loans to build rural electric distribution systems; (2) finances the purchase of electrical equipment and appliances.

Both types of loans are granted to public utility companies, local governments, co-operative associations, etc., with the second type extended also to dealers, contractors, and electrical and plumbing appliance companies.

WATER FACILITIES ACT

This legislation enables farmers located in arid states to borrow from a special congressional appropriation and funds made available by the Farm Security Administration for pumps, wells, and other small irrigation facilities.

REVIEW QUESTIONS

1. Who are the major private farm credit lenders?
2. What is (a) a produce dealer, (b) a tenant farmer, (c) a livestock loan company, (d) a national farm loan association?
3. Why was the Farm Credit Administration organized? What is its administrative organization?
4. Distinguish among the functions of the federal land banks, the federal intermediate credit banks, and the production credit corporations.
5. Describe the procedure a farmer would follow to use the credit facilities of a federal land bank and of a production credit corporation.
6. What is "full parity"? How does the Commodity Credit Corporation seek to achieve parity?

✠

Consumer Finance

Services. (1) Consumer credit greatly enlarges public buying power and broadens the market for consumer goods to absorb industry's current mass production. (2) Consumer loan facilities have minimized loan-shark activities to the public's benefit.

Specialized Nature of Consumer Credit. (1) Small sums are borrowed as compared with the amounts borrowed for productive operations. (2) The borrowers, unlike business credit seekers, are relatively unknown. (3) The small size of loans means a heavy cost of administration and a consequent higher rate on these loans as against the rates charged on productive credit accommodations. (4) Consumption credit loans do not increase the borrowers' earning capacity. Frequently, repayment of such loans is made out of a new similar loan, or the loan is renewed.

History. (1) Prior to 1910, financially indigent people with low incomes could turn only to pawnbrokers and loan sharks to meet extraordinary expenditures like medical bills. Commercial banks considered such individuals unworthy risks, lacking thrift. (2) Loan studies of the Russell Sage Foundation developed a new attitude toward consumer credit; poor people must be offered loans at fair rates to escape the extravagant and illegal charges of loan sharks. Within a short time, consumer credit organizations like remedial loan associations, Morris Plan banks, credit unions, and small loan companies assumed an increasingly prominent financial role. Commercial banks organized personal loan departments after 1925. (3) Installment sales finance also became a desirable loan field once the general aversion to such loans, as contrary to thriftiness, was overcome.

PERSONAL LOAN INSTITUTIONS

History. (1) In ancient times, the demand for money loans grew chiefly out of temporary personal difficulties. Since money was thought unproductive, interest was considered unwarranted. Both the Mosaic Code, making no distinction between consumption and production credit, and the Church barred interest charges. (2) The commercial and industrial development in medieval days led to a demand for business loans, and interest-bearing commitments became the rule. Eventually, both civil and Church law permitted reasonable interest rates, prohibiting only usurious charges. (3) But before 1910, nonphilanthropic loan organization, small consumer loans were available only at usurious rates.

Loan Sharks and Pawnbrokers. (1) A loan shark is a person who lends at exorbitant rates of 20 to 40 per cent per month to meet the pressing financial needs of small wage earners and merchants unable to obtain funds from other sources. (2) A loan-shark loan is made on the security of personal property like furniture, or on a wage assignment, or by the purchase of a borrower's salary at a sharp discount. (3) Even in states regulating personal loans, the loan shark frequently escapes criminal prosecution through legal loopholes like the power given creditors to garnish all or part of a person's income without much legal difficulty, through slothful law enforcement, or through mortgage contracts drawn to avoid the legal restrictions. (4) A city-licensed pawnbroker makes secured loans or purchases financially hardpressed individuals' personal property at a low price with the understanding that he will resell it to the original owner at an agreed upon higher price within a certain period of time. The longer the original seller waits to repurchase the item, the higher is its resale price. Where the sale of loan collateral is regulated, public auction is required after due notice to the borrower. (5) The pawnbroker's profit or rate of interest is determined by the difference between the two prices. (6) The receipt for property sold or a secured loan is the pawnbroker's ticket indicating the time period during which redemption is permitted and usually the interest rate. (7) General usury laws in various states provide for a yearly contract rate of about 10 per cent; in those states where pawnbroker rates are legally established, the usual charge is 3 per cent per month. But rates higher than the legal limits are everyday occurrences. (8) Pawnbrokers are regulated in some states, and must pay a general license or occupation tax. Many states also require the pawnbroker to post a bond guaranteeing proper conduct of his business and protection for his customers.

Remedial Loan Societies. (1) About 1910, public-minded citizens, under the leadership of the Russell Sage Foundation, organized remedial loan associations to eliminate the loan shark. (2) Loans are made on either chattel mortgages or mere pledges out of capital provided by public-spirited people. (3) The dividend on capital is limited usually to from 6 to 8 per cent.

Morris Plan Banks. (1) In 1910, Arthur J. Morris, a Norfolk lawyer, interested in adapting the principles of European co-operative industrial banking to American economic life, established the first industrial bank at Norfolk, Virginia, to lend to people of limited means without access to normal banking facilities. His successful efforts led to the organization of comparable banking institutions like the Citizens Finance Companies, the Modern Loan and Investment Corporation, and the Industrial Banking Corporation of America. (2) Shortly after a few Morris Plan banks had been established, Mr. Morris founded the Fidelity Corporation to handle the affairs of the banks. (3) In turn, it was succeeded by the Industrial Finance Corporation which supervised bank operations and subscribed for about 25 per cent of the capital stock of each new bank. Local people bought the rest of the stock issue. (4) The Industrial Finance Corporation, also engaged in automobile financing, became a holding company when it organized the Morris Plan Corporation of America to assume its interests in the Morris Plan banks and the Industrial Acceptance Corporation to handle automobile financing. The latter was subsequently liquidated. (5) Morris Plan banks are organized under state or national charters, offer general banking services and grant credit for both business and personal needs. (6) Many Morris Plan banks have dropped the words "Morris Plan" and become independent enterprises by purchasing the stock owned by the Morris Plan Corporation of America.

LOAN PURPOSES; AMOUNT; COLLATERAL. (1) Some business and installment credits have been granted, but most loans are still consumption loans for emergency expenditures or the purchase of necessities. (2) Loans of $25 to $500 or more and averaging $250 are made to good character risks, whose financial position and earnings warrant, on different types of security as one or two co-maker notes, stocks and bonds, chattel mortgages on durable goods like automobiles, and real-estate mortgages. (3) In some cases, unsecured single-name promissory notes evidence productive and consumptive loans to high-grade credit risks. (4) Industrial banks also finance retail installment sales by purchasing installment buyers' promissory notes.

LOAN PROCEDURE. (1) If an application is approved by a bank's loan committee, the borrower and indorsers make out a note discounted at a rate of 6 to 8 per cent per annum. They pay a $1 investigation fee for every $50 borrowed, but the fee cannot exceed $5. (2) The borrower must purchase an investment installment certificate for every $50 borrowed, paying $1 weekly. At the end of the twenty-fifth week, the money paid in on the certificate draws interest at 4 per cent and at the end of fifty weeks when the $50 is fully paid in, the certificate is turned in cancelling the loan. (3) If the loan is repaid with funds other than the weekly installment deposits, the installment certificate is exchanged for a full-paid investment certificate yielding 5 per cent interest and redeemable in cash on thirty days' notice. (4) Full-paid investment certificates are also sold to investors like banks desirous of a safe investment for their surplus funds. Most Morris Plan bank capital is provided by the sale of such investment certificates and the receipt of deposits.

ADVANTAGES. (1) Borrowers obtain credit on a business basis and need not resort to unscrupulous loan sharks. (2) Repayment is easy through the purchase of installment loan certificates. These certificates have facilitated payment of insurance policy premiums written by the Morris Plan Insurance Society, established in 1917 by the Industrial Finance Corporation. Account receivable and acceptance debtors can purchase certificates to pay off obligations discounted by creditors at Morris Plan banks. (3) Borrowers without access to commercial banks can secure character loans. Losses on such loans have been less than one-fourth of 1 per cent.

DISADVANTAGES. Since loans are paid off weekly, reducing the average outstanding balance, the nominal 6 per cent rate, plus investigatory and other charges, actually is an effective rate of about 19 per cent yearly. The states have legalized this rate by either suspending the usury law on these loans or holding the deposit-payment arrangement unrelated to the loans.

REGULATION. (1) State laws regulate industrial bank incorporation, capital requirements, the sale of investment certificates, the receipt of deposits, state examinations, and reports of condition. (2) Loan powers are circumscribed through limitations on the maximum amount to a single party, or the proportion to paid-in capital and surplus, and loan charges. (3) Morris Plan banks were allowed membership in the Federal Reserve System in 1933, but this privilege has been little used. (4) New York State declared industrial banks state banks, so that investment certificates are considered certificates of deposit, insured by the FDIC, with the interest thereon fixed by the insurance corporation.

Personal Loan Companies. (1) Personal loan companies are organized by private stockholders under state law to grant consumption loans principally to small borrowers for about two years. (2) The Russell Sage Foundation is responsible for the writing of a model law, the Uniform Small Loan Law, regulating businesses making small loans. Suggested to state legislatures, it was used as the basis for the Massachusetts small loan law passed in 1911. Since that time other states have passed the same or similar laws.

RATES. (1) Small loan laws exempt personal loan companies licensed and supervised by state banking departments from usury law restrictions. (2) Loan charges average 3 or 3½ per cent a month to attract capital investment in a business marked by (a) heavy overhead and operating expenses, (b) special investigation problems, (c) little security protection or poor market collateral, (d) installment payments calling for expensive collection techniques over the life of the loan.

OPERATION. (1) Most loans are secured by chattel mortgages on house furniture, wage assignments, and comaker notes; a few credits are unsecured. (2) A personal loan company scatters its loan offices over several states to obtain advantages like (a) a diversified loan portfolio under one management, (b) an interstate loan area enabling a quick shift of loanable funds to those areas where they are needed and can be put to work safely. (3) Since they are large companies, they can tap the central money market and borrow large sums at relatively low cost. (4) A few companies dominate this field.

REGULATION. (1) Lenders must be licensed and supervised by the state banking department. (2) Lenders must have a minimum capital of $25,000, must pay an annual license fee with the state vested with authority to revoke the license. (3) Borrowers are protected by requiring lenders to give them a loan contract, payment receipts, and the right to repay the loan at any time with interest charged only for the time the loan was used. (4) Wage assignments and chattel mortgages must be written and signed by a borrower and his wife. (5) Only 10 per cent of a borrower's wages can be collected by a lender, provided he presents a copy of the assignment to the employer attested to by the lender as to the unpaid loan principal.

Commercial Bank Personal Loan Departments. The National City Bank of New York took the initiative in the late 1920's in developing a department to push personal loans repayable on an installment basis.

DEVELOPMENT. The National City's example was followed by other commercial banks, for: (1) the banks were surfeited with idle funds during the 1930's and lacked the usual commercial and industrial loan outlets; (2) when business loan rates dropped, the higher level personal loan rates attracted bank management; (3) customers were cultivated by personal loan service.

OPERATION. (1) Comaker loans are most prominent, followed by loans on unsecured notes, and single-name paper collateraled by life insurance policies, chattel mortgages, stocks, bonds, and savings bank passbooks. (2) The customer's paper is usually discounted at 6 to 8 per cent, but since he must repay in monthly installments accumulated in a savings bank deposit or applied directly to the loan, the actual interest rate is ordinarily about 12 to 16 per cent. Personal borrowers must also pay service and investigation fees and delinquency fines. (3) The purchase of consumer installment notes from retail dealers and loans to sales finance and personal finance companies indirectly finance the consumer by directly financing the finance companies. Small sales finance companies pledge installment paper and other collateral with trustees as protection for bank loans. The financially powerful sales finance companies usually borrow without pledging collateral.

Credit Unions. They are co-operative organizations, state or federally incorporated: (1) to develop thrift habits in their members who have a common bond of interest like occupation or community; (2) to lend to them or member co-operative societies and similar organizations out of a common pool of savings for remedial or productive purposes.

HISTORY. (1) Credit unions were first established in Germany in the middle of the nineteenth century and spread over the European continent. (2) The first American credit union was organized in New Hampshire in 1908. (3) The states then enacted credit union laws during the next twenty-five years. (4) Mr. Edward A. Filene, prominent Boston merchant, pushed the credit union idea vigorously and stimulated its modern development. His sponsored organization, the Twentieth Century Fund, set up the Credit Union National Extension Bureau in 1921 to aid the movement by publicity, advice in union establishment, and by urging permissive legislation. (5) Congress passed the Federal Credit Union Act in 1934 authorizing a Federal Credit Union System, with federal credit unions chartered by the Farm Credit Administration.

SOURCES OF FUNDS. (1) Each credit union member must purchase at least one share of stock with a usual par value of $5 or $10. No matter how many shares a member owns, he can cast only one vote in electing officers and determining policies. (2) The second major source of funds is member deposits. (3) Entrance fees and bank loans also contribute to an organization's resources. Although borrowing rarely occurs, a federal credit union may borrow up to 50 per cent of its capital and surplus. (4) The fund built up out of stock subscriptions and deposits is a revolving fund for loans to any union member. A good portion of the members never borrow and are interested in the income from their shares and deposits.

LOANS. (1) Small personal loans average $50 to $125, but loans to small businessmen reach higher figures. (2) Loans are made on single-name promissory notes, on comaker notes, on mortgage collateral, and on wage assignments. (3) A lien is obtained on the shares of a borrowing member or a member who has indorsed loans. (4) A federal credit union can lend an individual borrower at most $200 or 10 per cent of its capital and surplus whichever is the larger, and loans above $100 must be secured. (5) State and federal laws establish maximum loan rates of 10 to 12 per cent annually on unpaid balances. These rates are lower than personal loan and industrial bank charges because union costs of operation are lower; their activities are subsidized by philanthropic and other agencies; they may be exempt from state taxes; close knowledge of borrowers means easy, low cost credit investigations; little or no compensation is paid to credit union officials; and business organizations whose members belong to credit unions usually offer financial assistance.

FEDERAL CREDIT UNIONS. (1) The Federal Credit Union System and federal supervision enable the government to show federal credit unions how best to organize and operate the institution. (2) The powers of the Farm Credit Administration over federal credit unions were permanently transferred to the Federal Deposit Insurance Corporation in 1946. But the shares of these unions are not insured.

SALES FINANCE COMPANIES

Reasons for Growth. Organized installment sales financing, initiated in the automobile field in 1915, was encouraged by these influences: (1) Manufacturers and dealers were able to concentrate entirely on production and sales effort and avoid diversion of capital to sales finance. (2) Mass production of new commodities like radios and automobiles at low prices broadened the consumer market and encouraged installment financing. (3) The rising national income of the 1920's enabled individual purchases on a bigger scale. (4) The weekly or monthly regularity of family income assured a steady flow of buying power to the employed and offered a firm basis for retail credit extensions. People could now enjoy goods purchased on the installment plan if willing to save in order to meet overhanging debt obligations. (5) Manufacturers pushed sales on the easy payment plan. (6) Installment credit terms became easier as this type of financing became well organized and commonplace. (7) Commercial banks entered the sales finance field during the depression of the 1930's, seeking outlets for their excess funds and impressed by the small losses of sales finance companies. (8) The government, through the Federal Housing Administration, has insured sales finance companies against risk on different types of real-estate modernization loans.

NATIONAL AND LOCAL ORGANIZATION. (1) Three large finance companies do a national business. (2) Five companies finance sales in eight or more states. (3) There are several hundred local sales finance companies.

Wholesale Auto Finance. (1) Originally, auto dealers requiring working capital were not able to purchase cars on credit from manufacturers needing cash. (2) Commercial banks, skeptical in the 1920's of the automobile market, were unwilling to finance dealers. (3) Therefore, wholesale dealers used the finance company to finance their retail sales out of finance company borrowings at commercial banks.

METHOD. (1) The auto manufacturer draws a sight draft on the dealer, attaching the bill of lading. (2) Upon receipt of the bill of lading the finance company pays off the manufacturer. (3) The dealer obtains the bill of lading in exchange for a promissory note due in one to six months, secured by a direct lien on the cars. (4) A finance company lends a dealer from 80 to 90 per cent of his note, the percentage being greater on cars in a warehouse than on the dealer's floor and greater against passenger cars than trucks because of the shorter financing period. (5) The finance company receives a trust receipt for cars on the dealer's floor and a warehouse receipt for cars stored in a warehouse. (6) As the cars are sold to the public, the buyers' installment notes are given to the finance company with the proceeds of the sale used partly to discharge the dealer's debt to the finance company and the remainder pocketed for his own use. (7) A trust receipt does not give the manufacturer the right to recover a car against an innocent buyer as does a registered chattel mortgage or conditional bill of sale.

Retail Auto Finance. (1) A retail buyer applies to a dealer for the privilege of purchasing a car on the installment plan, supporting his application with references and a statement of his financial position. (2) If the application is accepted after investigation by a finance company, and a sale made, a down payment in cash or a used car of at least one-third of a new auto's retail sales price or two-fifths of a used car's price is required. The remainder is to be paid in twelve monthly installments evidenced by separate notes or acceptances. In addition, a "territory charge" covering physical damage insurance and graded according to the model and number of monthly payments plus a filing fee and a possible "carrying charge" are also imposed on the buyer. In all, the cost of finance company capital amounts to almost 12 per cent simple interest on the average of all unpaid balances. (3) The finance company discounts the buyer's notes at a rate determined by such factors as market conditions, recourse conditions, maturities, etc. (4) Since repossession means reclamation of a car whose resale value has greatly declined, the finance company usually calls for a down payment more than sufficient to offset the sharp depreciation in a used car, while each monthly payment is in excess of the monthly depreciation. (5) Car buyers are required to carry insurance against fire, theft, and collision to protect the finance company's equity. (6) The dealer holds a conditional bill of sale, lease, or chattel mortgage until all notes have been paid off. A default on any one of the notes makes all the notes due and payable immediately. (7) The dealer may be called on to protect the finance company's position by indorsing the customer's notes, thereby giving the finance company recourse against the dealer. Some finance companies do not require such indorsements, for the dealers object that the finance company alone has determined the financial position of the car buyer. (8) If a repurchase agreement is negotiated allowing the finance company to repossess a car in case of default on a payment, the dealer buys the car back from the finance company for the unpaid installments. However, the finance company loses its commitment if it is impossible to repossess the automobile.

Manufacturers' Finance Companies. (1) Originally, several automobile companies sought to stimulate sales by establishing their own finance companies, like General Motors Acceptance Corporation, and offering their services to their dealers. (2) Other manufacturers purchased an interest in an existing finance company and recommended it to their dealers. (3) Still other companies arranged for such finance companies as the Commercial Investment Trust Corporation to work with their dealers. (4) Attempts to show preference to affiliated finance companies by insistence on dealer use of these companies has ceased, and stress has been placed on attracting business through superior accommodations. (5) In some cases, auto manufacturers have abandoned the financing business to foster better relations with independent finance companies. (6) In 1938, Ford, Chrysler, and General Motors agreed to end their bias in favor of affiliated finance companies. (7) Big finance companies, independent of manufacturers, buy sales finance papers exclusively on their merits. Such a procedure is often typical, as well, of enterprises sponsored by producing units. (8) Small finance companies limit their area of operation to the local scene since a small overhead and greater familiarity of local risks and business conditions enable them to offer dealers and purchasers terms superior to those of the large finance company.

Capitalization. Sales finance companies obtain capital by: (1) the sale of common and preferred stocks, bonds, and collateral notes to the investing public; (2) commercial bank loans on lines of credit, borrowed on without collateral by financially strong companies (smaller organizations are often called on to pledge installment paper and other collateral); (3) the occasional sale of unsecured, open-market promissory notes by the bigger and stronger companies.

Credit Position. (1) Finance companies are considered good risks since their assets are liquid and their risks are spread over many loans each of which is only a few hundred dollars. (2) They have been able to borrow at lower rates than commercial and most industrial enterprises. (3) The return on capital investment has been high with few failures. (4) Installment paper was made eligible for rediscount at federal reserve banks in September, 1937.

Regulation. (1) The Federal Trade Commission has criticized automobile producers and finance companies for their claim that they charge only 6 per cent on unpaid balances. The National Association of Finance Companies prefers the use of the term "service" rather than interest charge on the grounds that it is necessary to cover such service costs as investigation, repossession, reselling, or resale at a loss on defaulted payments. (2) A few states now regulate retail installment financing concentrating chiefly on different phases of installment automobile sales. (3) In 1941, sales finance company consumption credit was brought within the scope of federal reserve regulations to curb the demand for scarce consumer goods. In the postwar period they were removed.

Advantages of Installment Credit. (1) Installment credit broadens the consumer market for mass production goods. (2) Consequent increased production means a lower cost of production. (3) The demand for seasonal goods is steadied, and such business enterprises are given greater stability. (4) The increased demand for goods stimulates the feeder industries and all industries in general. (5) Installment credit losses during the depression years were slight.

Disadvantages of Installment Credit. (1) The installment buyer often pays an excessive price for inferior articles. (2) Installment credit only shifts demand from necessities to luxuries and does not generate a new demand. (3) Since installment credit only anticipates future income, it creates the basis for a business downturn when future income is entirely anticipated. (4) People are encouraged to incur debt without consideration of their ultimate ability to discharge these debts. Many critics fear that banks, financing a good portion of installment credit, will suffer heavy losses when business declines and does not enjoy the stimulus of further increases in demand. (5) Service charges offset mass production economies.

ACCOUNTS-RECEIVABLE FINANCE

Sales finance companies also lend against accounts receivable which may have resulted from sales on the installment plan. In recent years commercial banks have entered this field.

Borrowers. Borrowers against receivables include: (1) business concerns without bank connections, or with a poor credit rating (some small entrepreneurs cannot secure bank loans but may be aided by finance companies); (2) clients desiring to do a larger volume of business than their capital allows—for example, seasonal business firms may need additional funds at the height of their season; (3) businessmen whose capital is frozen in plant and equipment; (4) dealers whose current capital is tied up in accounts receivable and inventory; (5) entrepreneurs who do not wish to sell stock and assume additional obligations; (6) applicants whose profit outlook is good but who lack current capital.

Method. (1) The finance or discount company agrees to discount a certain amount of accounts receivable under agreed upon terms and conditions. Since the discount company realizes that it probably will not be able to collect the face value of all the accounts receivable, it advances about 80 per cent of their face value. (2) The discount company obtains title to the accounts. Debtors on these accounts are usually advised of their assignment on the bills sent them and that payment is due the finance company. (3) Payments received by a borrower on assigned accounts are forwarded to the finance company. (4) The finance company can indorse the assigner's name on all credit instruments like checks and drafts received from his debtors. (5) It may hold an account receivable until sixty days past its maturity date when the borrower is required to repurchase it, usually by assigning another account. (6) A limited loss clause is included in some contracts and limits the assigner's liability to a small percentage. (7) Discount rates vary from 12 to 18 per cent annually while other charges for investigation, etc., add to the loan costs.

Capital. Capital is obtained by: (1) the sale of stocks and bonds, like short-term collateral trust certificates secured by discounted receivables; (2) bank loans; (3) open-market borrowing.

FACTORS

Large finance companies may also be factors. Some concerns are exclusively factors. This type of financial enterprise was confined originally to the textile industry, but in the late 1920's, it spread to such industries as furniture, clothing, paper, electrical appliances, etc.

Functions. (1) The factor purchases for cash at a small discount a manufacturing client's sound accounts receivable. The discount is used as a reserve against possible losses from returns of, or allowances for, damaged goods. (2) The debtors on the accounts receivable are notified that all payments are due the factor. He does business on a "notification" basis. (3) The factor bears all losses on, and pays all expenses of, collecting from the accounts receivable. (4) Since the financial burden is entirely the factor's, he supervises a manufacturer's sales, passing on the risks and the amount of credit sales that can be made. (5) Loans may be made against inventory to finance heavy seasonal needs.

Compensation. The factor is compensated by: (1) a commission varying with the type of account receivable from three-fourths of 1 per cent to more than 3 per cent on the customer's net sales; (2) 6 per cent interest on the sums advanced; (3) a possible additional commission of about 2 per cent for supplementary services, as advice.

Advantages to Manufacturer. (1) His cash and financial position are improved since he sells virtually for cash. (2) Financial difficulties growing out of credit losses are impossible. (3) A manufacturer is able to discharge bank obligations contracted to finance inventories and production. (4) A manufacturer can hold smaller cash reserves, and can use his cash to expand his business if conditions warrant. (5) A manufacturer can obtain cash discounts on his purchases and so reduce his costs and build up his profits. (6) Factors stimulate sales by providing storage and display space and shipping services. (7) Factors also push manufacturers' sales by arranging retail and jobber outlets and supplying expert advice.

REVIEW QUESTIONS

1. Distinguish between a loan shark, a pawnbroker, and a remedial loan association.
2. What are industrial banks? For what purposes and on what type of collateral do they lend?
3. Why are personal loan companies organized frequently on a national basis? Why have commercial banks organized personal loan departments?

4. What is (a) the Russell Sage Foundation, (b) the Uniform Small Loan Law, (c) a credit union, (d) a factor?
5. Describe the procedure of financing a retail automobile sale on the installment plan.
6. What are the advantages and disadvantages of installment credit?

⊞

American Financial Policy after World War II

AMERICAN FOREIGN FINANCIAL POLICY

One objective of American financial policy after World War II was the improvement of Europe's economic position.

At the close of the war Europe's industrial capacity was sadly impaired. Its transportation system had been badly damaged by persistent bombing; its industrial equipment was obsolete; its currency was so badly inflated as seriously to interfere with trade between city and rural areas. Consequently, governments used their meager foreign resources to purchase food at the expense of greatly needed heavy industrial equipment.

The Marshall Plan. Economic confusion was typical of the Continent in 1947. But the United States held a key to the development of an orderly and prosperous economy advantageous to both farmers and city dwellers. America's productive capacity had greatly expanded during World War II and required markets; these markets were available in Europe if Europeans could obtain the necessary dollar exchange to pay the American producer.

The problem thus became one of placing vitally needed American goods and services at the disposal of the crippled Continent. General Marshall, then Secretary of State, provided an answer in June, 1947.

"It is logical that the United States should do whatever it is able to do to assist in the return of normal economic help in the world without which there can be no political stability and no assured peace . . . [but] . . . before the United States can proceed much further in its efforts to alleviate the situation and help start the European world on its way to recovery, there must be some agreement among the countries of Europe as to the requirements of the situation and the part those countries themselves will take in order to give proper effect to whatever action might be taken by this government. . . . The role of this country should consist of friendly aid in the drafting of a European program and that later support of such a program so far as it may be practical for us to do so. The program should be a joint one. . . ."

All European countries except Russia and her satellites enthusiastically accepted the idea. To facilitate its initiation, the Committee of European Economic Cooperation was formed, to be replaced shortly by the Organization for Economic Cooperation.

The United States Congress passed the Foreign Assistance Act in April, 1948, and the Economic Cooperation Administration (ECA) was launched. While American aid provided Western Europe and the friendly areas of Asia and Africa with the necessary dollar exchange to purchase essential capital goods, the bulk of the European Recovery Program was financed by the Europeans. American foreign trade was stimulated by the plan, and simultaneously the living standards of the Marshall Plan countries markedly improved.

THE ORGANIZATION FOR EUROPEAN ECONOMIC COOPERATION. The Organization for European Economic Cooperation made most dollar-import decisions in Paris, where it studied plans of the member countries and after due analysis of the entire European economic problem drew up a master plan aimed at meeting the needs of all participating countries in the best manner possible.

THE COUNTERPART FUNDS. European buyers paid the price of desired American goods to their own governments in their own currencies. These governments reported the purchases to the Economic Cooperation Administration which provided the necessary dollars, the ECA paying the dollars to American producers, who then shipped the goods to the European buyers. The governments of the European purchasers then put an equal amount of their own moneys in special accounts called *counterpart funds*.

These funds were used in various ways. Each country had to turn over 5 per cent of its counterpart fund to the account of the ECA to cover the cost of the plan's administration in its country and to finance the purchase of scarce materials being stockpiled in the

United States. The other 95 per cent was used to assure internal monetary and financial stabilization, to stimulate production and the development of new sources of wealth. Some countries like Britain took their counterpart fund out of circulation to curtail the danger of inflation; others used their funds for internal improvements. No country could use its counterpart funds without ECA approval.

THE TECHNICAL ASSISTANCE PROGRAM.   This program, an essential part of the Marshall Plan, was designed to encourage the exchange of productive practices for the benefit of all participants in the plan. For example, the British Steel Foundry Industry sent specialists to the United States to learn how to stimulate steel production.

THE DOLLAR GAP.   The Marshall Plan also attempted to close the "dollar gap," a lack of dollars available to Europe with which to pay for America's huge export surplus to the Continent. Some idea of the dollar gap can be gathered from the fact that between July, 1914, and December, 1948, the United States exported $101 billion more than it imported. The dollar gap grew so large because Europe's trade with other areas of the world had slumped sharply while its purchases from the United States continued at a high and rising level. European countries sought to minimize their reciprocal trade obligations through tariffs and other restrictions that paralyzed the exchange of goods on the Continent. Elimination of these obstructions to trade was first attempted by the Intra-European Payments and Compensations Agreement. Claims of one country against another were settled through "drawing rights." Nations with a trade surplus made goods available to other countries suffering from a deficit on their daily international trade operations. The ERP aided the Intra-European Payments and Compensations Agreement through grants of financial assistance to those nations that afforded drawing rights to other powers. This plan was replaced in 1950 by the European Payments Union.

THE EUROPEAN PAYMENTS UNION.   This union facilitated international trade on the Continent by establishing a noncirculating currency unit called an ecu. Ecu claims between different nations were guaranteed by $600 million of ERP funds. Thus multilateral rather than bilateral trade was encouraged, for the ecu was protected by the dollar. When a nation earned a certain number of ecus, it was empowered to change a part of them into dollars, and this convertibility encouraged world-wide trade.

Mutual Security Program. The Mutual Security Program was initiated in October, 1951 as a continuation of the Marshall Plan Program, the Technical Assistance Program, and the general effort of the democratic world to thwart communism. (Although superseded by the Foreign Operations Administration, explained below, one should be aware of the scope and purposes of the Mutual Security Program.)

PURPOSES. According to the terms of the Mutual Security Act, the purpose of the program was "to maintain the security and to promote the foreign policy of the United States by authorizing military, economic, and technical assistance to friendly countries (for example, the French in Indo-China) to strengthen the mutual security and individual and collective defenses of the free world, to develop their resources in the interests of their security and independence and the national interest of the United States and to facilitate the effective participation of those countries in the United Nations system for collective security." The broad scope of the program was indicated by the range of its functions, among which were military aid, health advice, and assistance in the development of tax programs.

FINANCING. The Mutual Security Agency put dollars and counterpart funds at the disposal of its defense organization to pay for debts on contracts negotiated prior to December, 1951, by the Mutual Security Organization or its forerunner, the Economic Cooperation Administration. Funds were also provided for the security agency's defense branch to purchase strategic materials, especially for stockpiling in the United States. Millions of dollars of the Mutual Security Agency funds were lent to participating nations. They used these funds for American equipment and services; counterpart funds covered local expenses assumed in connection with materials-development projects. The loans were repayable in the goods produced, and the United States had the privilege of buying additional quantities of the goods.

Foreign Operations Administration. In August, 1953, the Foreign Operations Administration was established for the purpose of integrating several foreign assistance programs into a single agency. The functions of the Mutual Security Agency, as well as those of the Technical Cooperation Administration, and the Institute of

Inter-American Affairs, were assumed by the Foreign Operations Administration. Through acts of 1954 and 1955 this administration has had its powers expanded on the one hand and limited on the other, but generally it retains much of the scope of the agencies it absorbed.

The Foreign Operations Administration is designed to promote the security, foreign policy, and general welfare of the United States by providing military, economic, and technical aid to friendly countries in the promotion of international peace. It is responsible for coordinating all foreign aid programs and for conducting mutual security operations, except mutual defense assistance. Organized on a regional basis—with offices in Europe; Latin America; Near East, South Asia, and Africa; and Far East—this administration performs its activities under the guidance of the secretaries of State, Defense, and Treasury. The mutual security program is separated into seven major categories: two of these are concerned with military defense of the democratic world; two categories deal with technical cooperation and economic development; one is concerned with both of the preceding categories; one copes with problems of relief, rehabilitation, and East-West trade controls; and one deals with special emergency programs.

United States Operations Missions are maintained in participating nations in order to develop programs in cooperation with the local governments and the Foreign Operations Administration.

DOMESTIC MONETARY POLICIES OF THE UNITED STATES AFTER WORLD WAR II

The Controversial Monetary Situation. The American domestic monetary picture after World War II was highly controversial. Inflation was typical. Notwithstanding price and wage controls and rationing, prices and wages showed a decided upward trend. When controls were abandoned, prices continued upward. Inflationary factors appeared during the entire period between April, 1939, and August, 1948; a 60 per cent rise in the cost of living took place after the end of hostilities. The public had accumulated enormous savings in cash or readily convertible savings bonds. These savings were in part made possible by government emphasis on deficit financing during the war and a tax structure incapable of withdrawing the spending powers created by this deficit financing.

Treasury-Federal Reserve Monetary Conflict. Initially federal reserve policy, in accordance with Treasury directives, was aimed chiefly at restricting any rise in the yield on government securities. In order to accomplish this aim the Federal Reserve System held itself ready to buy an unlimited amount of federal securities at support prices agreed upon with the Treasury. Such action meant that the system's government security portfolio could increase without limit, but meanwhile the amount of bank reserves and money in circulation was unrestrained. Thus a plentiful supply of credit at no increased cost was made available to private industry.

The Treasury and the Council of Economic Advisors favored this easy money program for several reasons.

(1) A low level of interest rates would hold down the carrying cost of the public debt. (2) Particularly in the case of large institutional holdings of government securities, price stability seemed necessary to assure confidence in the government's obligations, to prevent any capital depreciation in these securities and to forestall heavy losses and the danger of fear-selling should the government's credit deteriorate. (3) It was feared that any slight rise in government yields would discourage inflation if federal bond prices slumped. (4) Easy money would stimulate reconversion to a peacetime economy and encourage business activity.

Federal Reserve Policy. Convinced of the logic of these arguments, the Federal Reserve System continued to buy government bonds in the open market at fixed prices and so maintained a generally low level of interest rates. Actually the Treasury set short-term government security yields, with the Federal Reserve System merely serving in an advisory capacity. Likewise the price of long-term government bonds was supported by the Federal Reserve System to maintain its above-par market quotation.

The Federal Reserve System exercised certain credit control powers during the early postwar period (1945–1948). Fearful of continued inflation, it raised reserve requirements on several occasions in 1948 and increased member bank required reserves to the detriment of the banks' lending power. It also eliminated the preferential discount rate on credits secured by short-term government securities. The only rate of discount was 1 per cent and in 1948 this was raised to 1½ per cent. The federal reserve authorities and the American Bankers Association warned banks and public of the inflationary effect of the excessive use of bank credit. Strong controls were exerted through high margin requirements on stock market loans, and consumer credit was limited.

The Treasury used surplus tax funds (and also money obtained from security sales and from withdrawals on its commercial bank balances) to liquidate excess bank reserves by repayment of debts which it owed to the federal reserve banks and by the accumulation of deposits at the reserve banks. However, all these maneuvers in an anti-inflation program were counterbalanced by the federal reserve open-market policy of buying all federal securities offered to it at high prices and low yields.

When the recession of 1947 occurred, the Federal Reserve System sought to stimulate business by easing member banks reserve requirements and consumer credit controls. It also continued support of the government bond market at even higher prices and lower yields than previously. The conflict between the Treasury and the Federal Reserve System subsided, for a low interest rate on the national debt was in keeping with the objective of an upward business trend. However, this truce was only temporary. The inflation following the beginning of the Korean War led the federal reserve to urge a restrictive credit policy, although the Treasury still desired a low interest-rate policy. While they were at odds, the federal reserve continued to support government bond prices and short-term securities at yields satisfactory to the Treasury.

Agreement between the Treasury and the Federal Reserve Policy. In March, 1951, both governmental monetary powers came to an agreement on policy whereby the federal reserve could permit marketable federal bonds to vary in value and yield. The fact that federal reserve policy could be managed to increase the cost of new money to the Treasury as open-market federal securities dropped in value created general monetary uncertainty. The federal reserve had once again recaptured to some extent its ability to curb credit. Nevertheless, the federal reserve pledged itself to maintain an "orderly" government bond market and to prevent erratic and uncertain government bond prices and yields. What a disorderly market is, has yet to be decided.

REVIEW QUESTIONS

1. What was the purpose of the Marshall Plan?
2. What is a *counterpart fund* and how is it used under the Mutual Security Agency setup?

3. Why did the United States Treasury desire to keep money rates low during World War II?

4. How did the Federal Reserve System use its credit control powers after 1945 to support government bond prices?

5. What is the purpose of the Foreign Operations Administration? What agencies did it absorb?

Bibliography

This Bibliography provides sources of detailed information on selected topics. Students should also consult the standard textbooks listed in the cross-reference tables on pp. xi–xv.

American Institute of Economic Research. *Counterrevolution, American Foreign and Domestic Policy and Economic Aspects of National Defense,* 1952.

Arkin, H. and Colton, R. R. *Statistical Methods,* College Outline Series. New York: Barnes & Noble, Inc., 1955.

Babb, Hugh W. and Martin, Charles. *Business Law,* College Outline Series. New York: Barnes & Noble, Inc., 1952.

Bach, G. L. *Federal Reserve Policy-Making: A Study in Government Economic Policy Formation.* New York: Knopf, 1950.

Beatty, J. Y. *Basic Principles of Bank Credit.* Cambridge: Bankers Publishing Co., 1952.

Bogen, J. I. *Financial Handboook.* New York: Ronald, 1948.

Bremer, C. S. *American Bank Failures.* New York: Columbia University Press, 1934.

Brown, W. A., Jr. *The International Gold Standard Reinterpreted, 1914–1934.* 2 vols. New York: National Bureau of Economic Research, Inc., 1940.

Burns, A. R. *Comparative Economic Organization.* New York: Prentice-Hall, 1955.

Cassel, G. *Postwar Monetary Stabilization.* New York: Columbia University Press, 1928.

———. *Downfall of the Gold Standard.* Oxford: Clarendon Press, 1936.

———. *Money and Foreign Exchange After 1914.* New York: Macmillan, 1922.

Chalmers, Henry C. *Foreign Trade Policies: The Changing Panorama, 1920–1953.* Berkeley: University of California Press, 1953.

Chandler, Lester V. *Inflation in the U. S., 1940–1948.* New York: Harper, 1951.

———. *Introduction to Monetary Theory.* New York: Harper, 1940.

———, and Wallace, D. H., eds. *Economic Mobilization and Stabilization.* New York: Holt, 1952.

Chapman, J. M., et al. Commercial Banks and Installment Credit. Princeton: Princeton University Press, 1940.

Clapham, Sir John H. Bank of England, 2 vols. New York: Macmillan, 1945.

Clark, George L. Trusts: Cases and Text. New York: Bobbs-Merrill, 1954.

Comptroller of the Currency of the United States. Annual Reports, 1934 to date.

Dewey, D. R. Financial History of the United States. New York: Longmans, Green, 1931.

de Veigh, I. Peace Aims, Capital Requirements, and International Lending. American Economic Review, XXXV, No. 2. May, 1945, pp. 253–261.

Duggan, I. W. and Battles, Ralph V. Financing the Farm Business. New York: Wiley, 1950.

Ellis, Howard S. Exchange Control in Central Europe. Cambridge: Harvard University Press, 1941.

Ellsworth, P. T. The International Economy. New York: Macmillan, 1951.

Enke, Stephen and Salera, Virgil. International Economics. New York: Prentice-Hall, 1947.

Farm Credit Administration. Annual Reports.

Federal Deposit Insurance Corporation. Annual Reports.

Federal Home Loan Board. Annual Reports.

Federal Housing Administration. Annual Reports.

Federal Reserve Bulletin.

Fellner, W. "The Commercial Policy Implications of the Fund and the Bank," American Economic Review, XXXV, No. 2, May, 1945, pp. 262–271.

Goldenweiser, E. A. American Monetary Policy. New York: McGraw-Hill, 1951.

Guthmann, H. G. and Dougall, H. E. Corporate Financial Policy. New York: Prentice-Hall, 1948.

Halm, G. N. Monetary Theory. Homewood: Irwin, 1946.

Hansen, A. H. Fiscal Policy and Business Cycles. New York: Norton, 1941.

———. Monetary Theory and Fiscal Policy. New York: McGraw-Hill, 1949.

Hanson, A. W. and Cohen, Jerome B. Personal Finance. Homewood: Irwin, 1954.

Hayek, Frederick A. Capitalism and the Historians. Chicago: University of Chicago Press, 1954.

Harold, G. Corporation Finance, College Outline Series. New York: Barnes & Noble, Inc., 1950.

Harris, S. E. *Exchange Depreciation*. Cambridge: Harvard University Press, 1936.

Hawtrey, R. G. *Capital and Employment*. New York: Longmans, Green, 1954.

————. *Towards the Rescue of Sterling*. New York: Longmans, Green, 1954.

————. *Cross Purposes in Wage Policy*. New York: Longmans Green, 1955.

Hoagland, H. E. *Corporation Finance*. New York: McGraw-Hill, 1947

Kelley, Pearce C. *Consumer Economics*. Homewood: Irwin, 1953.

Kemmerer, E. W. and Kemmerer, Donald L. *ABC for the Federal Reserve System*. New York: Harper, 1950.

————. *Gold and the Gold Standard*. New York: McGraw-Hill, 1944.

Kennedy, Ralph D. and McMullen, S. Y. *Financial Statements: Form, Analysis and Interpretation*. Homewood: Irwin, 1952.

Keynes, J. M. *The General Theory of Employment, Interest, and Money*. New York: Harcourt, Brace, 1936.

————. *A Treatise on Money*. New York: Harcourt, Brace, 1950.

————. *Economic Consequences of Peace*. New York: Oxford, 1946.

Killough, Hugh B. and Killough, Lucy W. *Economics of International Trade*. New York: McGraw-Hill, 1948.

Leavitt, J. A. and Hansen, Carol O. *Personal Finance*. New York: McGraw-Hill, 1950.

Lutz, F. A. and Mints, L. W., eds. *Readings in Monetary Theory*. Homewood: Irwin, 1951.

Mills, F. C. *Statistical Methods*. New York: Holt, 1940.

Mints, L. W. *The History of Banking Theory*. Chicago: University of Chicago Press, 1945.

McGowan, G. B. *Trust Receipts*. New York: Ronald, 1947.

Money, Trade, and Economic Growth. A collection of essays in honor of J. H. Williams. New York: Macmillan, 1951.

Nadler, M., Heller, S., and Shipman, S. S. *The Money Market and Its Institutions*. New York: Ronald, 1955.

Nurkse, R. *International Currency Experience*. Geneva: League of Nations, 1944.

Paris, J. D. *Monetary Policies of the United States, 1932–1938*. New York: Columbia University Press, 1938.

Prochnow, H. V. *American Financial Institutions*. New York: Prentice-Hall, 1951.

————, and Foulke, R. A. *Practical Bank Credit*. New York: Prentice-Hall, 1940.

Ritter, L. S. *Money and Economic Activity*. Boston: Houghton Mifflin, 1952.

Sawyer, R. A. and Day, P. M. *Federal Reserve Banking System.* N. Y. Public Library, 1928.

Securities and Exchange Commission. *Annual Reports.*

Schultz, W. J. and Harriss, C. L. *American Public Finance.* New York: Prentice-Hall, 1954.

Shaterian, W. S. *Export-Import Banking.* New York: Ronald, 1947.

Shaw, Edward S. *Money, Income, and Monetary Policy.* Homewood: Irwin, 1950.

Silverstein, N. L. "Effects of the American Revolution on Prices and Export Trade." American Economic Review, XXVII, June, 1937.

Sloan, Harold S. and Zurcher, Arnold J. *Dictionary of Economics,* Everyday Handbook Series. New York: Barnes & Noble, Inc., 1953.

Taus, E. R. *Central Banking Functions of the United States Treasury, 1789–1941.* New York: Columbia University Press, 1943.

Taylor, Jack. *Business and Government,* College Outline Series. New York: Barnes & Noble, Inc., 1952.

The Trust Bulletin.

Towle, Lawrence W. *International Trade and Commercial Policy.* New York: Harper, 1947.

United States Congress Joint Committee on the Economic Report: Subcommittee on Monetary Credit and Fiscal Policies. *Report,* 1950. Washington, D. C.: U. S. Government Printing Office, 1951.

Vest, G. B. "The Par Collection System of the Federal Reserve Banks," Federal Reserve Bulletin, Feb., 1940, pp. 89–96.

Ward, W. and Harfield, H. *Bank Credits and Acceptances in International Trade and Domestic Trade.* New York: Ronald, 1948.

Whittlesey, C. R. *Readings in Money and Banking.* New York: Norton, 1952.

Williams, J. H. *Postwar Monetary Plans and Other Essays.* New York: Knopf, 1947.

Youngman, A. P. *The Federal Reserve System in Wartime.* New York: National Bureau of Economic Research, 1945.

Final Examination

This examination is composed entirely of multiple-choice questions. Place a check by the phrase which correctly completes each statement. On page 255 there is an answer key by which you may check your responses.

1. Among the following, the two most important functions of money are
   (a) standard of value
   (b) store of value
   (c) medium of exchange
   (d) standard of deferred payment
2. Price advances
   (a) help a borrower to repay his debt
   (b) hinder a borrower's capacity to repay his debt
   (c) do not affect a borrower's ability to repay his debt
3. Legal tender
   (a) must be accepted in payment for debts
   (b) consists of only certain types of money
   (c) is identical with lawful money
4. Among the following, the two most important forms of money in circulation in the United States are
   (a) federal reserve bank notes
   (b) federal reserve notes
   (c) demand deposits
   (d) United States notes
5. Credit money in the United States does not include
   (a) silver certificates
   (b) federal reserve notes
   (c) gold certificates
   (d) gold
6. One type of managed money is
   (a) the gold coin standard
   (b) the gold exchange standard
   (c) the inconvertible paper standard
7. The gold exchange standard prohibits
   (a) a free gold market
   (b) the use of drafts on gold reserves held abroad
   (c) the establishment of a fixed gold content in the money unit

8. The United States gold dollar contains
    (a) 25.8 grains of gold
    (b) 16 grains of gold
    (c) 13.714 grains of gold
    (d) 3 grains of gold
9. The standard money of a country consists of
    (a) all types of money, whether legal tender or not
    (b) the money of ultimate redemption
    (c) representative money
    (d) funds held abroad on deposit
10. A gold standard
    (a) is an automatic check on inflation and deflation
    (b) has been widely accepted in most countries
    (c) assures stability of prices
11. The world-wide abandonment of the gold standard during World War I was due to
    (a) the equitable distribution of the world's gold reserves
    (b) the general adoption of the silver standard
    (c) the paralyzing effects of trade restrictions
    (d) the wide adoption of the bimetallic system
12. The "crime of 73" was eased by the passage of
    (a) the Gold Reserve Act of 1934
    (b) the United States silver program during World War II
    (c) the Bland–Allison Act of 1878
13. Gold devaluation was aimed at
    (a) lowering commodity prices
    (b) stabilizing commodity prices
    (c) raising commodity prices
    (d) retarding investment activity
14. The American colonist traded primarily
    (a) through barter
    (b) with inflated paper money
    (c) with the British pound
    (d) with continental currency
15. The Coinage Act of 1792 established
    (a) the gold standard
    (b) the gold exchange system
    (c) fiat currency
    (d) bimetallism
16. The mint par of exchange is typical of the nations operating on
    (a) fiat standards
    (b) managed currencies

(c) inconvertible currencies
(d) the gold standard

17. Under a fiat currency system, the mint par of exchange is fixed by
    (a) government order
    (b) international agreement
    (c) purchasing power parity
    (d) the Federal Reserve Board of Governors

18. Long-continued currency depreciation encourages
    (a) international trade
    (b) monetary chaos
    (c) price stability

19. The American Stabilization Fund was created to
    (a) stabilize farm prices
    (b) stabilize the dollar
    (c) fix the value of land
    (d) stabilize the value of corporate securities

20. The International Bank for Reconstruction and Development is intended to
    (a) correct disequilibriums in international balances of payment
    (b) modify the gold values of currencies
    (c) stimulate international loans
    (d) restore the gold standard internationally

21. The value of the currencies of the member nations of the International Monetary Fund is expressed in terms of
    (a) the British pound
    (b) the American dollar
    (c) all currencies of the world
    (d) foreign exchange

22. The initial par value of the currency of a nation belonging to the International Monetary Fund can be changed as much as
    (a) 10 per cent
    (b) 20 per cent
    (c) 30 per cent
    (d) 50 per cent

23. A nation which runs short of a foreign money can buy such money through
    (a) its citizens
    (b) its government
    (c) its central bank
    (d) its commercial banks

24. The International Bank for Reconstruction and Development can call in 80 per cent of its members' subscriptions to its capital stock if needed for
    (a) development loans
    (b) paying off its borrowing and guaranties
    (c) operating expenses
    (d) loans to governments

25. Investment credit instruments include
    (a) open book accounts
    (b.) promissory notes
    (c) bills of exchange
    (d) bonds

26. Preferred stock
    (a) may be a draft
    (b) may be a check issued by the company
    (c) may provide for participation in earnings
    (d) may be an income bond

27. Bank notes should possess the basic quality of
    (a) elasticity
    (b) parity
    (c) redeemability

28. Commercial banks are not known chiefly for
    (a) the granting of business credit
    (b) the monetization of credit
    (c) their savings departments

29. Free banking refers to
    (a) dual banking
    (b) branch banking
    (c) the privilege of entering the commercial banking business if the organizers meet certain tests
    (d) group banking

30. Bank stockholders today are subject to
    (a) double liability
    (b) direct management of their bank by the government
    (c) loss of their investment if the bank fails

31. Branch banking is superior to unit banking because it usually provides
    (a) superior management
    (b) close contact with its customers
    (c) a limited number of services
    (d) a duplication of routine operations

32. Bank failures
    (a) have recently been large
    (b) were large prior to 1934

(c) have been concentrated in the big cities
(d) have chiefly been due to fraud

33. A commercial bank's assets do not include
    (a) United States government securities
    (b) cash and balances due from banks
    (c) acceptances outstanding
    (d) corporate securities

34. Checks have the advantage of
    (a) nonnegotiability
    (b) increasing the community's means of payment
    (c) forgery
    (d) no service charges

35. Local checks are cleared through
    (a) the federal reserve Interdistrict Settlement Fund
    (b) the federal reserve banks of the 12 districts
    (c) the local clearinghouse
    (d) correspondents

36. Deposit currency is vital to the business welfare of the United States for
    (a) it is a restraining influence on business
    (b) it is identical in appearance to the federal reserve note
    (c) it is always certified
    (d) it expands and contracts with business requirements

37. Primary deposits result from
    (a) bank loans and investments
    (b) increasing bank capitalization
    (c) cash deposits
    (d) the growth of bank earnings

38. The FDIC guarantees bank deposits up to
    (a) $1,000
    (b) $10,000
    (c) $5,000
    (d) $50,000

39. The consumption loans of commercial banks include
    (a) loans for the purchase of durable consumer goods
    (b) loans for the purchase of securities on margin
    (c) working-capital loans
    (d) loans to finance the short-term working capital needs of business

40. National banks cannot legally make loans secured by
    (a) the bonds of the corporation
    (b) FHA mortgages
    (c) marketable securities
    (d) their own issues of common stock

41. Bankers' acceptances largely finance
    (a) international trade transactions
    (b) commercial paper operations
    (c) call loans
    (d) "term" loans

42. "Term" loans grew out of
    (a) the fear of nonrepayment of short-term loans
    (b) the need for long-term capital market loans
    (c) the marketability of federal reserve loans on any sound asset
    (d) the high cost of short-term loans

43. Open-market commercial paper consists of
    (a) stocks
    (b) bonds
    (c) promissory notes
    (d) bankers' acceptances

44. Primary reserves of a commercial bank consist of
    (a) commercial paper holdings
    (b) cash on hand, deposits with other banks, and legal reserves with the federal reserve bank
    (c) bankers' acceptances
    (d) corporate security assets

45. The ability of a commercial bank to increase its loans and investments depends on
    (a) its required legal reserve
    (b) its cash position
    (c) its excess primary reserves
    (d) its outstanding loans and investments

46. The size of a bank's secondary reserve depends on
    (a) instability of its deposits
    (b) the risks of deposits to capital
    (c) business fluctuations

47. Bank investment policy has been criticized because
    (a) bond portfolios are built up at high prices
    (b) of sound bank management
    (c) bank management is a good judge of fluctuations of interest rates

48. Banks are officially supervised by the
    (a) Comptroller of the Currency
    (b) Secretary of the Treasury
    (c) Treasurer of the United States
    (d) state governors

49. The federal reserve banks are bankers' banks because
    (a) they borrow from the member banks

(b) they own the commercial banks

(c) they lend to the public directly

(d) they carry on their credit operations through the other banks of the country

50. The immediate cause for the establishment of the Federal Reserve System was the

    (a) Bank Holiday of 1933

    (b) suspension of the American gold coin standard in 1933–1934

    (c) banking and monetary panic during the economic crisis of 1907

    (d) stock-market crash of 1929

51. The federal reserve banks

    (a) cannot have branches

    (b) have branches which are member banks

    (c) have as one branch the Treasury

    (d) can organize branches

52. The Board of Governors of the Federal Reserve System

    (a) consists of 8 members chosen by the Comptroller of the Currency

    (b) consists of 10 men chosen by the Comptroller of the Currency

    (c) consists of 7 members chosen by the President with the approval of the Senate

    (d) includes the Comptroller of the Currency

53. Open-market operations of the Federal Reserve System

    (a) can decrease member-bank excess primary reserves

    (b) do not influence member-bank excess primary reserves

    (c) necessarily are correlated with the power of reserve banks to lend directly to industry

    (d) cannot be carried on directly with the United States Treasury

54. Qualitative credit controls of the Federal Reserve System

    (a) influence the volume of federal reserve credit in use

    (b) are used to influence federal reserve credit through rediscount-rate policy

    (c) influence the uses to which federal reserve credit is put

    (d) influence federal reserve credit through open-market operations

55. The sale of newly mined gold to the Treasury decreases

    (a) bank deposits only

    (b) bank primary reserves only

    (c) both deposits and primary reserves

    (d) bank cash assets

56. The Treasury is important in the establishment of national monetary policy since it
    (a) maintains deposits with commercial banks
    (b) maintains "tax and loan accounts" with the banks
    (c) keeps gold in its own vaults
    (d) holds currency in its own vaults and can shift its funds from the commercial banks to the federal reserve banks and back again

57. Increased government spending to take the place of a declining volume of private spending is called
    (a) pump priming
    (b) deficit financing
    (c) the acceleration principle
    (d) compensatory spending

58. Heavy taxation may force
    (a) heavy personal borrowing at the commercial banks and a rise in their deposit balances
    (b) reduced personal bank borrowing
    (c) a decline in bank deposit balances
    (d) high interest rates

59. The first Bank of the United States
    (a) offered foreign exchange services
    (b) financed the United States government
    (c) issued nonlegal tender paper money
    (d) financed businessmen's needs

60. Deposit banking was not a result of
    (a) the development of urban business centers
    (b) the proximity of the business public to banks
    (c) the development of a national transportation and communication system
    (d) weak state-banking organization

61. The Federal Reserve System was an outgrowth of
    (a) a large number of bank failures
    (b) big-city banking
    (c) a par collection of checks
    (d) national bank rediscount powers prior to 1913

62. The banking crisis of 1933 resulted from
    (a) strong state-banking systems
    (b) the business and real-estate depression of 1929–1933
    (c) a strong system of national branch banking
    (d) the unit banking system

63. Since 1934 commercial bank failures
    (a) have been phenomenal in number
    (b) have been few in number

(c) have been of great business significance
(d) have been entirely prevented by the FDIC
64. When the value of money rises
    (a) the buying power of money increases
    (b) the buying power of money falls
    (c) the gold value of money increases
    (d) the silver value of money falls
65. The factors determining the forces composing the equation of exchange are
    (a) the public propensity to consume
    (b) disinvestment
    (c) government issuance or retirement of money
    (d) the business outlook
66. Investment is
    (a) the purchase of securities
    (b) the acquisition of new capital goods
    (c) the acquisition of old capital goods
    (d) the spending of savings
67. If savings exceed investment
    (a) labor's income is reduced by the amount of the savings
    (b) money and bank credit are spent liberally
    (c) capital goods industries expand
    (d) investment expands
68. Rising prices benefit
    (a) bondholders
    (b) stockholders
    (c) landlords
    (d) laborers
69. A mutual savings bank is managed by
    (a) a board of directors
    (b) the stockholders
    (c) a board of trustees
    (d) the state in which it is located
70. The Savings Banks Trust Company serves as
    (a) a source of investment information for savings banks
    (b) a trust company for the general public
    (c) supervisor of activities of the FDIC
    (d) protector of the soundness of the United States Government savings bond issues
71. United States savings bonds were sold
    (a) to increase the public debt
    (b) to minimize monetization of the public debt
    (c) to divert public buying of these bonds
    (d) only to banks

72. The savings departments of commercial banks can invest their depositors' funds only
    (a) in legal list securities
    (b) in local government obligations
    (c) in real-estate mortgages
    (d) in the same ways as the other deposits are invested

73. Postal savings depositors hold
    (a) transferable certificates
    (b) negotiable certificates
    (c) nonwithdrawable deposits
    (d) sums as large as $10,000

74. Private placement of securities is identical with
    (a) the joint account
    (b) the stabilization process
    (c) direct sales of securities to institutional investors
    (d) a "bull" market

75. An investment banking syndicate
    (a) underwrites securities
    (b) does not underwrite securities
    (c) is appointed by the SEC
    (d) consists of brokerage firms exclusively

76. A security prospectus
    (a) is the underwriting contract with the investment banker
    (b) summarizes the registration statement
    (c) is the registration statement
    (d) is the only means of advertising a security for sale

77. A stock exchange is identical with
    (a) a money market
    (b) a new-issues or capital market
    (c) a market for trading already issued securities
    (d) a commodity market

78. Brokers' loans discourage
    (a) speculation
    (b) trading in securities
    (c) trading on "margin"
    (d) brokerage operations

79. A trust company performs these services for individuals:
    (a) it acts as an executor
    (b) it serves as a transfer agent
    (c) it acts as a registrar
    (d) it serves as a paying agent

80. A trust company is superior to an individual trustee in that
    (a) it has a determinate life

(b) it is governmentally examined
(c) it seeks to avoid the law
(d) it enjoys smaller financial resources

81. Commercial banks enter the trust business
   (a) by establishing trust departments with the approval of the Board of Governors of the Federal Reserve System
   (b) without state or federal approval
   (c) with the sanction of a trustee
   (d) with the approval of the bankruptcy courts

82. Trust companies
   (a) protect private properties against waste
   (b) keep production funds idle
   (c) do not arrange for property transfer
   (d) do not serve as liquidating agents

83. Savings and loan associations obtain their loan resources from
   (a) Federal Home Loan Banks
   (b) commercial bank advances
   (c) the sale of shares
   (d) contributions

84. The Federal Savings and Loan Insurance Corporation assesses each member institution
   (a) $\frac{1}{12}$ of 1 per cent of its liabilities and creditor obligations
   (b) $\frac{1}{24}$ of 1 per cent of its liabilities and creditor obligations
   (c) $\frac{1}{2}$ of 1 per cent of its liabilities and creditor obligations
   (d) $\frac{1}{8}$ of 1 per cent of its liabilities and creditor obligations

85. The function of the Federal Home Loan Bank Administration is to
   (a) provide high-cost housing facilities
   (b) stimulate home construction
   (c) depress the real-estate market
   (d) accumulate scarce materials for the armed services

86. An objective of the Federal Housing Administration is to
   (a) discourage employment in the building trade
   (b) slow down home modernization
   (c) insure privately held mortgages
   (d) encourage federal building activities

87. Agricultural credit reform was demanded in 1916 and 1923 to
   (a) raise interest rates
   (b) make loan renewals more certain
   (c) narrow the market for farm loan securities
   (d) squeeze out the small farmer

88. Production Credit Corporations are owned and capitalized chiefly by
    (a) the joint-stock and banks
    (b) the Federal Farm Mortgage Corporation
    (c) the federal government
    (d) the federal land banks

89. Federal land bank borrowers must subscribe to their local land banks for stock equal to
    (a) 10 per cent of their loans
    (b) 5 per cent of their loans
    (c) 15 per cent of their loans
    (d) 50 per cent of their loans

90. The Farmers Home Administration aims to
    (a) lend to farmers to buy supplies
    (b) lend to farmers to purchase farm property even if they cannot make the first down payment
    (c) reduce livestock fees and seed loans
    (d) increase farm debt

91. The objective of the Commodity Credit Corporation is to
    (a) lower farm prices
    (b) stabilize farm prices at parity
    (c) raise farm prices far above parity
    (d) reduce land values

92. Most Morris Plan bank capital is provided by
    (a) the government
    (b) the Reconstruction Finance Corporation
    (c) the sale of bonds
    (d) the sale of investment certificates

93. Loans made by a credit union
    (a) average $1,000
    (b) are made on single-name paper
    (c) carry charges of 25 per cent
    (d) can average 20 per cent of its capital and surplus

94. The loans of personal loan departments of commercial banks are usually made
    (a) on comaker notes
    (b) on discountable customers' paper
    (c) only to finance the finance companies
    (d) after imposition of service and investigatory fees

95. Sales finance companies grew during the 1920's because
    (a) manufacturers pushed sales on the easy payment plan
    (b) production was at a low level
    (c) the national income was low
    (d) personal income was not regularly received

96. Federal reserve government-bond support was intended to
    - (a) lower government security prices
    - (b) reduce the nation's gold reserve
    - (c) maintain the low yield on government securities
    - (d) decrease the liquidity of the banks
97. The Treasury-Federal Reserve monetary conflict concerned the
    - (a) yield on government obligations
    - (b) excess reserves of the member banks
    - (c) deficiency of member bank reserves
    - (d) level of business activity in the United States
98. The Marshall Plan was intended to
    - (a) rehabilitate American-Asiatic political alliances
    - (b) combat the economic breakdown of western Europe
    - (c) speed the flow of private American capital abroad
    - (d) retard the investment of private American capital abroad
99. The Mutual Security Agency is the successor to the
    - (a) Dawes Plan
    - (b) Young Plan
    - (c) Export-Import Bank
    - (d) Marshall Plan
100. Counterpart funds finance
    - (a) military defense in the United States
    - (b) civilian waste in Europe
    - (c) the internal administration of the Marshall Plan
    - (d) internal European monetary and financial stabilization

Answers to the Final Examination

1. a, c	18. b	35. c	52. c	69. c	85. b
2. a	19. b	36. d	53. b	70. a	86. c
3. a	20. c	37. c	54. c	71. b	87. b
4. b, c	21. b	38. b	55. c	72. d	88. c
5. a	22. a	39. a	56. d	73. a	89. b
6. c	23. c	40. d	57. d	74. c	90. a
7. b	24. b	41. a	58. a	75. a	91. b
8. c	25. d	42. a	59. c	76. b	92. d
9. b	26. c	43. c	60. d	77. c	93. b
10. a	27. a	44. b	61. a	78. c	94. a
11. c	28. c	45. c	62. b	79. a	95. a
12. c	29. c	46. c	63. b	80. b	96. c
13. c	30. d	47. a	64. a	81. a	97. a
14. a	31. a	48. a	65. c	82. a	98. b
15. d	32. b	49. d	66. b	83. c	99. d
16. d	33. c	50. c	67. a	84. d	100. d
17. c	34. b	51. d	68. b		

Index